UNDER THE MEDITERRANEAN

Under The MEDITERRANEAN

MARINE ANTIQUITIES

by

HONOR FROST

PRENTICE-HALL, INC
Englewood Cliffs, N.J.

Library of Congress Catalog Card Number: 63–9710

Printed in Great Britain

93568–T

CONTENTS

PLATES

IN COLOUR

MONOCHROME

FIGURES IN TEXT

INTRODUCTION

NEW methods of exploration and discovery invite speculation. My own journey to the bottom of a well has been continued under Mediterranean waters, and very gradually the things I have seen have cohered in my mind and taken on significance. In this book I have treated the ideas that emerged in order of complexity: stone anchors, for instance, are relatively easy to interpret; harbours are more difficult, while the problems of wreck excavation in deep water have to come last because they can be apprehended only after a considerable experience of submarine conditions. This is therefore a journey of ideas that follows its own specious time. A chronological list of my own peregrinations in Mediterranean countries would not only be tiresome, as I have revisited the same places so often, but in view of the subject matter it would also be irrelevant. In a narrow sense my diving life has spanned a period of ten years, but my interest in and familiarity with the Mediterranean dates back to earliest childhood.

As a subject, underwater archaeology remains conjectural. As 'black currants are different from Wednesday', so marine remains differ from those we know on land. Sites beneath the sea present problems that cannot be resolved by a well-intentioned application of the current methods of scientific excavation, because these were devised to answer other kinds of question. Only people familiar with the established principles of underwater work can make the effective transposition of land techniques of digging and recording for this different element.

Any excavation must be undertaken by a professional archaeologist, but no professional archaeologist can be a professional diver as well. With, at best, amateur status as diver, the archaeologist will be at a disadvantage at marine levels. The solution must be a collaboration between the two professions. A diver with twenty years' experience of scientific research has remarked: 'A gulf separates the professional, grounded in all the disciplines of underwater work, from the amateur who dives sporadically for the purposes of hunting or exploration.' The import of this statement is realized by anyone who has seen craftsmen-divers on a job. I count myself lucky to have had the opportunity of watching those who dive regularly, whether engaged in picking sponges or conducting scientific research. In addition to their technical efficiency, the men I speak of also have a wide experience of Mediterranean conditions and are, incidentally, familiar with submarine remains; a familiarity which has often allowed me to understand the implications of puzzling phenomena that I myself had uncomprehendingly observed.

Most underwater sites are half buried under sediment and concretions. Their excavation involves heavy manual labour and the use of specialized machinery. On the wreck of a 40-metre ship several hundred tons of cargo will have to be lifted to the surface, and the same weight again of sand will have to be displaced on the bottom; all this in a controlled manner that will permit of recording. This is the problem that faces the archaeologist. Other scientists: geologists, biologists and ichthyologists, can easily pursue their research under the sea, because their work depends on observation and the taking of samples, tasks which are well within the scope of any good amateur diver. Moreover, should they make a mistake, their experiment can be repeated. This is not so with archaeologists, for excavation entails destruction, and antiquities may be unique. When, for instance, an ancient ship is to be reconstructed from its broken and buried remains it can be done only by recording each consecutive layer of excavation before it is removed, and by later interpreting the records taken.

If archaeologists were to collaborate with professional divers in evolving a standard technique of excavation, and in training a generation of young archaeologists to carry on the work, the present problems would be solved. No pilot excavation on these lines has as yet been carried to completion. Nor is the initiation of such an excavation as simple as it may appear, for in planning a rational campaign, both archaeologists and specialist divers would have to have a comparative knowledge of wreck-formations before they could anticipate the problems likely to occur on a specific site.

A ship is a mobile, integral mechanism: it reaches the sea-bed only by accident. As a wreck it undergoes a sea change before it becomes stabilized within the local geological environment. Buildings, by contrast, are imposed on the ground by man's will; even in decay they maintain this direct relationship with the earth. These are differences which must be taken into account in marine excavation. A collapsed machine can be reconstructed if, first, we understand the way in which its parts have been redistributed, and second, we examine its remains in their entirety as a once functional unit. The excavator's approach to architectural remains is quite different, for the size and character of a ruined building can be assessed by trenching through its foundations at strategic points.

Harbours, though they are imposed by the will of man at a certain spot, are also machines. They are machines designed to ensure an area of calm water while preventing a deposit of silt. In consequence, the excavation techniques used on a town will be inapplicable to its adjacent harbour.

The complexities of these mechanisms are obvious, but other kinds of marine remains, such as the apparently meaningless, ancient jetsam found on offshore anchorages, look simple. Appearances are deceptive: these artifacts should not be moved without considerable thought, for they mark stratified sites containing evidence of a changing pattern of trade with the hinterland. As yet no technique has been devised for excavating these sites. They may disappear before this is done, for the present tendency is to raise any antiquity found on the sea-bed.

In this book I am not attempting to draw archaeological conclusions—indeed, this would be beyond my capacity—but rather to describe the different kinds of underwater remains I have seen in the Mediterranean. Though individual experience is necessarily limited, the present need for a comparative standard by which to judge this newly accessible type of site is urgent enough to justify any contribution, however small.

My intention in reproducing underwater drawings, such as details of Roman wood, is not so much to throw light on the structure of ancient ships but to demonstrate that, given favourable working conditions, it is quite possible to make archaeological records even under 30 or 40 metres of water. Since I travelled alone, unaffiliated to any expedition, official or otherwise, the conditions in which I had to draw were never really favourable. When planning a wreck I had neither the assistance nor the equipment which any land surveyor would require. Further, the time I could spend on any one wreck was limited by the boat owner's other commitments, which were never archaeological. The plans reproduced in the following pages are based on the overall measurements of the site, later checked against the known size of individual units of cargo, such as tiles or amphorae. The general appearance and disposition of the finds and their orientation (by compass bearings) were drawn underwater. There were occasions when I had sufficient time to measure strategic parts of a wreck and fix the interrelationships by triangulation. None of these drawings, however, is put forward as a substitute for the accurate survey that would have to be made as a preliminary to methodical excavation. Nevertheless, some form of visual description of the appearance of a wreck is useful, especially since no camera, used underwater, can record an area of more than a few square metres. Even if large areas of the sea-bed could be photographed, the resulting pictures would be difficult to interpret, because sea growths and lack of cast shadow camouflage even those shapes which, to a diver's eye, are intelligible and clearly defined.

A diver who wants to describe what he has seen cannot rely solely on his camera; in many ways he is like a traveller before the invention of photography. On land, and with a camera, the traveller finds little that is unknown: even in remote parts there are excellent picture postcards which automatically limit his scope to the personal, anecdotal or 'artistic' type of photograph. A diver is faced with opposite problems. In the sea there is everything to record; very often drawings, and to a limited extent photographs, will be his only means of communicating what he has seen.

Where diving is concerned I would stress that the first thing to strike the novice is his own 'weightlessness' in water. Possibly the last thing that the experienced amateur will realize is that, in accordance with the laws of underwater gravity, other bodies behave in the same way as his own: the sand he raises or the organic matter he uncovers becomes seemingly lighter than water. Water is an active element: that is a truism—yet it takes experience and a particular type of training before a diver can calculate the effects these factors will have on his own working efficiency, and then control and even use the force of water in his work.

Sensational reports of wreck 'excavations' in the popular Press have led to misconceptions. People with only a theoretical knowledge of the subject are therefore prone to draw analogies between land and sea archaeology. When, for instance, the looting of ancient wrecks is discussed it is frequently said that the same sort of pillage takes place on land, but this is a half truth. Traffic in looted amphorae is a regrettable fact in many parts of the Mediterranean; it is less often pointed out that, at the bottom of the sea, one false move by a well-intentioned amateur can destroy, in the fraction of a second, some delicate find preserved for centuries in marine conditions. On land the same effect could be produced only by hard work implying deliberate destruction, gross negligence, or grosser ignorance.

Until recently, Mediterranean divers held the monopoly of submarine remains. Like retriever dogs, they laid their finds at the feet of land archaeologists, who, in turn, became intrigued and are now taking to the water during their brief seasons of field-work. Although the divers' shortcomings are perhaps more manifest than the experience they have gained, there is no reason to dismiss this corpus of experience. Perhaps the most useful contribution any individual diver can make to the nascent science of underwater archaeology is to record his own observations, for the benefit of those about to embark on a more specialized stage of research.

ACKNOWLEDGEMENTS

In writing this book I have drawn on the experience and knowledge of those divers mentioned in the text and of many others whose names do not appear. I am in particular indebted to Georges Barnier for the early training he gave me and also for the photographs he has allowed me to reproduce. Frédéric Dumas, whose first exploits as a pioneer of the aqualung are mentioned in every book on diving, is less known to the general public for his scientific research. His unparalleled knowledge of ancient wrecks in the Mediterranean and the analyses he has made of these formations constitute the most important contribution yet made to the development of underwater archaeology. I personally have to thank him for advice, for many of the photographs in this book and for reading the text. As well as to those divers I have been able to mention by name, I owe much —indeed, this book could not have been written without their help—to all those who have allowed me to see their finds and have offered me the hospitality of their boats.

For assistance in obtaining both material and illustrations I would like to thank M. Seyrig and M. Daux, the Directors of the French Schools of Archaeology in Beirut and Athens respectively; also M. François Clouzot, editor of the *Bulletin* of the French Diving Federation, M. Georges Beuchat and many others mentioned in the text.

It would seem that few authors of works pertaining to the sea are not in some way indebted to Mr George Naish of the National Maritime Museum, and I am no exception. He has given most generously of his wide knowledge of so many aspects of marine history. I am also most grateful to Miss du Plat Taylor, Librarian of the Institute of Archaeology of London University, for her unfailing help in obtaining books, and to Messrs R. W. Hutchinson and L. Biek, and Professor King and Dr Vevers for their good counsel.

Lastly, I owe particular thanks to David Wright for reading my first draft, to Alan Neame for his constant help in literary matters and, at a later stage, to Alexander Walton. Needless to say, whatever shortcomings remain in the text have slipped through despite their expert advice.

SWITZERLD
AUSTRIA
HUNGARY
FRANCE
Venice
ITALY
YUGOSLAVIA
Albenga
Cannes
Anthéor
Toulon
Agde
Marseille
Corsica
Rome
L. Nemi
ALBANIA
Naples
Pompeii
Sardinia
Mediterranean
Motya
Sicily
Sousse
Mahdia
Sfax
Malta
TUNISIA
0
100
200
300
400
Scale of Miles
Land above 2,000 ft.
LIBYA

MANIA
LGARIA
Black Sea
Istanbul
Sea of Marmara
Ankara
TURKEY
Afyon
C. Artemision
Izmir
Chios
Athens
Bodrum (Halicarnassos)
Karabağla Is
Ceramic Gulf
Cos
cenae
Aspendos
Antalya
Adana
Seleucia
SYRIA
C. Gelidonia (Anadolou Burnu)
Rhodes
Heraclion (Knossos)
Mallia
Mochlos
Crete
Phaistos
Komo
Matala
Cyprus
Ruad
Byblos
Tabarja
Beirut
Sidon
Tyre
LEBANON
Damascus
Jericho
Jerusalem
ISRAEL
JORDAN
an Sea
Alexandria
EGYPT

PART I

INITIATION CEREMONIES

O litus vita mihi dulcius, o mare! felix
cui licet ad terras ire subinde meas.[1]

[1] 'O seashore sweeter to me than life, O sea, happy am I who may go down at once to my own lands.' Petronius.

CHAPTER 1

Well Baptism – Psychological Effects of Diving – Mediterranean Beginnings – Diving Craft

THERE were 6 metres of black water above my head and I sucked air through a mouthpiece, connected by hose to a pump on the surface. Sometimes I forgot and breathed through my nose which meant drawing out the negligible quantity of air in my suit as opposed to the supply to my mouth. A full moon shone on the snow-covered garden, but I was no longer conscious of that world. This first crazy experiment reduced the act of diving to its essentials. My mind was confused neither by exotic surroundings nor the beauties of subaqueous light and landscape, for the baptism took place in a well in Wimbledon.

I had been invited to try a suit, of the type used for shallow-water work during the war. It was entered legs first through a hole in the belly, this orifice being surrounded by an 'apron' of soft rubber. The final touch was to gather the 'apron' in a bunch in the left hand and close it with an elastic band, like fixing one's own umbilical cord. After the visor had been screwed down and lead hung round my neck I climbed into the well holding a watertight torch.

It was not as easy to sink as I had supposed. The suit was full of air, which had to be let out. Those on the surface helped by pushing me down with planks. Eventually bubbles escaped through a valve on top of the helmet and the heavy canvas closed in, welded to my body by the pressure of the water. A moment before I had been buoyant and struggling helplessly; now, for the first time, it seemed to me that I was free from the laws of gravity. Suspended in black water, I relished the sensation; the pressure of a finger against the side of the well was sufficient to send me up or down. In the silence it crossed my mind that no telephone could reach me here. The only moment of claustrophobia came when actually getting into the suit.

Peter Pan has a strong influence on most children, even on those born, as I was, by the Mediterranean. Eternal youth hardly concerns a child; the immediate effect of Barrie's play is to make him jump off the highest piece of furniture and, with arms flapping, defy the force of gravity. Usually this yearning to be free from weight is satisfied in dreams; by flying out of bedroom windows, over rooftops or, using breast stroke, by swimming round the clerestory of a cathedral. The diver fulfils the urge in the flesh, by wearing just enough lead to allow him to ascend a few inches as he fills his lungs and sink proportionately as he exhales. It is one of his psychological satisfactions.

I reached the bottom of that well in a state of euphoria and sat, until I remembered I had promised to give four flashes to show I was all right. There ensued a Thurberian struggle with the torch, which I had not examined on the surface. When the light finally shone I became so fascinated by my surroundings that I forgot the signals. Had those on the surface been nervous, there was nothing they could have done, beyond trying to draw me up by the rubber tube, like Degas' lady acrobat, who hangs by her teeth and a string from the Big Top. I touched the walls of the well, air bubbles, like quicksilver, adhered to the undercut surfaces. The floor was a cushion of dead leaves in every stage of decomposition. There were red, yellow and brown ones in shiny completeness, while others were no more than fragile skeletons. Air came short and I surfaced; I was told that I must, unconsciously, have changed over to breathing through my nose. I dived again. The second time a trickle of water ran down my neck, gathered momentum and filled one of my shoes. The leak was subsequently traced to a screw on the visor. When I remarked that I had only been under for a few minutes the first time and even less the second, the man on the pump corrected me. He had been working for twenty minutes and a quarter of an hour respectively.

Later, when I took to the bottle and became a 'free-diver', not one dependent on the surface and joined to it by a pipe, I sometimes regretted this light suit with its hand-pump. A cylinder that looks like a bomb is not the easiest of travelling companions, nor is compressed air always available. On the other hand, at such tempting places as the 'ginger-pop' spring at Pammukale and elsewhere in the Levant there is always surplus labour only too willing to man a hand-pump.

Consciousness refocuses under water, but one never loses the thrill of breaking past the surface and penetrating another world. I learned at the bottom of the well that diving involves odd psychological reactions. The mind loses its habits of anxiety, while powers of contemplation increase. Sea diving with an aqualung confirmed these impressions. Even after I had acquired some theoretical understanding of the reactions of the body to pressure, my mind continued to refocus itself. I exercised greater conscious control, but still enjoyed an enhanced awareness of the things I saw. This sense of calm is quite distinct from the 'rapture of the depths', a kind of drunkenness which attacks anyone who goes down a bit too far. Addiction to diving gives one an understanding of one of the treatments for lunacy, which consists in strapping the sufferer and immersing him in running water. Far from providing a thrill, the effect of immersion is to soothe. Later experience taught me that it was also an anodyne. Diving when unwell is forbidden, but there are few divers who, put under oath, would not admit to having done it. For Andersen's 'Little Mermaid' every step on dry land was agony, but she did not suffer in the water. Since reactions would be poor in an emergency, the treatment is not recommended.

Glancing through jottings in an old diary, I find my first account of wearing a mask in the sea. It brought me what Proust calls '*cette qualité inconnue d'un monde unique*' and happened just after the war, in Italy. It also somehow convinced me that time spent on the surface was time wasted, though the unique quality is apparent even to one who floats face down looking through a mask and breathing through a tube. I conclude from these jottings that it is easier to dive than to write about it:

> Masked under water is like going home to a forbidden land. The body, being horizontal, is somewhere behind; out of sight out of mind. No module to measure by. Surrounded by creatures with which one can have no contact. Peace! Fish look coldly in the eye . . . are they larger or smaller than oneself? Suspended above a landscape of forests, massives and sandy plains. The forests sway, but there is no wind against one's flesh. Progress slow as in a dream. Like being drunk underground or in a smoky night club . . . no, because it's clean. Reluctance to raise my head; contrast of worlds too violent. Prefer steering by the landscape below. Things enlarged by a quarter because of mask. Not pleasant to feel like Gulliver. Nearest thing to life after death. . .

and so the diary runs on, but this extract is sufficient to evoke first reactions.

On that occasion I had been on the surface of shallow water, so my shadow continued to swim below; that was not comforting either, because, since I felt I did not exist, it became a peculiarly sinister doppelgänger, a *memento vivere*. In depth there are no shadows. Light is magically defused as in a cathedral. Of course, a cathedral is like a ship, not only in the sense Charles Péguy meant

CONTRASTING SEASCAPES BY NATURAL AND ARTIFICIAL LIGHT

I (opposite). Corbs *or corvina between rocks covered by Mediterranean moss-like growths and gorgonia. Picture taken by flash.*

II and III (centre pages). *In contrast, an Atlantic jungle near Vigo Bay. The brown and green Laminaria are much larger than any Mediterranean growth; their stems being sometimes as thick as a man's arm. The photographer, coming as he did from the south of France, was attracted by what seemed to him to be a brilliant yellow flower belonging to this weed; Laminaria, however, does not flower, so the yellow growth remains unexplained. Nevertheless, surrounded as it is by starfish, and with a jellyfish floating above, it enhances the dream-like quality of this scene so different from anything we might see in the enclosed sea.* (Above right). *A diver under the palm-like fronds of Laminaria.*

IV and V (verso). *In the Mediterranean, a friendlier sea, where divers are not allowed to hunt while wearing a bottle, men develop a harmonious relationship with marine life.* Above: *one diver breaks sea urchins to feed* girelles *or rainbow wrasse while another watches in the background: the fish flock to the feast like sparrows. Taken in less than 15 metres of water, by natural light, this photograph shows the colours a diver would actually see at that depth.* Below: *hunting with a camera is allowed, and here a marine crawfish has been caught in his hole; notice the coral trees in blue 'flower' (expanded polyps) above the cave. Taken at over 40 metres the camera's flash transformed, for the fraction of a second, what to the diver had been a monochrome subject into a blaze of colour.*

1. G.E.R.S., photo P. Tailliez

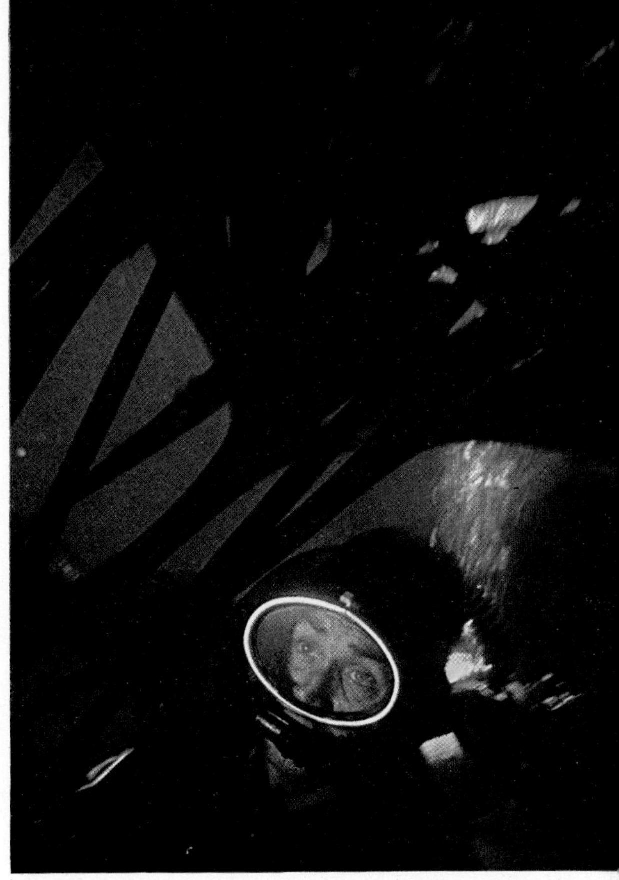

II & III. G. Barnier

IV. G. Barnier

V. G.E.R.S., photo F. Dumas

when he described *Notre Dame au Grand Galère*: as Notre Dame seen across the Seine looking like a galley of souls with the flying buttresses as oars . . . no, a cathedral from inside is like a sunken ship. Light in diving is somehow illustrated by a cathedral: for the first few metres where the windows are there is colour, but the floor below is in shade, though there is still quite enough light and one can read if one wants. The explanation of the gradual disappearance of colour underwater is, of course, that as the sun's rays diminish with increasing depth, so the world goes into monochrome. Red disappears first, after about 15 metres, yellow is the last to go at about 30. I discovered this for myself when I cut my finger at 50 metres. My blood oozed out black as ink, and when I looked at my nail varnish it was black too. I can now gauge the depth at which I happen to be swimming by the colour of my nails.

It may seem irrelevant to go back to these jottings about first reactions which took place in special circumstances. Nevertheless, they point to exact, if intuitive, conclusions. How frequently in everyday life one regrets not having acted on intuition; in a strange element it can be fatal. When the senses are dulled one learns to rely on those parts of the mind which, in the normal way, are too strictly subjected to reason. Of course, in time one adjusts oneself to a certain extent to the new element. Some people lose their sense of direction under water because of either bad visibility, diffused light, or because they are moving three-dimensionally and 'landmarks' are difficult to recognize; later they may adapt themselves. What is more serious, when there is a job to be done, is that the mind does not work normally below about 20 metres. It is possible to compensate for, but never to overcome, this difficulty; amateurs seldom realize the full extent of the handicap. Only the veteran, or someone who has had a sound professional training, will have the experience to realize that he becomes like a child of six at 30 metres. The dulled mind cannot formulate questions, but as soon as one returns to the surface questions pose themselves.

Many excellent books have been written on the physiology of diving, so that it is unnecessary here to do more than mention those particular factors which affect the diver's work. Making plans of wrecks, for instance, is more intellectually exacting than picking sponges, or most salvage jobs. Accurate measurements have to be taken, artifacts camouflaged by sea growths must be examined and diagnosed and their interrelationship noted. Furthermore, archaeological excavation of an underwater site has to be continuous, and may last for years, whereas salvage jobs are automatically limited. The known value of goods to be salvaged is set against diving fees, the hire of machinery, boat and crew; once found, the goods are immediately lifted. In archaeological excavation lifting comes as the climax to a series of delicate operations, and relative to these, takes only a small proportion of the total working time. Using an aqualung at a depth of 30 metres or more, time on the bottom is limited to two dives of 20 minutes or less per day. This, of course, is a very rough estimate of what can be done without having to undergo stage decompression. It is therefore essential not to waste a moment and to plan each dive so that no operation which could possibly be done on the surface is attempted in depth.

I count myself lucky to have been French trained, in the Mediterranean. This implies no slur on the prowess or skills of Northern divers, but a profound difference of approach. There was no difficulty in adapting French training to my eventual interest in making underwater archaeological records. The only drawback was that it took me years to understand why Northern divers reacted so differently to Mediterranean conditions. I first used a bottle in the South of France, where I had been sent to convalesce, at a time when the post-war British travel allowance was at its lowest ebb. I was living with friends, but even so, had very little money to spend on expensive sports. I used to watch a man at the local beach giving swimming lessons and occasionally teaching the use of an aqualung. One day as I swam across him when he was giving a lesson he shouted: 'There's nothing I can teach you!'

'Oh, yes, there is! You could teach me how to dive.'

He told me to meet him afterwards, as he had some half-empty bottles in his car (refills were costly) and would allow me to try one. It seems my fate to be given faulty apparatus. This first lung I ever wore had a twisted mouthpiece, an almost unique occurrence. The thing turned outwards and had to be gripped between clenched teeth, thus distorting my face muscles, so that water leaked into the mask, which, at that time, I did not know how to clear. My instructor turned out to be Monsieur Georges Barnier, a *Moniteur* of the *Club Alpin Sous-Marin de Cannes*. Despite this bad beginning, he recognized the fanatical gleam in my eye and arranged to take me with him and let me practise when he had other more lucrative pupils. He did, however, stipulate that I must join the Club, which entitled me to borrow apparatus, and, after a medical examination, to an insurance policy.

In those days, during the season *Moniteurs* used to dive groups of tourists at submarine beauty spots all along the coast. Some of these places were even listed in the Michelin guide. It was a hard and rather dangerous job for a conscientious man. He had to keep close watch on his charges, who, like most novices, swam off in all directions. At Cannes they seldom dived to less than 30 metres. Tables for cumulative decompression, that is to say several dives in one day, were only being formulated, and what safety regulations did exist were not as closely followed as they are now. Apart from the risk of 'bends', it was very exhausting for a *Moniteur* to dive so often. Photography was the other incentive for professionals. The market was not yet glutted, and underwater shots sold well; indeed, a dive without a camera was regarded as a waste of time. Luckily for me, the pictures had to include a model, to give scale to the unfamiliar seascape, and a female was a definite commercial advantage. As usual, I did not grasp the full implications, and turned up one day with my hair cropped as short as a boy's. The gesture was received with horror; '*sirènes*' had to have long hair. I promised to buy a wig the following year. On the occasions I dived alone with Monsieur Barnier I learned more than when the water seethed with tourists. The next few months were spent doing the classic dives around Cannes: The *Arc de Triomphe*, a great arch at the foot of a 30-metre, submarine cliff, *Nôtre Dame de Trayas*, a deep, blue, tunnel-like cave, and the magnificent *Tombant du Vengeur*, another submarine cliff of over 40 metres, covered with rich growths of sponges, gorgonia and coral. The *tombant* ended in a sandy plain; a burial ground for anchors of all periods, shapes and sizes, which had dragged off the shallow shelf above, broken their cables and fallen to inaccessible depths.

I associate two particular memories with the *Arc de Triomphe*. We were diving alone, Barnier, of course, with his camera and, as usual, I served as a yardstick. But first, I should explain that I have a bad eustachian tube, which means going down slowly. The ear-drums become concave as the pressure of water increases; most people can hold their noses and blow the drums back into place, but I am forced to dilly-dally until the internal and external pressures have equalized. Knowing this, we started off together and made a rendezvous at the arch below. Barnier in the interim went to collect a lost anchor and saw two gigantic pasternaca rays, lying close by on the sand. He photographed them automatically, but without a scale it was impossible to prove that they had measured almost 2 metres from wing tip to tip. By the time I joined him they had gone. He explained all this later, on the surface.

These rays are flat, roughly lozenge shaped and, like most of their species, weird and beautiful in motion (Plate 6). They flap along slowly, their long tails straight behind them. I was told that Dumas, a diver whose prowess is legendary, never missed an opportunity of catching the harmless extremity of a passing tail and going for a ride. The natural habitat of these fish is sand, where they are almost unnoticeable. If approached from above they instantly erect a sharp, bayonet-like spike, which is not quite as long as the tail itself and carries in its saw-teeth the same poison as a viper. This is jabbed into the attacker. Fishermen have a healthy respect for these rays, and books on sting fish abound with lurid descriptions of the wounds they inflict.

Barnier's appetite had been whetted. Here was the photograph of the season: a *sirène* sitting between rays. I was not so sure, and rehearsed in my mind possible methods of approach. Should one crawl along the sand at their own level, then sit up between them and pose? or would they turn and jab one from the side? For two days we chased the creatures, but though they usually stay in the same place, the *Mistral* blew, bringing cold water to the depths, and very sensibly they left for warmer parts. I was much relieved, and for years afterwards experimented inconclusively with smaller, sitting rays to see in what circumstances they would attack.

All this seems a long time ago. In those days cold mattered to divers as well as rays. I was not one of the real aqualung pioneers, but I was among the first of the many at Cannes. Pleasure diving was still unknown in America, and only a few of the yacht-owning tourists joined us at the *Club Alpin Sous-Marin.* The bottles we used had reserve taps at the bottom, which meant that one had to be very careful when putting them on.[1] This particularly affected me, as I could hardly stand upright under the weight of the equipment, while dressing and undressing in a sitting position was liable to damage the vital taps. Once in the water, weight ceases to matter, and muscular strength is irrelevant unless the diver does heavy work. Age and sex, in my experience, are not very important. I have seen a man of seventy-six learn to dive, and as for women, they have certain definite advantages. Their layer of subcutaneous fat allows them to stand the cold better than men, while their smaller lungs enable the limited air supply to last longer.

The tideless Mediterranean can be as cold in depth as the Channel in November. In England we not only benefit from the Gulf Stream but tides and currents also make warm surface water circulate in depth. Foam-rubber suits (in which

[1] French bottles have a reserve tap which, when the rest of the bottle is empty, gives enough air to get back to the surface and decompress in shallow water.

the water that leaks in soon takes on body-temperature) had been invented when I started diving, but they were rigid and cumbersome. I once borrowed a specimen and nearly drowned or, in the local euphemism, I 'drank several cups'. Movement became almost impossible, and as the suit was too big, it was very buoyant and I had to struggle to submerge. Because they were supposed to be skin-tight, suits had to be filled with talcum powder before one could get into them. The wearer's heads emerged white, and afterwards their whole bodies were covered with blotches of powder and crystallized salt. Being allergic to talcum, I came out in a rash. I did own a couple of dry-suits, such as frogmen wore during the war, but naval frogmen used the closed-circuit oxygen apparatus (which leaves no tell-tale bubbles on the surface). Oxygen is unsafe below 6 metres, whereas wearing aqualungs we rarely dived to less than 30. Here the pressure of the water clamped heavy, dry-suits to the skin, chafing it and causing weals. Cousteau (the inventor of the aqualung) designed a constant-pressure dry-suit, the appropriate amount of air being introduced into the suit according to depth; but it was never really successful.

All things considered, I returned to woollen ballet-tights and jerseys until the invention of the present Neoprene wet-suit, which is completely satisfactory. It fits like a second skin and does not deteriorate in the same way as rubber. Air bubbles in the material retain the heat of the body, and what little water penetrates takes on body-temperature. The first Neoprene suits, being skin-tight, were liable to tear, and were consequently an expensive luxury for divers who had to have them made to measure. Naval divers were issued with new suits every few months, but few amateurs could afford this. The problem has now been solved by nylon jersey lining which not only reinforces the Neoprene but obviates the use of talc.

In those early days I was still too bemused by the beauty and unfamiliarity of my surroundings to understand very much. Once, at the Arc de Triomphe, even Barnier made an error of judgement. He told me he had seen a man-made object in the rocks at a fairly shallow place near by. It might be the drum of a marble column, such as the Cannes Club had found at St Tropez; this would imply the possibility of a Roman loot ship with statues. I asked whether I might look at it; rather diffidently, since I knew that it was important enough to be kept secret. On the next dive I repeated the request. He had been back in the interim.

'Actually, I'm pretty sure it's a mine.'

Naturally I let the subject drop, and we set off in the opposite direction. I think it was on this dive that I had further proof of how a lack of general knowledge and not having one's wits about one detracts from one's usefulness underwater. We swam over a very unusual landscape of large, circular formations with concave centres, about 2 metres in diameter, like huge ashtrays. They appeared chalky and strangely free from weed. It was not until I was walking in Queen Mary's Garden in Regent's Park some months later that I noticed a similar object beside some fossilized trunks, labelled 'concretion formed around fossil tree'. We must have been swimming over a prehistoric forest.

We still had some air when we got back. As I was about to turn to the place where we had left our things, Barnier pulled my sleeve and beckoned me to follow him along the rocks. I was filled with forebodings: 'large and cylindrical' he had said. Perhaps the mine was magnetic. Nervously I counted over our metal appurtenances: lead . . . O.K., aluminium . . . query . . . but there, to my horror, was Barnier unsheathing his bayonet and scraping at the concretions to prove the cylinder was not a column. I nodded politely and backed away. Equally courteously, he took hold of my arm and swung me over, so that I landed astride the thing, then handed me a dangling excrescence which I assumed to be the fuse. He backed and took a snap. Something must have shaken, because the film showed the top part of me with the 'thing' in my hand: the cylinder itself was out of the picture.

Barnier gave me another lesson about this time that was to prove invaluable in my later, less orthodox submarine life. On these dives, which we made together between his working hours, we never had a boat above us and the sea was often rough. Though muscle doesn't count for much underwater, if a diver has to surface he becomes a swimmer hampered by 20-odd kilograms of bottles and lead, as much as the air-travel allowance. I, for one, might not have been able to get my equipment back to the shore. Barnier took an inner tube attached to a ball of string which he wound or unwound as we swam. In an emergency we would have come up to the tube and been able to hold on to it while we paddled back to land. Later, when I had either to dive alone or not at all, I always used this device.

Mines are common in most waters, but apart from this reminder of humanity, the character of each sea varies enormously. Even the symbolism of their mythical inhabitants differs: Glaucus and sea-nymphs rule the Mediterranean under Poseidon, though his subjects in northern waters are more likely to be Forsaken Mermen and Sad Selchies. This, by analogy, goes for divers.

The fundamental difference between northern and Mediterranean diving techniques stems from the clarity of the water and the fact that diving followed on spear fishing in the south: an historical sequence which is explained in *The Silent World*. The mask was invented before the war, and in those early days primitive weapons were constructed, such as a trident or an arrow with elastic which worked like a sling. During the war, when the South of France was particularly affected by food shortages, people who had no boats but who had started spear fishing as a sport practised it in earnest. If the harpoonist is skilled it is an efficient and selective method of hunting. So much so, that local *Syndicats de la Pêche* became the sworn enemies of spear fishermen and later of divers. To a certain extent this situation still persists in France. The fact remains that there can be no better training for the diver's eye than to learn, from the outset, to distinguish creatures or objects beneath Nature's elaborate camouflage.

When Commandant Cousteau (as he then was) invented the aqualung in 1943, with the help of an engineer called Monsieur Gagnan, he, Dumas, Tailliez and the other pioneers, all fished while wearing bottles. After learning how to use a harpoon while holding one's breath, it was like shooting a sitting bird when fish were met on equal terms, but food rather than sport counted during the war. There were also luxuries to be had from the sea: coral, sponges, *violets*, sea-urchins. After tourists returned to the '*Côte*' and diving became a sport, ability to fish was the qualification demanded of the novice. One of Cannes Club's rules stipulated that all members should have had several years experience as spear fishers. I had neither experience nor interest in that sport, so my sponsor guaranteed that I was a competent swimmer and the rule was waived.

It is impossible to overstress the importance of the diver's having a trained eye. In my own case my whole education had been visual, and I had a good bump of locality, so that by a different method I reached the same stage as a hunter. I absorbed this part of the training unconsciously from Barnier. As we swam along a cliff he would pause by a hole where there was a pile of shells and an unnatural arrangement of pebbles. I took it for a cache marked by some previous diver; perhaps he had hidden coral or had left his knife there, but when I put my hand inside it was gripped and shaken gently by an octopus. These animals are home-loving; they sometimes embellish their front doors with lintels and push out garbage in the same way as cottagers put their tins on a rubbish dump. Barnier would point to a tree of red coral growing on the roof of a cave. Roofs are much more rewarding than floors (Plate V). Coral, sponges and *cigales de mer* hang there, but the landsman's inherent consciousness of the force of gravity tends to make him examine the floor instead of the rock above his head. Once, as we surfaced, near the concrete steps of a fashionable bathing establishment, Barnier picked a slimy ball off the rock. 'How strange, hundreds of people with masks must have passed and no one noticed this sponge,' he said.

The ability to distinguish man-made objects beneath marine camouflage comes later. Jetsam lying on rocks: an eighteenth-century cannon, amphora sherds, a marble column off a Roman loot ship, sea mines or even the chassis of a car which has plunged from the *Corniche d'Or* into deep water below become covered with concretions, sponges and sea plants within a few months. Sometimes the material itself is distorted or metamorphosed to such an extent that it is indistinguishable, except to a trained eye, from its surroundings. Some ancient wrecks are marked by their cargo, which lies half hidden in poseidon grass, others are betrayed only by a subtle change of gradient in a sandy expanse and perhaps the protruding neck of a jar.

In the diffused light of this world without an horizon the diver has to develop a new sense of direction. It is important for him to be able to make his way back to the boat or shore when his air runs out. He can surface to take bearings, but only as a last resort, because frequent changes of depth are inadvisable for physiological reasons. Moreover, as we have seen, it is difficult to swim for long distances on the surface. A sense of submarine direction is almost as inexplicable as the sensitive line on a fish. It is acquired gradually, like the ability to gauge depth. Analysis might show a bump of locality to be based on visual observation: of the way the sand is ribbed and of infinitesimal changes in gradient. Divers differ in their adaptation to environment. I think I rely on observation for my orientation under water, but others say they carry in their minds a picture of the coast, even if they are far from it and think, 'Now I am swimming away from Marseille, out to sea off Cassis', and so on.

Such is the Mediterranean diver: even professionals differ in the north. This is noticeable in their conversation, which often runs on mechanical solutions to their problems: 'Have you heard of the latest gadget? You stick a homing device into your ears. It goes pip, pip. The pips tell you where you are in relation to the boat. So simple.' Diving in England, I was astonished to hear a salvage man say that he didn't know what a sponge looked like, for calcareous varieties grow even in the Channel. These differences are not hard to explain. In waters where visibility is limited to a few feet and where professional work amounts to specific jobs, like cutting a propeller off a wreck, there is neither the opportunity nor the reason for acquiring skills which are basically visual.

Northern amateurs are also different in kind: they are trained in swimming-baths for ultimate sorties into turbid water or a fortnight's holiday in the Mediterranean. Training in a pool would be boring if stunts were not invented to keep the pupils amused. Most of these are based on legitimate safety precautions. People are taught how to take their apparatus off and put it on again under water and encouraged to swim around without their masks, bravely getting chlorine into their eyes and up their noses. Their training may stand them in good stead, for they will survive loss of equipment and perhaps be less subject to '*affollement*' or sudden panic in depth, which causes quite a few accidents among novices in the south. They will not, on the other hand, be very useful on jobs which require that adaptation to surroundings inherent in Mediterranean training.

The swimming-bath contingent also acquire tricks less easy to justify. Once, on returning to Lebanon, I visited the French-trained divers who ran the local air compressor. In awe they told me, 'Another English woman passed through since your last visit. She was a marvellous diver. We went out with her, and she opened and drank a bottle of beer at 15 metres!' A reverent silence followed this anecdote. None of us had dived with anyone who ate and drank under water, nor had it ever occurred to us to try. We did know that it could be done, because Lotte Hass had once gracefully swallowed a banana in front of a film camera. The two schools of divers seldom mix. It takes time to realize that people who can do such clever things are not able to perform duties which come naturally to a novice in the south.

A more serious aspect of this situation is the training of scientists, who, in increasing numbers, are extending their field of research to the sea. Until the invention of the aqualung, ichthyology was virtually confined to the study of corpses in bottles. This was unrewarding, as many fish are like chameleons in life and all change colour after death. Moreover, it is impossible to observe the habits of a living creature out of its natural surroundings. Geologists too have reason to work underwater and now, in theory, all these people have the opportunity. Practice is another matter; unless scientists train in marine research centres on the coast, they cannot hope to become familiar even with one type of sea. However, in those sciences where field-work consists mainly in observation and the taking of samples, centres of specialized underwater research are coming into existence, notably in America, where diving is becoming an accepted part of a scientist's training.

Without entering into a discussion about whether or not archaeology is a science, we must recognize the fundamental difference between the practice of excavation and the kind of research mentioned above. Archaeological work involves the displacement underwater of several hundred tons of sand, rock and, in the case of a wreck, cargo. Not only a sizeable boat and equipment are needed for this heavy labour but also skilled seamen and divers practised in the handling of tools. The scientist himself cannot hope either to rival or to dispense with the services of trained divers. Furthermore, all underwater sites bear a peculiar geological relationship to their surroundings, which it is essential that the excavator should understand. Lastly, for all practical purposes, ancient wreck-formations are a Mediterranean phenomenon, so the peculiarities of this sea have to be appreciated.

The reader may wonder what is the explanation of the many reports of 'excavations of ancient wrecks' that have appeared in the popular Press. Allowing for their sensationalism, I think the answer is to be found in semantics: on land the word 'excavation' implies a limited and methodical investigation of certain buried remains with a view to their being reconstructed, later, on paper. The aims and results of land digs are published in reports, and these, and the methods used, are open to verification. The sites being accessible, other archaeologists are in a position to form an opinion as to how the work was conducted.

Before the aqualung was invented wreck 'excavation' amounted to the salvage of treasure by sponge divers from cargoes such as those which sank off Mahdia and Anticythera; the diver's aim was never to reconstruct the ship itself. Owing to their ignorance of wreck-formations, the first 'excavations' by free divers followed a similar pattern. Their work might be described as a series of exploratory soundings on a wreck site. So far no excavation of an ancient wreck consisting of a buried ship complete with cargo has been carried to conclusion and, of course, no complete archaeological records have ever been published. However, these so-called excavations have made both archaeologists and the public aware of the potentialities of wreck sites. A certain category of diver, but not alack of archaeologist, has gained a comparative experience of submarine remains.

The crops are now ripe, but they will have to be gathered by a combined harvester; archaeologists are not versed in maritime problems, and divers are ignorant of archaeological requirements. Inexpert work by either party would produce a certain amount of evidence, but the great danger is that neither being aware of what he does not understand, neither will know how much he has inadvertently destroyed. The miracle of being able to reach a wreck can turn the strongest head. Ancient wrecks are not inexhaustible, so further amateur experiment should be discouraged.

A diver who makes a technical mistake has the opportunity of recognizing it and correcting himself, since he dives regularly, but a scientist devotes only two months of the year to field-work, and the rest to research and 'writing up'. He may never find out that an operation could have been more efficient. His salvation lies in an intellectual grasp of the problem and an ability to seek out and take professional advice. It is one thing to dive and another to be able to work efficiently underwater. In the first throes of enthusiasm free-diving has been made to look too easy. A sponge diver serves for years as a dresser, ship's boy and life-line tender before he is allowed to go down, but no one has yet written a book called *The Intelligent Scientist's Guide to Underwater Work*! The first professional aqualung divers took hints from salvage men who used standard apparatus. Since then, a generation has grown up which can train its own apprentices. A skilled craftsman clearing a delicate object can, for instance, work in a cloud of mud and at the same time keep a stream of clear water before his eyes by moving his hand in a figure of eight. He draws in the clear water from above his head and simultaneously controls the flow of the sand below with the same movement. This sort of thing has to be taught; it would take years to discover by accident. If a group of objects on an ancient wreck have to be freed from sand and mud so that they can be photographed and drawn the amateur will be unsuccessful, even if the area is no more than a metre square. He will make a series of rabbit holes which it would be disaster to record. On the other hand, a professional diver can peel sand evenly, layer by layer to the appropriate depth.

One solution is, as suggested above, that archaeologists should have an intellectual grasp of diving problems. Mechanization is often put forward as an alternative. Could not a group of objects be cleared by water jet rather than by hand? Possibly they could, but instruments, when indeed they exist, are themselves hard to control. I once heard two well-known divers discuss an electronic device which when used on the bottom might give an accurate assessment of the depth below the sand of the keel of an ancient wreck. Both were educated men, one American and the other French. The latter spontaneously remarked, 'I could tell you that without a machine. I have done it a dozen times and never been wrong.' Their nationalities are significant. Diving reminds one of ballet: Americans have a natural aptitude for both, but just as their classical dance is now recognizably different from the European or Russian tradition, so it is with diving. U.S. divers do have some home waters as clear as the Mediterranean, and spear fishing is popular. All the same, they tend to be more highly mechanized than their European counterparts. It is, however, too early to draw definite conclusions. Universities never seem to flourish by sunny seas, so that an archaeologist from either continent is faced with the same training problems.

Diving scientists are rightly interested in gadgets which will help their work or compensate for their lack of time. Unfortunately, most machines which can be used in depth are both big and, at present, in an experimental stage of development. Big machines are expensive and need a large boat, but worst of all, it takes considerable seamanship to use them. This is yet another skill which scientists cannot expect to possess, but they do appreciate its existence more easily than the craft of diving. The sea revenges ill-advised attempts at mechanization: gadgets are torn from inefficient moorings, pounded and swallowed up. Instruments can be replaced, but the damage inflicted by their inappropriate use is permanent: a Minoan wreck is unique. Instead of listing gadgets for his expedition, the scientist should set aside some of his money to pay for a man who can use them. He should also be prepared to follow that man's advice, even if it sounds unorthodox.

CHAPTER 2

The First Wreck – 'Suckers' – Underwater Propulsors

ARCHAEOLOGICAL method had not started to trouble me when I saw my first wreck. Some of my earliest dives were on a large Roman ship lying at the foot of a rock, now a safety beacon, called the *Balise de la Chretienne.* The *concession*, or permission to dig, had been given to the Cannes Club, which at that time numbered among its most active members such experienced divers as Broussard, Rebikoff, Charvos and Barnier. By the time I saw it, the surface of the site had already been turned upside down from the standpoint of excavation technique. This was in good faith, for there was a sad lack of archaeological guidance. Certain questions immediately occur to anyone who sees a wreck: where did she come from? how many amphorae was she carrying? was there any other cargo on board? what ports did she visit? what is the hull like? . . . and so on. All are valid questions, but archaeologically they have to be taken in a certain order and under strict excavation discipline. If no one puts this to the divers they cannot be blamed for going ahead 'every man for himself' in unbridled enthusiasm.

Before I saw the wreck Dumas, who was interested in hulls, had put down a trench. This was skilfully done, for he is too intelligent a diver to dig at random without first noticing the lie of the ship (see Appendix). Part of the wooden structure was examined, but the importance of the findings was cancelled by the absence of any excavation record and, of course, a disproportionate amount of destruction was entailed. It is impossible to make a vertical trench underwater; the sand falls back into the holes and only reaches equilibrium on a shallow gradient. This rules out the land archaeologist's concept of soundings or trenches with nice, straight walls. In order to see a few centimetres of wood buried under 2 metres of sand about 6 square metres of surface cargo has to be removed. In taking a trench across a section of the hull the destruction of evidence is proportionately greater, for the walls of the trench have to be at an angle of about

40° on either side. The problem is not insuperable. Since those early days Dumas himself has suggested several solutions compatible with archaeological method.

As I had never seen a wreck, I did not notice all this. We were moored above, with a shot-line going down to the part of the site that was being worked. Charvos and Barnier had been doing some job together, so, being a novice incapable of work, it was my lot to go down alone. I crossed Barnier on the line coming up and continued my descent nervously, because it was the first time I had been 'in the blue'. I reached a point when I could see neither surface nor bottom. The depth was about 25 metres where we were. The beacon rock was out of sight, there was no reassuring land mass and the light was dim (it was dawn). Around 15 metres I could just make out the wreck, or rather a tumble of amphorae extending as far as the eye could see. Curiously enough, my first reaction was to estimate the lie of the ship and, what is stranger, my guess proved right. There could have been no logical justification . . . and yet I still wonder. These first impressions are frequently correct. I had been made to swear that I wouldn't leave the shot-line at the bottom as there was current, and that I was carefully to examine a '*poulpe*' at the end where the rope was tied, as I might never see such another. I did not know what a *poulpe* was. Nor was I much wiser when I saw an amorphous, grey, roughly conical lump covering an amphora. Two enormous, dark eyes on top blinked slowly. It was soft, rubbery and immobile. I decided that it must be attached to the jar like a limpet, and resolved to look up the bilingual dictionary when I got home. No sooner was I inside the front door than the children of the house screamed, 'Octopus! It means Octopus!' We all went to bed and had nightmares. I dreamed that it snatched away my mask and tubes.

The object that day was to salvage a large, anchor stock which must have lain in the bows of the ship. As usual, the crew had not had time to drop it before she sank. That they had tried to do so was indicated by adzes and various cutting implements scattered round the anchor (such was our fanciful interpretation). No one but an expert would have noticed the tools, for they were covered with thick concretions. There were quantities of similar concretions in the rough sand under the poseidon grass, which at one time had grown over the entire wreck. Barnier lifted these particular lumps quite by chance, and when he realized they were hollow he cracked one open. The section revealed a blackened hollow of regular shape; to a layman it looked as though the iron implement had 'dissolved' in the water at the same rate as the concretions formed. Both concretions were perfect moulds, preserving within them the shape of the tool and even part of a wooden handle. He made casts and sent them to the Boreli Museum. This was the first observation of a phenomenon which is now widely known (Plate 2).

It was Barnier too who discovered the anchor. He had been pottering about in the tall poseidon grass when he came on a bit of lead; he pulled, but it did not yield a millimetre, even to his considerable strength. Realizing that it must be part of a very large and buried anchor, he decided, with other members of the Club, to raise it. All winter they worked on the spot at week-ends and whenever they had a free day. The poseidon grass had to be cleared and then the sand. They rigged a home-made suction pump. These things now tend to be called 'air-lifts', which is accurate, but in France they will always be known by the shorter and more vivid word: '*suceuse*'. Compressed air is forced down from the surface through a small, outer hose connected at the bottom to the larger tube. On the return journey the air expands as the pressure of water decreases. The principle involved is that when air is forced into the bottom of a half-submerged tube it causes, within the tube, an air–water emulsion which rises until the pressure of the column of emulsion equals at its base the pressure of the water at the same level. It is this force that carries to the surface sand or objects below the nozzle.[1] In theory the operation is simple, but in practice highly complicated. The machine does or does not work, according to the angle at which it is rigged in the water. At the surface it has, of course, to be attached to a low-powered compressor on the boat and is usually positioned in the water by floats, such as oil drums. The diameter of the pipe is very important, and must vary according to the consistency of the sand or mud on which it is used, and also according to the type of work intended: whether it is to free large objects, clear wood, dig a sizeable trench or any other of a number of possible uses. Further, the force is affected by depth, as air expands at different rates at different water pressures, so that the machine's performance varies from one part of a wreck to another. Taken together, these factors make an air-lift beyond simple mechanical control. Only expert judgement can modify its performance according to changing circumstances at the bottom. The effect which winds and currents have on this contraption can be left to the reader's imagination. With all its faults, the air-lift

[1] For a more detailed description of this machine and its adaptation for archaeological purposes see Frédéric Dumas' *Deep Water Archaeology* (Routledge, 1962), pp. 33–41. Dumas also gives an exhaustive bibliography for these machines.

EARLY DAYS AT CANNES

1 (opposite). *Cannes Club divers play with octopuses they have lured out of amphorae on a Roman wreck where these creatures had made their homes. Charvoz uses a torpedo-flash camera designed by Rebikoff (see p. 25).*

2 (verso; top left). *One of the concretions found by the lead anchor stock at Anthéor. A break showed it to be hollow and contain part of a wooden handle. This natural mould was caused when the metal 'dissapeared' and the concretions formed; when a plaster cast was taken an axe emerged (see p. 20 and Appendix).*

3 (bottom left). *Georges Barnier with the 6-foot lead anchor stock he found on the same wreck, known as the Chretienne A at Anthéor.*

4 (recto). *The same stock at the bottom of the sea with its wooden crown still in position (compare Fig. 13). The picture was taken after the find had been cleared of weed and concretions and just before it was raised. A diver's lead belt was left as a marker beside the central hole in the stock (see pp. 20, 21).*

5 (verso). *Barnier on* Pegasus *during its first sea trial in 1955.*

6 (below). *A more natural form of propulsion—a sting-ray in action. The dark spike at the end of its tail contains the same venom as a viper's.*

1. G. Barnier

2.

3. G. Barnier

4. G. Barnier

5. *G. Barnier*

6. *H. Broussard*

remains an essential tool for submarine excavation, because, unlike the gentler water jet, it is the only instrument which can remove several hundred tons of sand from one place and dump them elsewhere down current.

To be preserved at all, wrecks must lie in deep water beyond the ravages of winds and currents. They must also be buried in sand. On a rocky bottom wood is broken up or eaten by sea animals. Sand holds both wood and cargo together in a significant relationship. Since oxygen is reduced in certain layers of sand, it also helps to preserve organic matter. Sand burial is common in the Mediterranean, where ancient ships are found almost intact; in the Pacific a 'wreck' means something quite different, usually only the remains of a cargo. Lifting a hundred tons of sand on land would be a big undertaking, but under water the task is far more daunting. Recently Dumas and I were discussing an excavation which was to be run on strictly scientific principles: he said, 'I mustn't tell them (the archaeologists) how almost impossibly long and difficult submarine excavation really is, or they will never attempt it.' At that time good archaeologists, who are always fully occupied on land, were doubtful whether the type of evidence which could be had from wrecks justified any effort.

At Anthéor the Cannes Club certainly made their *suceuse* work, but it may have sucked up more than sand, and it took the whole winter to clear one anchor (Plate 4). By the time I arrived I saw the huge lead stock lying loose. There was something else in the sand, at right angles to it, which looked like wood. The stock was about 2 metres along, and on land five men could hardly lift it (Plate 3). The divers spent all day roping, then floating it up to 6 metres below the surface. Being too heavy to get on to the boat, it had to be towed underwater to the nearest harbour. Sausage-shaped nylon bags (which were Barnier's speciality; he even used them in swimming lessons) and jerry cans were filled with compressed air under water and attached to the anchor to lessen its weight. Such floats are either filled from a spare bottle, which the diver takes down with him, or more often than not from the bottle he is wearing. He takes out his mouthpiece, puts it under the open bag or jerry can and keeps it there for as long as he can hold his breath.

At last the anchor was gently raised. We set sail for Agay, which was twenty minutes away, though it seemed more, so great was our anxiety that the floats might burst and the anchor plunge back into even deeper water. Another delay occurred at the port, for the annual *joutes* were in progress. These must be the last survival of medieval tournaments, a poor man's jousting. They are still run on the lines set forth in the *Livre du Roi René* of Provence. Boats with a projecting plank attached to their sterns are substituted for horses. Teams of fishermen, dressed in white, man the oars, while one of their number, holding a long lance, stands on the tip of the plank, braced against a rail. The two boats charge each other at full speed, and one of the knights is dislodged by the other's lance. He is fished out, his clothes dripping wet, and another man takes his place, until victory for one team is declared.

When this was over, we gingerly manoeuvred ourselves up to the jetty, where there was a crane. Most of our bottles were empty; I went down on a reserve and was surprised to see that the jerry cans were twisted and battered, while many of the nylon bags had collapsed under the strain of the journey. It was too late to take the anchor back to Cannes and, being heavy, it would have damaged the smart yacht which we were using, so it was left at Agay overnight. When the stock was examined Barnier noted that there was something very odd about the way it was cast. The importance of his observation was brought home to me later, when I myself became interested in anchors. Both inclination and policy led to a celebration in the form of a round of drinks with the fishermen at the local *bistrô*. They had enforced the law earlier in the day: within a few minutes of our arrival over the wreck they came out to demand our concession paper and would have given us short shrift had it been out of order. This done, they moored some way off and continued to watch us through binoculars, to make sure that we raised only antiques and not the odd grouper or lobster. Would that anti-pillage regulations were still as strictly enforced!

Later the anchor was brought to Cannes in triumph, on a suitable boat.

'What's that?' asked the Port Authority.

'A Roman lead anchor.'

'Well, you know you have to pay duty on stuff imported from Italy.'

The Museum at Marseille was notified and the anchor provisionally left in the Club meeting-room. Being an unwieldy white elephant, it was not claimed and remained for many years in the Martinez Hotel in Cannes, until the Club presented it to the local Souquet Museum. It was the largest lead stock found in France. Barnier had taken excellent photographs of the salvage, and these were published later in the *Illustrated London News*.[1]

There was always some excuse to go back to that wreck. The half-buried object I had seen lying at right angles to the anchor stock had been the crown of

[1] *Illustrated London News*, August 21, 1954.

its wooden stem. We raised this, but though covered with wet sacks, it broke in the boat. Looking back, I wish we had searched the sand more carefully for the other parts, but work was not systematic. Such anchors are not interesting in themselves, unless they are marked; this one was not. On other occasions we returned to the place to take photographs. American magazines were still in the market, and Rebikoff's big torpedo-flash cameras were themselves photogenic. On one occasion divers coaxed or frightened the octopus colony out of the homes they had made in amphorae, so that the fantastic mêlée of human beings and cephalopods could be recorded. These photographs, it was hoped, would sell particularly well, as there is a belief in the Mediterranean that octopuses guard wrecks. If so, they make bad watchdogs, for in their own surroundings they are graceful, playful and as sensuous as cats when tickled (Plate 1).

Dimitri Rebikoff, a brilliant marine engineer, is also well known for his books and films. When I returned to Cannes a year or so later, Barnier told me that Rebikoff was about to give his 'Pegasus' its first sea trial, and there might be room on the boat for me. 'Pegasus' was a torpedo-shaped underwater motor (Plate 5). We set off for the Ile Ste. Marguerite in the late afternoon. Rebikoff's converted fishing-boat was filled by a compressor and piled with delicate machinery. He and Barnier were, in turn, to try out the propulsor while Rebikoff's wife and I kept close to it with the torpedo-cameras. Whichever man was not actually riding 'Pegasus' was to photograph the three of us.

The new machine was almost perfectly balanced, that is to say, though it was slightly larger than a tall man, it weighed nothing in the water; even I could pick it up and bring it back to the boat, in a free dive from a depth of about 5 metres. Its rear had a tendency to sink, which Rebikoff corrected by tying on cork floats. In motion, it could reach uncomfortable speeds, enough to tear a diver's mask off his face. Since this prototype the design has been perfected; there are enclosed models, and others with television cameras, which are directed by remote control from the surface. The torpedo-cameras were slightly smaller, one took colour slides and the other cinematic film. Both had floodlights in the nose, little electric propellers in their tails and two hand-controls. You pressed one to start shooting with the floods and the other for the propeller. Rebikoff, not without reason, was nervous about my competence to handle these machines. On the boat he would shout 'Elephant!' as one of us tried to ease his cramped position and leaned on something delicate. When I was about to get into the water with a camera he said earnestly: 'It's quite simple, you just use it like a machine-gun. This controls the floods and that the propeller. If you touch the former you will waste five pounds worth of film per minute.'

Under the water we started to deploy, Mme Rebikoff and I trying to keep close to Barnier on the 'Pegasus'. Night fell and the rocks took on an even weirder loveliness than by day. When it was quite dark they were lit by the strong floodlights. Suddenly I realized that I was being left behind. I saw Ada Rebikoff with her floodlight on near Barnier, and Rebikoff with his camera cocked, waiting for them to pass. I must have had a sort of brain-storm, for I gripped both controls and zoomed into the picture. Someone poked me and, conscience-stricken, I took my hands off the light control; after all, I had never used a machine-gun! It had been a wasteful but glorious moment. Rebikoff, I gathered, had suffered from other inconsiderate hangers-on and was generous in his forgiveness. But all this has nothing to do with the wreck at Anthéor and happened a year or so later.

To return to the wreck: despite the fun and games, questions nagged at us; divers would suddenly be seized by an urge to know more about this Roman ship and dig furiously for an intact wine-filled jar or a marked stopper. It was a tradition in the Cannes Club, told to all new members, that one such stopper had been found and traced back to a merchant who had been staying at Pompeii when he received a letter reporting the loss of his ship. Disaster followed at Pompeii itself, but the letter was preserved.[1] Systematic research was out of the question. The ship's rigging, for instance, must have lain as it fell and become buried in sand or covered by concretions, but all trace of it had been dispersed or destroyed with the surface layers of the wreck. Nor was it possible to see the way in which the cargo of amphorae had been loaded. Everything was turned upside down.

I am narrating the way in which certain ideas developed out of an accumulation of experience, so it would be premature to finish the story of this wreck, a story which I can now piece together, having revisited the place nine years after the events described. It has become known as the 'Chretienne A', being the first of three wrecks discovered around the base of that safety beacon off Anthéor. The history of wreck 'A' makes sad reading; I include it as an appendix, where it comes appropriately after the final chapter on wooden hulls.

[1] Monsieur M. Heurgon has traced the stopper bearing an Oscan inscription, through a memorial at Pompeii, to the Lassii family.

PART II

ANCHORS AND ANCHORAGES

'Four anchors were cast out from the stern and others were to be cast out from the foreship.' [1]

[1] St Paul's Wreck, Acts xxvii. 28.

THE ANCHOR DRAWINGS IN PART II

The relative sizes of the ancient anchors which I have drawn are significant; unfortunately the format of this book makes it impossible to reproduce them all to the same scale. The later composite anchors have had to be reproduced at half the scale of the stone anchors; that is to say the 1-metre drawn scales on the first group of figures are the same size as the 2-metre scales on the second. Even so, the Nemi anchors fill an entire page, whereas several stone anchors (printed twice as big) could be grouped together in the same space. To remind the reader of this change, I have included a representative stone anchor (drawn to the same scale) with the Nemi anchors.

This discrepancy in size and weight of the anchors does not necessarily imply a difference in the size of the ships from which they came. It is apparent that the Nemi anchors could not have been used on a small ship, but the converse need not hold true of stone anchors. The discrepancy does, however, imply differing methods of navigation and of port facilities over the period covered by these anchors.

CHAPTER 3

Road to Damascus – Anchorages – Information from Fishermen – Lebanese Divers – Stone Anchors – Byblos – Adonis' Cave

AFTER Anthéor, some form of diving became a necessary part of my life. In the circumstances archaeology had its uses for me. I took the subject for granted, as a result of being brought up in the Levant. Coming to Europe as a child, I visited museums as others the cinema and invented a solitary game of 'Happy Families', or finding relationships between Egyptian mummies. A point was scored by proving the specimen in, say, a convent in Fiesole, to be the uncle of another in the British Museum; my criteria were vague, though I treasured a book on Egyptology. The Coptic mummy in the British Museum, crouched and with golden curls, cured (so the attendant ghoulishly explained) in a 'different way', was my despair. He had no family and distressed me as an outsider.

To begin with, submerged remains were only an excuse to get underwater. I discovered that since I could draw, archaeology was a means of earning a return ticket to the Middle East. Working as a minor technician does not necessarily enlighten: the draughtsman is told to measure a few stones, draw them with a nice, thick line, hatch and cross-hatch, then hand over the finished result. After that, unless pursued by a hound of heaven, he is free to go to a café, or have a swim. The archaeologist knows what it is all about, but the draughtsman need have no idea unless he deliberately reads the subject or comes across the excavation report some years later.

After deep diving in France circumstances threw me into the shallow waters of ancient harbours, where I learned that there was more to submarine archaeology than sunken ships. Indeed, wreck excavation must come later, with a better understanding of marine conditions. It requires not only consummate diving technique, but if records are to be made (and these are the *sine qua non* of archaeology), it is bound to take years and be proportionately expensive. On land the archaeological interpretation of a wreck is simple, for it is a hoard of contemporary objects. By contrast, harbour excavation has fewer diving problems, but baffles the individual workman and presents archaeologists with a series of complex questions relating to both method and scholarship. In my case I went on amassing experience without realizing the implications until a certain land dig forced me to reassess the past.

In 1957 I reported for work at Jericho, for the last of six seasons of excavation by Miss Kathleen Kenyon. Four months later I flew back to Lebanon. Normally, I would have returned by the Damascus road, but at that time the Syrian frontier was closed to British passports. Though I was high above the scene of Paul's conversion, it happened that I, too, experienced a minor change of heart. There were two archaeologists from Jericho on the same plane, and one of them had a copy of Cesnola's *Antiquities of Cyprus*. He read out a passage about a ship laden with Cypriot bibelots destined for the Metropolitan Museum in New York which sank somewhere off the Syrian coast. Very interesting; Cesnola had good taste, it would be a lovely cargo to salvage, and yet it now seemed great fun but irrelevant. At Jericho I had caught a glimpse of scientific archaeology on a grand scale.

From a personal point of view the months of hard work were not entirely enjoyable, nor had they been unpleasant. The experience was analogous to my first dive in a well. I already knew Jericho, so the impact of the surroundings was not overwhelming. The previous year, when I was in the district, I became interested in the possible sites of Sodom and Gomorrah under the Dead Sea and intended to look at them, with my bottle, after Jericho. The scheme was intriguing, because of problems raised by the buoyancy of the water, but for various reasons it never materialized. The tombs where I worked at Jericho were underneath the refugee village, a dispiriting place. On top of this, I do not particularly enjoy community life and I had been ill. Yet at the end of it all I found my attitude changed. I had, during the Jericho excavation, seen a huge machine being driven with almost superhuman and impersonal determination. Like some electronic brain, it had, within its limits, given answers to the questions submitted, divulging no less than twenty-seven civilizations. The machine was not an end in itself; there is often more merit in being able to pose a question than in finding the answer. Then again, when answers are found, they have to be co-ordinated and interpreted.

The Jericho to which I refer is a *tell*, or artificial hillock, created by a series of mud-brick towns, each built on the ruins of the last. By slicing into, or through, this formation at strategic points the number, sequence and characteristics of successive civilizations were revealed. The face of the deepest trench, some 50 feet, was stuck with little paper tags indicating almost imperceptible strata.

Though it was the machinery which produced the evidence now recorded in Miss Kenyon's books that struck me, I cannot resist a reference, however impressionistic, to the results. Some types of settlements were comparable with existing sites, others were unknown. In the lower levels there were houses with burnished plaster floors, or with walls made of curiously shaped 'hog's-back bricks'. Skulls with the mandibles removed, the remainder covered with painted plaster and cowry shells for eyes, were found in groups under certain houses. What had they meant? As yet no one can say, but they antedate known forms of sculpture. At the very bottom, on bed-rock, was a walled town with an almost medieval-style defence tower. According to the carbon 14 tests, it dated at the latest from 9000 B.C. Before this discovery it had been assumed that men did not live in organized, settled communities at such an early period.

Archaeologists toiled in the dust of these trenches, endlessly recording, surrounded by workmen and basket boys who carried the earth up to dumps. At the camp there was more recording. Each sherd and bead was numbered, photographed, drawn, described and entered into a register. Physical anthropologists, a mining expert, zoologists, preservation technicians and a host of others sifted the evidence in improvised laboratories. The tombs were some distance from the *tell*. In these would be found the personal furnishings and accoutrements that the dead had been allowed to take with them. Houses on the *tell* could be refurnished, at least hypothetically, from this evidence. Interpretation would go on for many a long year; the job of the field worker was to record in such a way as to make this possible.

Most of the tombs found when I was there were sizeable, rock-cut chambers, giving off a vertical shaft about 6 metres deep. Usually one could stand upright. Their contents varied from sixteen skeletons well provided with jewellery, food and furniture to a few long bones and vertebrae mixed with animal remains. These latter tombs were in the majority, and very depressing they became. What aberration had prompted such baffling arrangements? The chambers were just as large as those containing more rational forms of burial. What had happened to the rest of the body, and why had a lamp been left? for this invariably remained on a shelf near the entrance. Crazier still were tombs where there were quantities of large, family teapots and very little else.

Though far from cool, the chambers were relatively quiet places to work in. Sometimes they reminded me of wrecks. Sometimes, as I stretched the measuring tapes across a floor crowded with bones and delicate bric-à-brac, I longed not only for a sensation of water against my flesh, but for the weightless mobility of diving. In these tombs I was seeing objects representing a civilization, but each had been selected by the people who buried their dead. The motives behind the choice were apparent and all too human. Fine weapons and jewellery denoted generosity; in other tombs the relatives had been mean and provided only a minimum required by decency. The pots had been flawed or cracked in antiquity. How different from wrecks, where everything had been in current use! Both are instances of closed groups, or objects which were sealed off at a given date and preserved by chance for posterity.

However, the importance of a tomb, fascinating though its contents may be, is only relative to the information about its date and background civilization wrested from the *tell*. It followed that the same must go for wrecks. There would be a kind of equation: as tomb furnishings are to the *tell*, so wrecks are to . . . well, what? The simple answer is: to the economic history of their period, but what archaeological evidence is there of this in the sea? Ports of course; then the pattern made by wrecks on the sea-bed, if this could be recorded. Finally, there is ancient jetsam in the sea; lost anchors and, when these are grouped on shallows, anchorages. Here was, perhaps, the meaning of the *Tombant du Vengeur* with its cemetery of anchors . . . the *Plâteau des Chêvres*, the long submarine reef off Marseille, and *Paşa Rock*. Were they not evidence of trade routes and methods of navigation?

We are now in a position to investigate these places; Jal, the nineteenth-century historian, was not. He was, however, a naval man with a fund of common sense. Though his *Archéologie Navale* was published in 1840, in it he anticipates the discovery and explains the existence of offshore anchorages. He reasons that, for a vessel of 500 tons to carry twenty anchors, as they were known to do, seems absurd, but when the construction of early ships was taken into account, it would be seen that they could neither get under way fast enough when caught by a storm near land nor could they sail against the wind (which is liable to change in the course of a single day in the Mediterranean). They were therefore forced to turn about and cast anchor where they might. He continues:

> What quantities of anchors they would lose, for they often had to moor fore and aft, having no room to swing in those forced anchorages which were frequently in the middle of shoals, or on dangerous reefs which they could not avoid.[1]

Frédéric Dumas has made an analysis of submarine archaeological sites, founded on his wide experience as one of the three pioneer free-divers. He differentiates between offshore reefs and shoals, where ships dropped anchor and waited for a change of wind, and the sheltered creeks where they took refuge during severe storms. The latter he describes as follows:

> At certain points along the Mediterranean coast, the sea bed is littered with ancient débris: broken pottery, anchors and other objects. At first glance one might suppose they came from a wreck, but the way in which the sherds are dispersed and their differing dates, indicate that we are looking at a place where the ancients dropped anchor, either in order to take shelter or to transact business with the land. Their mooring was marked by certain accidents: things fell overboard or were jettisoned, while the seamen took advantage of calm water to tidy their load.[2]

This distinction between sites is important, because objects found on an inshore anchorage will probably be on a sandy bottom, and if so, they will be stratified. Their disposition will throw light on the changing pattern of trade with the land. If, however, a diver now lifts what he sees on the surface of the sand, evidence, and indeed the situation of the site itself, will be lost for future and more methodical research. Even if he tries to plot at a certain point an amphora neck which he is removing, such a record, made in a wide expanse of deepish water, would not be sufficiently accurate to allow the sherd to be replaced on the same spot a year or so later.

Professional divers, either naval or commercial, are familiar with such anchorages, but so far they are unrecorded and have never been subjected to archaeological investigation. On offshore sites sometimes stone anchors and sometimes lead stocks preponderate; the latter, often caught on the side of a cliff, are seldom found below 30 metres. The more we know about ancient anchors, the better our understanding of these sites in relation to sea lanes and methods of navigation at various periods.

In France gentlemen-divers acquire more prestige from a lead anchor stock than an amphora, though the latter looks nicer in the home and has commercial value. In some of the poorer countries of the Levant divers melt down Roman

[1] A. Jal, *Archéologie Navale*, Vol. II, p. 169.
[2] Frédéric Dumas, *Deep Water Archaeology*, Routledge and Kegan Paul, London, 1962.

stocks and use them for their own leads; I have never seen a lead stock in Turkish waters. This snatching of objects from their context destroys much historical evidence. On the other hand, the sheer quantity of anchors fished up in the last twenty years gives importance to a rather recondite subject: anchors take on archaeological significance. It is now evident that many stones found on land, hitherto described as 'pierced', 'cult objects' or even 'loom weights', are really anchors. Sufficient quantities have been amassed for a scholar to busy himself on a type-series. Were this done, future underwater archaeologists would be able to deduce from ancient anchors, found on a wreck, something of the structure, size and date of the ship that lies below the sand.

Dr Moll was unfortunate, for he published his *History of the Anchor*[1] in 1927, when sources were mostly documentary. Ironically, it was the year that Mussolini started to drain Lake Nemi, an operation which eventually revealed not only two Roman ships but also their anchors complete with component parts—metal, wood and rope, *in situ*. The discovery disproved some of Moll's theories.

After my conversion at Jericho I started to take notes on ancient anchors as I saw them, in their context, either on land or sea. When compared, the results were interesting. The bottom of the Egyptian Harbour at Tyre in Lebanon and the small, natural anchorage at Tabarja, where I was staying after arrival from Jericho, were littered with stones of various shapes and sizes, pierced with one or more holes. It was likely that they were anchors, but were they ancient and, if so, of what date? Of greater interest is that the stones fell into two categories: those round or triangular, pierced by a single hole, and a smaller, flatter, rectangular variety with up to five holes. The fishermen had no doubt as to their use: the first were rock- and the second sand-anchors.

The single, itinerant diver has an advantage over archaeologists because of his special relationship with the locals. He is not even potentially their employer. In the Levant, where archaeology has been practised for a century, looting and forging antiquities are profitable industries; peasants quickly size up any individual examining sherds on a seemingly disinterested afternoon walk. When an archaeologist actually hires a team of labourers he may be on very cordial terms with them. On occasion they explain an artifact that puzzled him, but which is still in use in the district or has been used within living memory. However, such opinions must be taken with a pinch of salt, because they come from men who want to keep their jobs. Further, the courtesies of the East require that people

[1] A. Moll, 'History of the Anchor', *Mariner's Mirror,* Vol. XIII, p. 4.

should say things they think their visitor wants to hear. Levantine seamen do not yet regard archaeology as potentially profitable. A diver, once he is accepted, and he is accepted only after some sort of test, is on equal terms with fishermen or sponge-men, with whom he shares some of the same skills or vocation. He may also be their guest. In countries with a Moslem tradition the guest is not under the same obligation to his hosts as he would be in the West. His presence may or may not entertain them, but it allows them to discharge their religious duty of hospitality.

Diving, like war, is 90 per cent boredom, for there are long delays. The boat leaves before dawn and arrives over the sponge bed at first light. The captain tells his men the order in which they are to dive. Each diver has to be dressed; then while he is on the bottom one man tends the life-line while the others sit round and talk. Conversation on board is not brilliant, but it is less inhibited than in the home, and ranges widely from technical matters to politics.

I remember one exquisitely calm morning in Lebanon when I went out with sponge divers. The 'Chief', a Maronite Christian, was, like most of his compatriots, called Georges. The sponge bed was somewhere off the mouth of the Dog River. To locate it, Georges put his ear to the bottom of the boat, even though the depth was 40 metres. Sponges grow on rock; if he heard a swish-swish, it meant we were over sand, whereas a crack-crack meant rock. At last we found the bed and anchored. We could see Beirut to the south, over oil-calm sea. The mountains of Lebanon rose straight from the coast beside us. Diving was by *narghilé*, that is to say, though they used a similar type of Cousteau–Gagnan valve as free-divers, air was supplied through a hose from a low-powered compressor on the boat. This had the advantage of allowing longer working time on the bottom and a boat uncluttered by bottles. The first man went down with his sponge basket and the '*telephoniste*' played out the hose. There was, of course, no telephone communication. Lebanese, like Swiss, are by law bilingual: in any case words applying to modern mechanics are, in most Arab countries, borrowed loosely from the erstwhile 'Imperialist' language. I once asked a Jordanian working in Lebanon whether he found the colloquial Arabic very different. 'Oh, yes,' he replied, 'in Jordan we say "lorry", whereas they say "*camion*" here.'

That morning conversation was desultory; we watched the diver's bubbles on the surface of the water and the hose being played out or rewound as he moved about the bottom. In Lebanon they are up to date and the country is rich enough to import the newest equipment. It is the only place I know where sponge men use *narghilés*. Theoretically, diving time was not limited as it would have been by a bottle. In practice, it was restricted to half an hour by an old alarm clock in a glass-fronted box in the prow. Unlike other sponge divers, Georges was aware of decompression laws, though the tables he used would not have passed muster at the Admiralty. He made me promise, quite rightly, to spend five minutes at 3 metres when I came up, though I was using bottles and could not have exceeded the danger limit. On other boats casualties among divers were pretty high.

We gazed across at the town and lazily picked out landmarks; the Lazzareah building, a local skyscraper, St George's Hotel on the point, the Campus of the American University. 'That's Ashrafeah, where I live . . . on the hill,' said Youssef. As he pointed a white cloud started to form over the central part of the skyline. It was 1958, at the time of the troubles in Lebanon. The morning mist had dispersed, the cloud grew like a cumulus. Three aeroplanes, jets, hovered over the Moslem quarter of Basta. 'It is American snow,' said one of the men, but the Americans had not yet landed, and did not do so for another fortnight. 'If the Americans had not prevented the French and the British from going up to Cairo and finishing Nasser we would not have this trouble now,' said another. 'They are killing each other while we sit in the sun. If only everyone were like us.'

The cloud took about three hours to disperse; it seemed incredibly remote. On that calm sea it was almost impossible to imagine violence; moreover, the drama was played out as far as we were concerned in complete silence. Maroun was preparing to dive: either to mitigate or to convince himself of the reality of what was happening, he observed, 'Fanatical boys jump over the barricades shouting "Allah!" They don't bother to shoot straight, because Allah will guide their hand.' He disappeared and probably forgot about it in the cool detachment of the sea. I do not think these remarks have any profound, political significance. Indeed, the mention of the British may have been prompted by the aforesaid Oriental politeness, but at that particular time none but divers in open sea would have dared to comment freely in quite the same tone. We raised anchor, fished on two more beds, exchanged bread and olives, tomatoes, sardines and my chocolate and then returned to Tabarja in the evening and I to my subject of anchors.

Stone anchors are not the only puzzling objects which divers find on the bottom. When I was in Crete with an underwater expedition organized by the British School of Archaeology in Athens we picked up a marble quoit. Was it ancient and what possible use could it serve? Happily, as I have said, divers get on friendly terms with local seamen, but their chances of eliciting reliable information diminish if they belong to an organized group. However, on this occasion a Greek member of the team did get the answer. The quoit was modern; the fisherman said he had some on his own boat and used them to slip over fouled lines, which they disentangled as they fell. After this I started to see quoits all over the place (though never out of Greece) and even met one in a cellar of the Athens Archaeological Museum, lying with anchors and pottery which had been raised, together with the famous bronzes from the wreck at Anticythera. The quoit had probably been dropped from a modern *caïque*, like an iron grapnel also found on the wreck and catalogued with the antiquities.[1]

Lebanese sponge divers and others like them explained the difference between primitive rock- and sand-anchors, and demonstrated their use. Caïques and other small craft in the Eastern Mediterranean do not, in the normal way, sail at night. They put in at creeks where there is a well, since they carry only one jar of fresh water, which has to be refilled. Boats lie at anchor as near as they can get to the shore and usually over sand. The men sleep on board; sometimes they climb down into the shallow water and wade ashore to get water, and sometimes they use the dinghy. Sponge boats leave their port and fish in this way for months on end. I have never heard of one of these boats being beached while on a cruise. If the weather were rough they simply did not work, and if calm the tiniest sand-anchor was sufficient mooring. If the light were dim or the water cloudy they listened, as they did on sponge beds, to see whether they were on rock or sand and anchored accordingly.

However, my first lesson in the use of sand-anchors came when I found one in the bay at Tabarja. It was small and made of concrete (Fig. 1). Edouard, one of the divers, explained it to me. A rope is passed through a hole cut diagonally across one corner. The remaining holes are pierced vertically and bits of wood stuck through them. These sticks project on either side and grip into the sand. A stone weighing around 10 kilograms is sufficient to engage this type of anchor and hold a boat about 6 metres long. These anchors can be dismantled and stowed. They are also cheap and simple to make, but they do have to be made. In a

[1] See also that invaluable book *Diccionario de Artes de Pesca de España y son Posesiones*, by Benigno Rodrigues Santamaria, Madrid, 1923. Stone rings are still used in the Balearic islands and Algeciras, while lead rings of the same size are found at Cartagena. The latter have an outer diameter of 30 centimetres, and a square cut, pierced protuberance for their rope. From this information we can distinguish the function of the two sizes of lead rings found on Roman wrecks: the smaller were attached to the sails to take the guide ropes, while the larger were for freeing fouled ropes underwater.

country as prosperous as Lebanon most fishermen can afford a metal anchor. Moreover, a metal anchor bought in a shop may be a 'status symbol'; in any case, the stone or concrete sand-anchors are disappearing. A similar type of stone anchor is in current use in the Persian Gulf. Its survival there is explained by poverty, and its form by the shortage of wood and readily available metal.

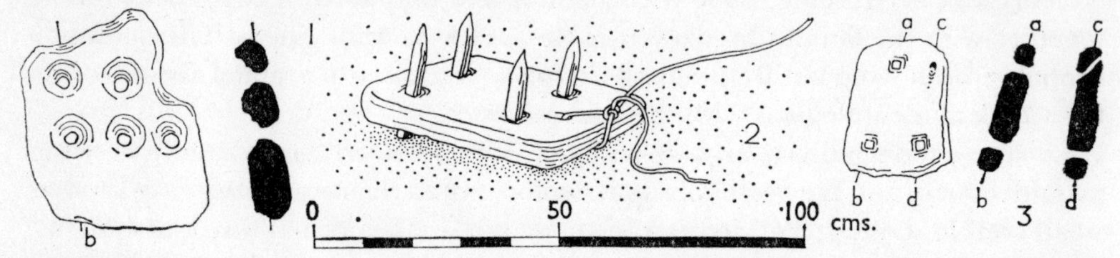

1. (1) Pierced, grey pebble-stone found in the sea at Mochlos in Crete; possibly a sand-anchor. (2) A sand-anchor in use: wooden spikes, stuck through the holes in the stone, grip the bottom. (3) The modern concrete sand-anchor found in Tabarja harbour.

The modern concrete Lebanese sand-anchor immediately reminded me of a stone which I had found some years earlier near a Minoan settlement in Crete [Fig. 1 (1)]. One corner had been broken, an occurrence easily explained if it had been weakened by the usual diagonal rope-hole. Once broken, it was probably put to another use. Because it was found in a rock-cut fish tank it was described in the official report as a 'stone grille'[1] which allowed water to flow while keeping the fish in the tank. It seemed odd at the time that in a region where there had always been so much wood this grille should have been laboriously cut out of hard pebble stone.

Certainly when we left the place, which was called Mochlos, to return by *caïque* to Agios Nikolaos, a journey of about seven hours, it became apparent that most of the Minoan settlements along that part of the coast were by beaches where a sand-anchor could have been used. Indeed, we stopped and dropped a small anchor on the sand at more than one of these bays. The sad moral of this story is that it will be difficult to collect a body of evidence about ancient sand-anchors owing to their very nature. They were used on sand, and only in shallow water; consequently, if they were lost it would be on sand. Other anchors which come from the sea are not only bigger but they are also found on rock, or on sandy bottoms at considerable depth, usually on wrecks. A small, flat stone in

[1] John Leatham and Sinclair Hood, *Journal of the British School at Athens*, Vol. 53–54, 1958–59, p. 263.

shallow water is not going to show after a few thousand years: it will be covered with silt. The only hope of finding datable sand-anchors will be in Bronze Age wrecks, assuming that these sank undisturbed to the bottom. Far easier to trace and date are the heavy rock-anchors which I first noticed in Lebanon.

There was a collection of rock-anchors on land at Byblos, or Gebail (its Hebrew and Arabic name), which is a charming little Crusader town. Papyrus, one of its exports, took on the name of the town; later it came to mean books in general and finally the Book, or Bible. The modern village of Byblos surrounds a small creek; to the south, a *tell* rises from the sea. Today one reaches the ruins through the portcullis of the Crusader castle. As at Jericho, a series of towns are built one over another. According to a tradition quoted by Philo, Byblos is the oldest city in the world; certainly there are Neolithic levels in the *tell*. The glacis round one of the towns towards the bottom of the mound is comparable to an early fortification at Jericho. Whether the round harbour, now used by fishing-boats, is natural or man-made is not quite clear, but this will be discussed later.

Byblos became known in antiquity as a religious centre. Under the influence of Egypt the Phoenician Goddess Balaat was identified with Isis Hathor as the Lady of Byblos. The coffin of Osiris, killed by their brother Set, was washed up on the shore, where Isis, who had taken the form of a swallow, found it. Later, these two become identified with Venus and Adonis. Isis–Venus, the Lady of Byblos, saw and desired Osiris–Adonis one morning in spring. Their happiness lasted only a few days, for Adonis was killed, but her love resuscitated him. Adonis' tomb became a place of pilgrimage. He died in the nearby gorge of the Adonis River, which every spring flows with his blood or the red earth washed down with the melting snow. A pilgrim road, flanked by ancient shrines, leads up

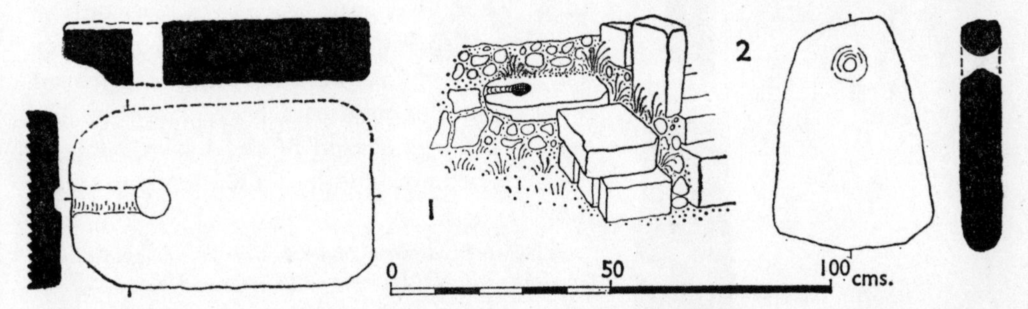

2. *Two rock-anchors from the Temple of the Obelisks at Byblos; both are of soft, buff coloured limestone, hammer dressed.* (*1*) *is built into the walls of the temple leading to the cella.*

the mountains to its source, which issues from the rock in a waterfall after subterranean meanderings through measureless caverns.

These have rather frightening personal associations; one day, after a particularly convivial lunch, John Carswell (who had also been an archaeological draughtsman before joining the staff of the American University at Beirut) and I were tempted to leave our party to their siesta, and with two hunters from the mountains go in search of underground lakes. We climbed into a hole in the rock under the waterfall, where the men left their guns. One of them had a stump of candle and I had a pencil torch with worn-out batteries (which I always carried for use in museums and tombs). With badinage about how we should have some of Ariadne's thread and assurance from the hunters that they knew the labyrinth like the back of their hands, we started wading along water channels into the mountain. Sometimes the water reached my waist, for the flow was swollen by the melting snow of spring. After half an hour the first hunter stopped and announced the water was too high; we would never be able to reach the lake. We turned round, John and the other man were now leading. Every few yards we were faced by at least three, identical entrances to channels which we had not noticed before. As the last centimetre of the candle spluttered, it became apparent that we were lost. Friends outside knew where we had gone, so it was only a question of sitting tight and waiting until they sent a search party, but the hunters disapproved this course. For months I bore bruises on the back of my legs caused by the heavy boots of the man behind, who had a tendency to stam-

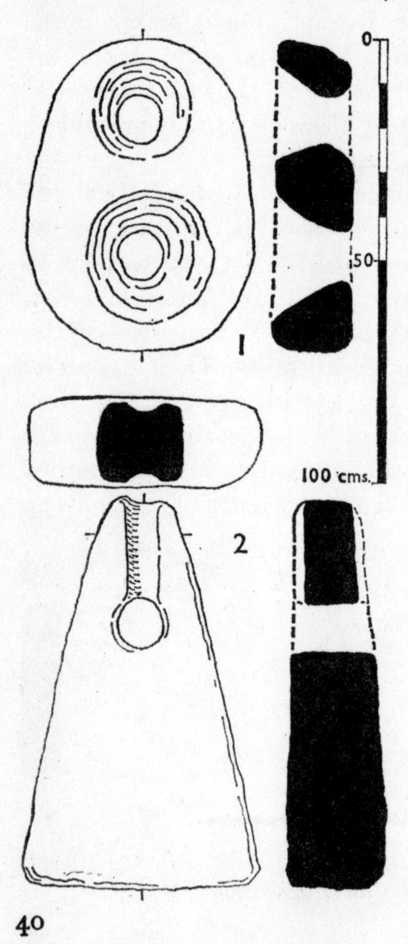

3. (*1*) *A pierced stone found beside the Temple of the Obelisks at Byblos* (*compare Fig. 19a and 24, 2 and 3*). (*2*) *Rock-anchor found against an outer wall of the same temple. Both are made of soft, hammer-dressed limestone.*

pede. At last we saw, in the darkness, something that looked like a glow-worm. It turned out to be the light of day.

It was back in the Temple of the Obelisks, dedicated to the Lady of Byblos, which had contained a treasure of votive offerings now in the Beirut Museum, that I came across the first clues to the dating of stone anchors (Figs. 2 & 3).

CHAPTER 4

Temple of the Obelisks – Tabarja Anchor – Stone Anchors: Votive, Maltese, Minoan, Round, Trireme and Byzantine–Arab – Documentary Clues – Lead-stocked Anchors, their Function and Variety – Iron Anchors

In, or built into, the Bronze Age Temple of the Obelisks at Byblos (nineteenth-century B.C.), M. Dunand, who was in charge of the excavations, found no less than six stone anchors. They were generally triangular (Figs. 2 and 3), and with one exception had a single hole, indicating that they must have been used as weight-anchors on rock. Here the stones were recognized as anchors, because one, which is now in the Beirut Museum, bore the incised drawing of an oar. M. Dunand thinks they were votive offerings to the Lady. It would be interesting to know whether they came from Egypt or were of local manufacture, offered by pilgrims leaving the shrine. I have noted the

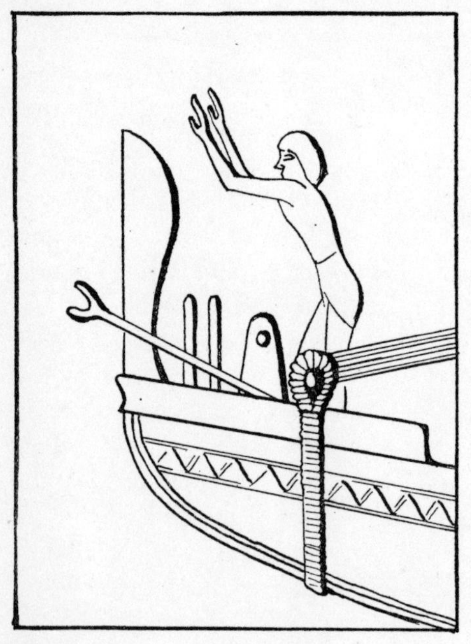

4. Egyptian rock-anchor standing in the prow of a ship, from the Vth Dynasty tomb of King Sahru-re (circa 3000 B.C.). *The cords round the bows of the ship strengthened the hull and prevented it from splitting outwards; they were held at either side by a pole which ran across the deck. The cords that disappear out of the picture to the right gave similar, longitudinal support to the hull.*

different types of limestone (see captions) which, as far as I could observe, might have come from the vicinity, but the stones have not, to my knowledge, been examined by a geologist. Nor do the shapes look Egyptian, for Egyptian paintings and bas-reliefs show pyramidal stone anchors standing on prows, though model ships of the dead occasionally have round anchors with a hole in the middle. The Byblos anchors might have been up-ended, but they could never have stood on the prow of a ship in motion (Fig. 4).

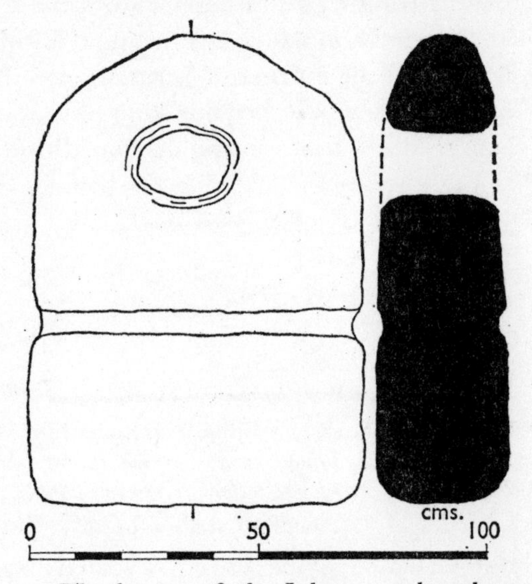

5. The largest of the Lebanese rock-anchors, found and drawn at the bottom of Tabarja harbour.

A larger version of one of these Temple anchors lies at the bottom of the sea at Tabarja, where, on land, there are traces of occupation dating from Early Bronze Age to Roman times. Nor is the anchor alone on the bottom: there are also small, unfluted, 'Phoenician' columns made of a hard black stone. Tabarja has never been excavated, but it is likely that there was a settlement there, contemporary with the Temple of the Obelisks. The Tabarja anchor (Fig. 5) is larger than the one in the Temple and has a groove around its waist; owing to its exceptional weight, a second rope tied in this groove must have been necessary to disengage it. It looks as though the Tabarja anchor could be dated by its counterpart, from a known level at Byblos.

The exception to the triangular or roughly rectangular anchors in the Temple of the Obelisks is an oval stone with two holes [Fig. 3 (1)]. It was so unlike any form I had seen that I put the drawing aside for some years, wondering whether or not I could call it an anchor. However, it came to my notice that a similar stone (Fig. 7) lay, together with several triangular Phoenician anchors, in the garden of the small museum founded in the last century by Mr J. Whitaker on the island of Motya off Sicily. Motya, built on one of a group of islands in a now silted lagoon, had been an important Phoenician port and trading centre, and the anchor stones came from its surrounding muddy waters. Both van Nouhuys and Rodrigues Santamaria[1] illustrate the use of similar stones (Fig. 12).

That anchors should be votive and found in a temple is not surprising, as they have always had symbolic significance. A local instance comes to mind in the anchor emblem which the Seleucid family used from 321 B.C. to A.D. 100. Legend has it that the mother of Seleucus gave her son a ring with an anchor on it and said that he would become king of that country in which he lost it. Another version recounts that, during his expedition against Babylon, Seleucus stumbled on

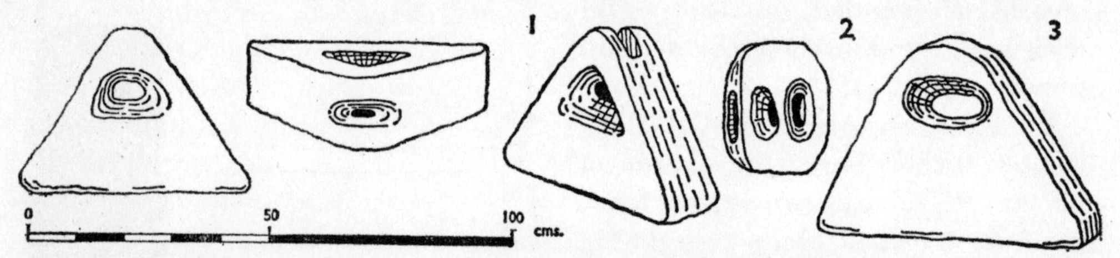

6. (1) Rock-anchor of soft limestone; apex pierced by an elliptical slit deep enough to meet a lower, transversal hole. Found in a Tarxien temple (Maltese Neolithic 1600–1500 B.C.) *compare with Fig. 10 no. 1. (2) Pierced stone from same temple, possibly associated with the sea. (3) Similar rock-anchor from Ta Hagarat temple (Maltese Megalithic).*

a stone which, when moved, revealed an anchor. Lead-stocked anchors were in use by this time, but one wonders whether it was not the stone itself which had a hole in it and so reminded Seleucus of an anchor and evoked for him security, or at least permanent residence.

Dr Moll suggests[2] that the anchor was connected with the cult of Heracles and might therefore be found in his shrines. Heracles had felled Cyzicus with an anchor (probably stone!); according to Greek tradition, the Milesians, following the directions of an oracle, found this at the fountain of Astacis, where the Argonauts had left it and took it to their own town, where they vowed it to Athena Jasonia. In Classical times miniature votive anchors were common: an example of such a hoard was found at Delos.[3] The lead stocks of anchors are occasionally inscribed. 'Zeus Soter' is not uncommon, and modern Greek sailors have been known to call upon Zeus as their saviour. There is also mention in classical texts of votive anchors being offered at Delphi. From the first to the fourth centuries A.D. we find the anchor as a crypto-Christian symbol, scratched on the walls of

[1] J. W. van Nouhuys, 'The Anchor', *Mariner's Mirror*, Vol. 137, January 1, 1951 and footnote on p. 37.

[2] See footnote on p. 34.

[3] Rhénée tombs: *Exploration Archeologique de Délos*, Vol. XVII, p. 198.

catacombs. It may be accompanied by 'spes in Christo' or the drawing of a fish. The sixteenth-century Emblem Books, which appeared after the Council of Trent, refer to anchors as a symbol of faith. We can take Dr Moll's word for the existence of a tract, in German, describing anchors as phallic symbols.

It would be an interesting but separate study to follow the meanings given to anchors in various civilizations. A glance at these sources blunts the surprise that might otherwise be felt when, in prehistoric times, stone anchors turn up in palaces, temples and shrines, where many hoards must still remain unrecognized, or undiscovered.

Further datable anchors have been found in Malta, on temple sites. One triangular example [Fig. 6 (1)] comes from the Tarxin Temple (Maltese Neolithic, 1600–1500 B.C.) and the other [Fig. 6 (3)] from a Megalithic Temple at Ta Hagarat.[1] The Stone Ages in Malta roughly correspond with the Bronze Ages in Palestine.[2] The curious pierced stone [Fig. 6 (2)] also from the Tarxin Temple may be associated with the sea. The triangular Tarxin anchor [Fig. 6 (1)] is interesting because the holes are pierced in such a way that they inter-communicate. This puzzled me for some time, until it was explained as usual by a sailor, from the Piraeus Maritime Museum [see Trireme anchors below, Fig. 10 (1)]. These holes allowed the extra security of double ropes and knots, which might seem unnecessary on such a small anchor, but we do not know what ropes were used in Malta at that date. Elsewhere, both Homeric and archaeological evidence agree that ropes were made of plant fibre such as papyrus or *pharagmites communis*, the common reed. If the Maltese lacked wherewithal to make strong ropes they compensated in ingenuity by anticipating the later system of double knotting.

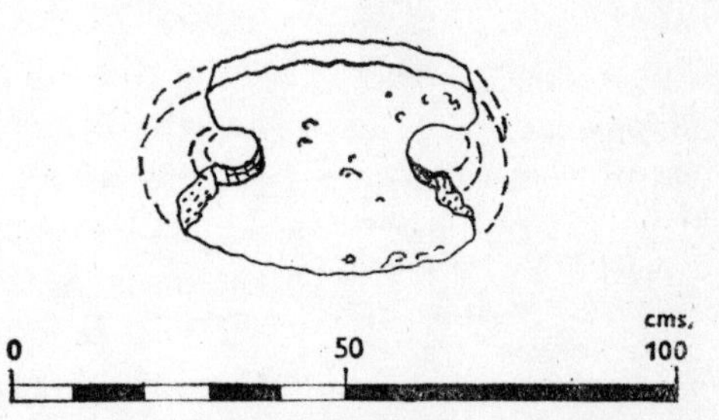

7. Anchor from the Phoenician harbour in Sicily, now in the Whitaker museum at Motya. Compare Fig. 3, 1 from Byblos and the modern drag-net anchors from the Balearic Islands Fig. 12 (2) and (3).

[1] Evans, *Prehistoric Malta*, p. 89, Fig. 16; *Bulletin of the Valletta Museum, Malta*, Vol. I, No. I.

[2] Pierced stones are also built into the recently excavated Tarxin Temple at Skorba in Malta, see *Illustrated London News*, August 12, 1961. Pictured in the entrance of this temple, two double-holed stones resemble the Byblos anchor [Fig. 3, (1)] and the Motya anchor (Fig. 7), the third, a triangular stone with one hole, is like Fig. 3 (2). A pyramidal, one-holed stone below the altar is described as a tethering post for sacrificial animals, but it, too, may have served previously as an anchor.

The Byblos and, from documentary evidence, Egyptian anchors reminded me of the elaborately carved, late Minoan example in the Heraclion Museum [Fig. 8 (1)]. Sir Arthur Evans had found this stone in the Palace of Minos and had called it a 'weight' because it happened to correspond in weight to the copper ox-hide ingots near by. Since ox-hide ingots are now known to be of no standard weight,[1] the coincidence has no significance. In any case weight is irrelevant, as other stone anchors have been found in Crete.

I returned to that island recently and came across an anchor, standing in the Palace of Mallia [Fig. 8 (2) and Plate 8]. Sir Arthur Evans' example was so elaborate that it might have been manufactured for votive use, whereas the Mallia anchor was roughly cut and still bore chisel marks. M. Dessenne, who excavated Mallia, very kindly sent me the following information:

> The anchors which you saw (*there had apparently been two, but one had disappeared*) were found in the Palace in a part which was next to a stone-cutter's workshop, excavated in 1956. It was some way from the sea . . . about 400 metres from the beach. The anchors were certainly not in a sanctuary, but in a building which, to judge from the general plan, the traces of burning and a bronze disk found there, was probably used for making fire in order to work bronze. All the objects in the stone carver's workshop date from the 1st Palace, that is to say, for Mallia, from Middle Minoan I to II.

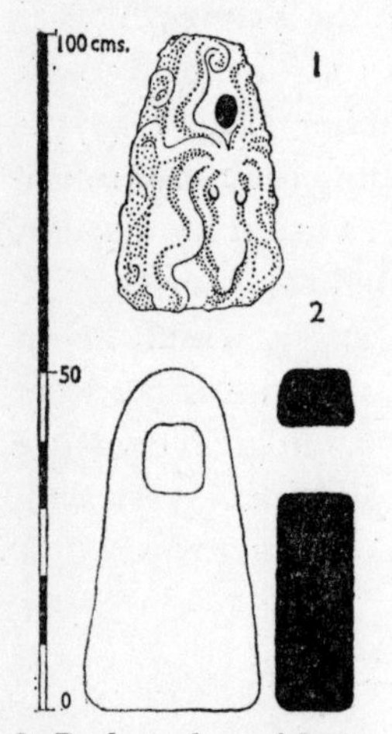

8. Rock-anchor with octopus carved in low relief on a hard reddish stone. Found in the Palace at Knossos, now in the Heraclion museum. (2) *Also from Crete, this anchor was found in the Palace of Mallia; chisel marks show on the soft reddish limestone* (*see also Plate 8*).

I am also indebted to M. Daux, Director of the French School of Archaeology in Athens, for a photograph of these two anchors (Plate 8). The broken example on the left closely resembles the Byblos anchor [Fig. 3 (2)] and the one in the Beirut Museum. Judging from the anchor which I saw at Mallia and the other in the photograph, the stone was freshly cut and neither had been used in the sea. It looks as though they may have been made in the same workshop as the more elaborately carved bowls and gems; perhaps they were the first, easy task given to an apprentice.

[1] Hans Von Günter-Büchholz, *Prähistorische Zeitschrift*, Vol. XXXVII, 1959.

Round stone anchors, which I have seen on the bottom of the ancient, disused port of Tyre and mentioned in connection with model ships of the Dead, have a single hole pierced through the centre. Their use is illustrated in the painting on a Cypriot vase of the eighth century B.C. (Plate 7). Other examples were found by a French expedition[1] in the bottom of Marathon Bay [(Fig. 9 (2) and (3)]. This expedition picked up a series of stone stocks from the same area [Fig. 9 (1)]; unfortunately none was associated with a wreck. It is impossible to say whether they represent a transitional stage between the stone anchor and the wood and lead variety used in classical times. They may be no more than a 'poor man's lead stock'. Similar, slightly smaller stocks are found along the French coast, but again out of context. Judging from the places where these lay (in

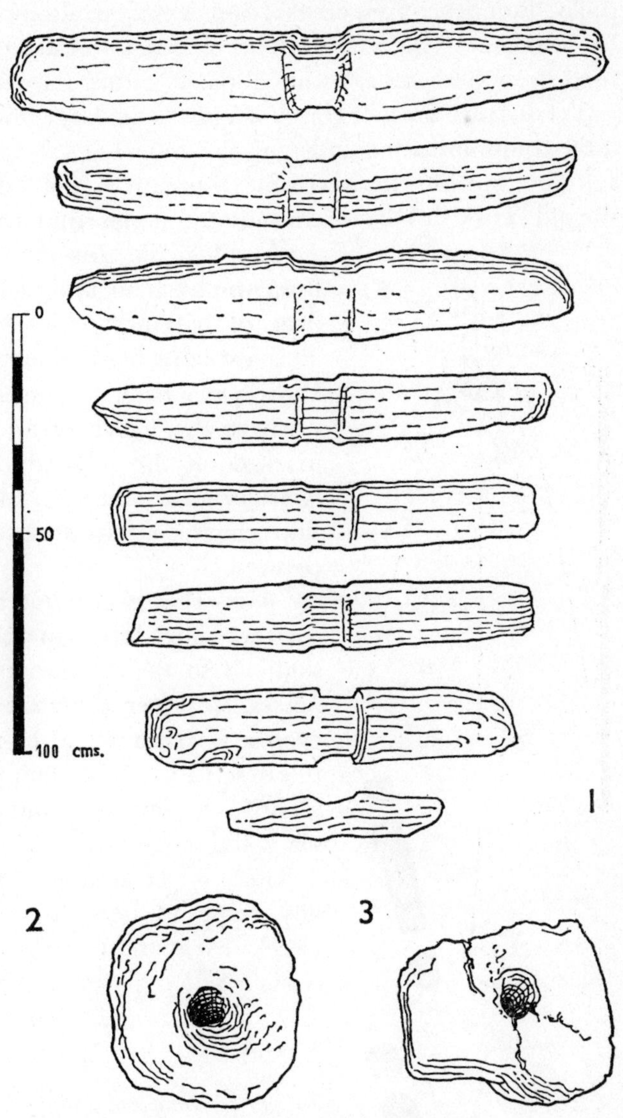

9. (1) Stone stocks found in Marathon Bay by F. Braemer and J. Mercadé in 1953. (2) and (3) Round stone anchors found on the same expedition; compare Cypriot drawing of a man dropping one of these anchors Plate 7.

[1] F. Braemer and J. Mercadé, *Bulletin de Correspondence Hellénique*, p. 145, 1953.

rocky but unsheltered creeks) and their resemblance to the long stones mentioned by Rodrigues Santamaria in his dictionary of fishing-tackle, they may have been used in modern times to anchor nets rather than ships.

Yet another form of Greek anchor is the large and heavy pyramidal stone with inter-communicating holes at the top [Fig. 10 (1)]. There are two examples standing outside the Maritime Museum at the Turko, now called Zia, Liman, the old 'Turkish Port' of Piraeus and no less than ten in the grounds of the nearby Archaeological Museum. All were lifted by dredgers from the harbour and were reputed to come from the fleet of triremes which used this port in antiquity. This explains why such anchors have never, to my knowledge, been found elsewhere, for we have yet to discover the wreck of an ancient warship. Wrecks are marked on the sea-bed by their imperishable cargo. Amphorae or statues stick out of the sand, but a warship which keeps its decks clear for action would become covered by silt. Further, since warships were dependent on oars, they were not subject to those vagaries of weather which forced merchant ships to moor on offshore shallows so their anchors would never be lost in these places. However, there are certain types of bottom where even a warship would be noticed, or at least a stone of this description. The anchor might, in the circumstances, identify the ship; it is only a matter of time before the sea will divulge this secret.

There is yet another type of anchor which may one day come to light as a result of skilled, methodical wreck excavation: this is the bag-anchor. Torr, in *Ancient Ships*, quotes Arrian[1] on a Roman method of

[1] Arrian, Anabasis V. 7.

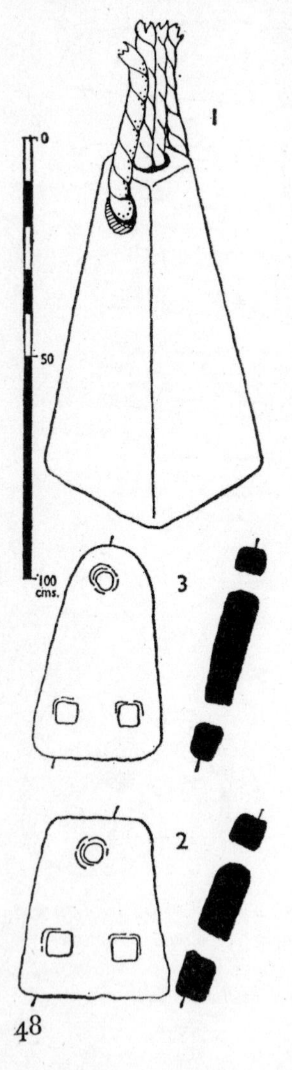

10. (1) An example of the trireme anchors from Zia Liman (Piraeus); compare the piercings with the Maltese anchor [Fig. 6 (1)]. (2) and (3) 'Byzantine–Arab' composite anchors from the submarine plateau near Marseille; now in the Boreli Museum. Compare Plate 9.

mooring by baskets filled with stones. In default of controlled excavation techniques it has not been possible to say whether the pebble stones found on some ancient wrecks were ballast, let alone whether they were bag-anchors.

To return to the stone stocks and before passing on to their leaden counterparts, there is a form of anchor which we can regard as transitional in design, linking stone weight-anchors and the metal and wood, fluked variety. I am going to call these 'Byzantine–Arab', because they were common in this period, though they may well have been used earlier. The stones were basically triangular, one hole at the top and two at the base. The lower holes (which were sometimes square) held wooden sticks, like the modern Lebanese sand-anchors and the abovementioned, almost identical, triangular stone anchors still used in the Persian Gulf. In design, the three-holed stones were a compromise between sand- and rock-anchors and could be used on any type of bottom. Stephanus Byzantianus, in his book *De Urbis*,[1] says that there was a town in Egypt which derived its name, Ancyra, from the manufacture of anchors at local stone quarries.

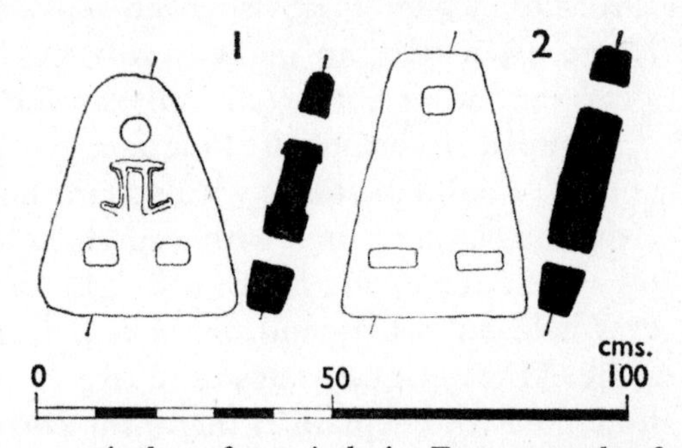

11. Anchors from Agde in France; made of the hard, volvic stone which in ancient times was exported in the form of mill-stones and later for building. These anchors have not yet been dated, but it should be possible to do so when the letter incised on both faces of (1) is traced. The design is difficult to justify, since wood oblong in section (in the lower holes) would be weaker than the round branches used in most other anchors of this kind; compare Fig. 12 (4).

This type of anchor is widely distributed and has been found in France and North Africa as well as the Levant. There are two examples in the Boreli Museum at Marseille [Figs. 10 (2) & (3)] which came from the submarine *Plateau des Chêvres*. Marseillais divers tell me they have seen others off the Ile Mayre and elsewhere. A similar design was made from local stone at Agde in the Hérault. Many specimens have been found there in the river and in the sea; but though one of these is marked [Fig. 11 (1)], the incised character has not as yet been identified, so the series remains undated. Stone anchors have no commercial or souvenir value, and as people do not know what they are, they are seldom lifted.

[1] Ed. Berkel, 1688, pp. 20–1.

I made enquiries about 'Byzantine–Arab' anchors in Turkey, but none cropped up when I was there. One year, however, just after I left, I got a letter from a Turkish friend saying that three were found off Bodrum, the ancient Halicarnassos, which had also been a Byzantine town. One example was raised (Plate 9); it bore an incised cross and the letters N and O, which point to a Christian, if not for certain a Byzantine, origin.

Grouped according to function, we now have three types of antique stone anchor: small flat stones with several holes pierced to take sticks which gripped into sand; larger stones with a single hole which, on a rocky bottom, held a ship by weight alone, and lastly, a weight anchor combined with two wooden prongs that held on either sand or rock. It would have been difficult to imagine how some of the antique stones were rigged and used, had it not been for the modern fishermen who explained them, the corroborative evidence of Rodrigues Santamaria and van Nouhuys[1] and collections of killicks in the Science Museum and the Maritime Museum at Greenwich. According to Rodrigues' *Diccionario*, most ancient forms of stone anchor are still in use in Spain and its dependencies, though they now hold fishing-tackle rather than boats. It is unlikely that the way wood and rope are combined in the pierced stones has changed (Fig. 12). Van Nouhuys gives further modern examples of stone anchors in use, from countries as far apart as Roumania, India, Indonesia, Brazil and China. In China we even find anchors, identical with the Roman lead-stocked variety, in current use. The principles of how ancient stone anchors were rigged can be established from these sources, but a great many details remain unexplained. In both shape and piercing, the holes in the stone anchors I have illustrated suggest surprising variations in their lost wooden components. The Bodrum anchor (Plate 9) would have taken rounded sticks, and the Agde anchors (Fig. 11) slats. Bevelled holes,[2] as on the oval Byblos anchor [Fig. 3 (1)], suggest a combination of rope and wood, while the 'girdle' on the Tabarja anchor (Fig. 5) indicates double ropes.

Tracing the gradual development of Mediterranean anchors from documentary evidence is even more difficult: The poetic term 'ευναι' used by Homer meant 'stone for anchoring', while 'ἄγκυρα' meant 'hook'. It is conceivable that, around 1500 B.C., it occurred to sailors that a rock-anchor might be more effective if it did not depend on weight alone, if it were combined with a hooked branch, a device still used by primitive people. If certain Bronze Age anchors

[1] See footnotes on p. 44 and p. 37.

[2] This also denotes a primitive method of piercing: borings started at either side, met in the middle of the stone.

were so adapted it would, in addition to the composite sand- and Byzantine-Arab variants, be a link in the development of wooden flukes and weighted stocks. Judging by the Levant today, all sorts of anchors must have been used contemporaneously. There was no clean break in development, but rather a change of emphasis at each innovation. A conscious distinction between rock- and sand-anchors persisted. Isidorus, writing in A.D. 600 (*Etymologia*, Book XX),

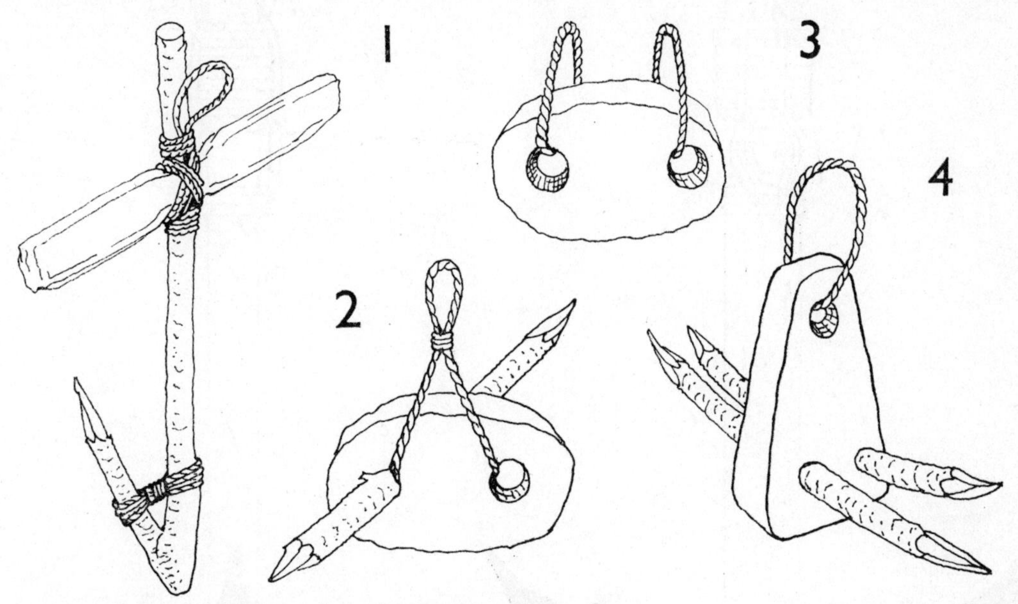

12. Arrangements of rope and wood on modern stone anchors.

Key: (*1*) *Branch with a stone stock from Malaya. There are many variations in rigging this type of anchor: sometimes the stone sinker is lashed between a frame of wooden battens and then to the stem.* (*2*), (*3*) *and* (*4*) *Stone anchors used on drag-nets in the Balearic Islands.*

gives the following definition: 'Anchor comes from the Greek, which, like a hand, grips *either sand or stone*' (the italics are mine).

This bring us back to the stone stocks (Fig. 9); did they antedate lead stocks?[1]

[1] Again ethnology gives a hint as to the use of these stones and the way in which they were combined with wood and rope. There is a model of a Chinese anchor in the Science Museum at South Kensington in which a slab of stone is lashed at both ends to wooden beams and used as a sinker. Quantities of long stones, usually slate, are found along the Mediterranean coast of France, often in rock crevices under cliffs where no ship would anchor; it follows that they must have been used by fishermen.

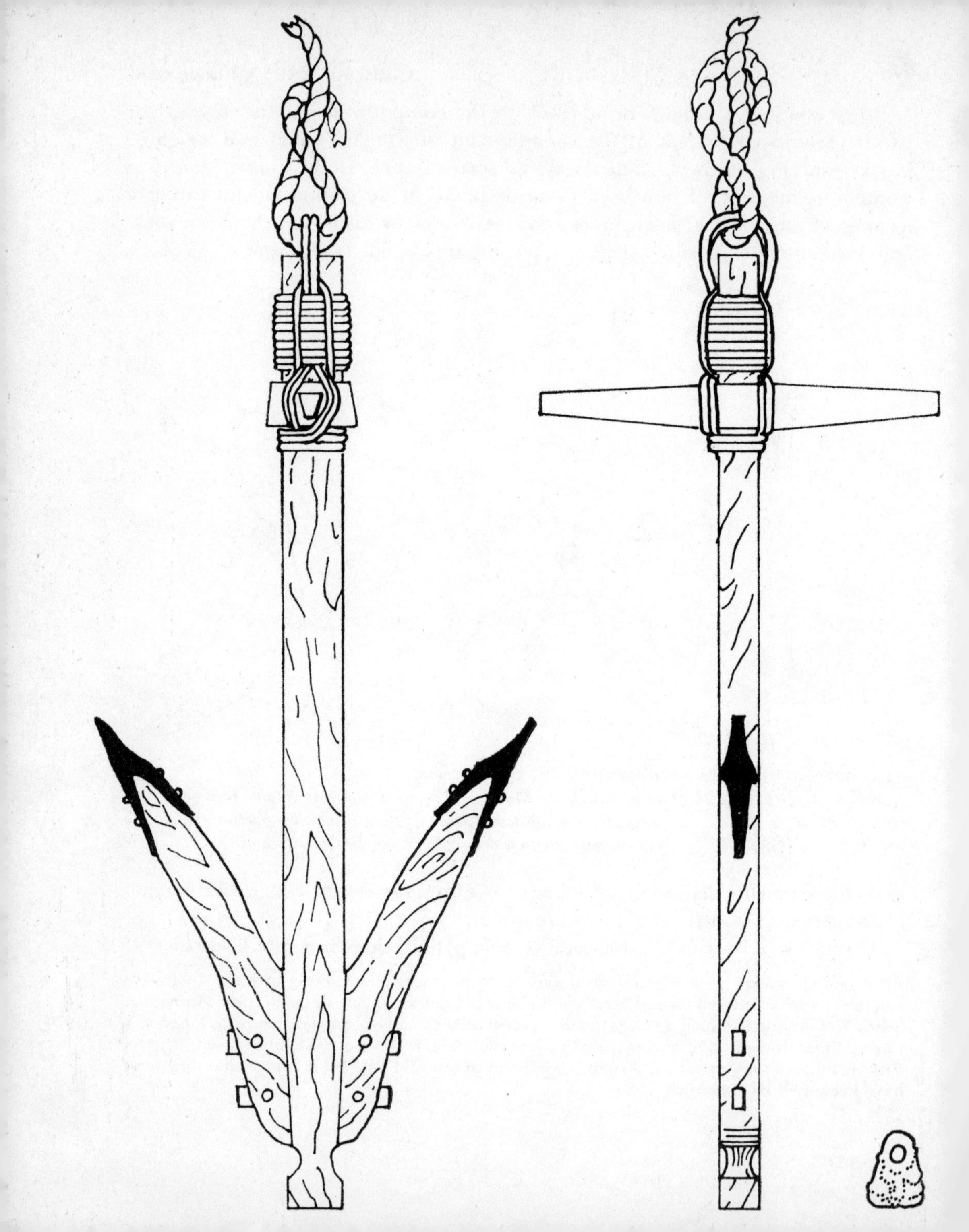

So far there is not enough evidence to hazard a guess, so it is prudent to go straight to an examination of the latter. Examples of lead stocks have been known for some time, they were found on land, or dredged up from the sea without their wooden components. The result was that discussion as to their function raged furiously among specialists of naval archaeology, whose research was based on pictorial and written sources (they seem to have ignored ethnological material).

13 and 14. Left: *the lead-stocked Nemi anchor.* Right: *iron anchor encased in wood; found complete in the mud of Lake Nemi. Compare their size with an average stone anchor drawn to the same scale (centre).*

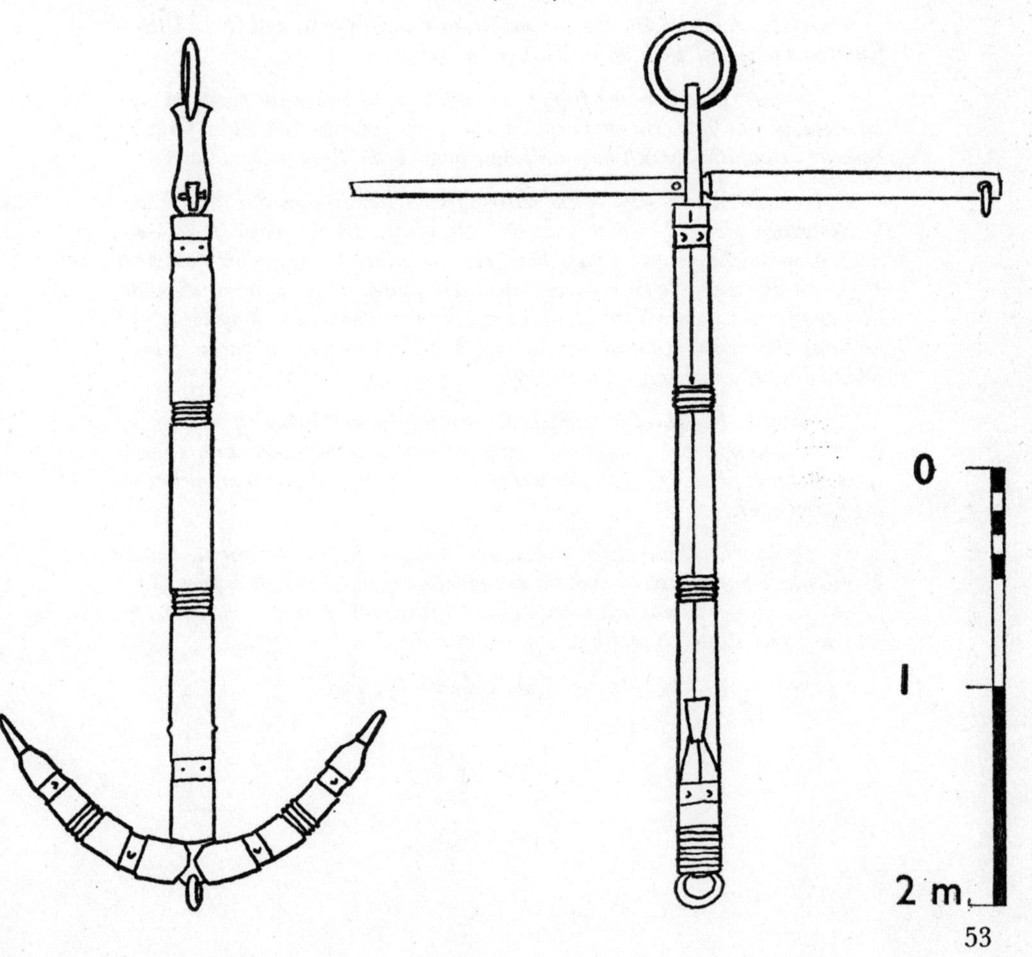

ANCHORS, HARBOUR INSTALLATIONS AND CONTRASTS IN EXCAVATION.

7 (opposite, top). *A round stone anchor [compare Fig. 9 (2) and (3)] being lowered by means of a mooring boom; note the amphora on deck. The scene is painted on a Cypriot jug of the eighth century* B.C.

8 (below, left). *Two Minoan stone anchors found during excavation at the palace at Mallia in Crete (see p. 46 and compare Figs. 3 and 8).*

9 (right). *A later form of stone anchor with incised cross and Greek letters, found in the sea off Bodrum in Turkey (p. 50).*

10 (verso). *Boat hanging from trees implanted in a rock-cut platform near an isolated hut in northern Crete. These arrangements hint at a form of harbour installation which may well date back to the Bronze Ages (p. 106).*

11 (recto). *Aerial view of the outer harbour, for foreign ships, at Sidon. Swell breaks along the south-westerly side of the island where a rock-cut wall protects the quays, which have been levelled to landwards (compare Figs. 18 and 19). Stone mooring bitts were found along the most sheltered northern quays; the swell which eddies round the southernmost tip of the island explains the submerged, but still visible mole, which was probably a later addition to this anchorage (see p. 89).*

12 (verso). *Façade of a complete Roman theatre in Turkey. It now stands in open country, but excavation could demonstrate whether the 10,000 spectators that filled its seats came from the town of Aspendos or from surrounding farmsteads.*

13 (below). *Underwater excavation by air-lift—a technique hardly applicable to buried cities—even the examination of wooden hulls is rare. This picture was taken on a wreck known as the* Titan, *which is also shown before excavation on Plate 16 and again in another stage on Plate 27.*

14 (bottom). *The baby seal from Lebanon (p. 120).*

7. British Museum

8. French School at Athens

9. J.-J. Flory

10. F. Dumas

11. Université St. Joseph, Beirut

12. F. Dumas

13. P. Tailliez

14. D. Parks

Unfortunately there were no pictures of these anchors, or rather, such representations as did exist were too formalized for it to be certain which part was wood and which lead. The generally accepted and erroneous opinion was that the lead part (Plates 3 and 4—the Anthéor anchor) constituted the flukes. This mistake would, in time, have been corrected by divers, but, as I have already said, it was discovered when the Nemi anchors were found (Figs. 13 and 14). The evidence was conclusive as regards structure, but it did not explain the design. For this we have to go to a seaman and, for a change, to a sophisticated professional. Capt. Cousteau has analysed the function of the lead stock:

> Why did the ancients put the weight at the top of their anchors? It was because they had no chains for mooring; instead, they had to use ropes. When a modern ship pulls on its chain, as a result of wind or current, the flukes of the anchor remain stuck in the bottom, because the heavy chain exercises a tangential traction, which is transmitted horizontally on the seabed. The light ropes, used by the Greeks and Romans, would lift the stock of a modern anchor and dislodge the flukes, so that the boat would drift. A heavy, lead stock neutralizes the upward pull of the rope. It keeps the wooden flukes in position and maintains that horizontal angle which ensures a good grip and firm mooring.[1]

Rope was both the principal factor in the design of classical anchors and their weak point. The stock was weighted to compensate for the movement of the rope; even so, the anchors were not completely efficient, and navigators sought safety in numbers. The other reason for the quantities of anchors was, as we have seen, that ancient ships were often forced to moor fore and aft in the most unlikely places.

Hundreds of lead stocks have now been found by divers. They range from those fitting dinghy-sized anchors, which can be picked up in one hand, to the 6-foot stocks of Nemi, Mahdia and Anthéor, which five strong men can hardly lift. Some are inscribed and some have Medusa heads, knuckle-bones and other talismans, but most are plain. There is already sufficient material for a scholar to classify, and this work has begun, as articles in journals such as *Gallia* and *Etudes Ligures* attest.

A complete anchor consisted of a wooden stem, which passed through a hole in the stock and ended in two wooden flukes which were, in plan, at right angles to the stock. The juncture of flukes to stem was another structural weakness. In the Nemi anchor the flukes were fixed with wooden pegs. Soon, divers started to

[1] J. Y. Cousteau, *Monde du Silence*, Editions de Paris, p. 139.

come across leaden contraptions with three slots (Fig. 15) which turned out to be a reinforcement for this part. These assembly pieces fitted over flukes and stem, holding them together and also adding useful weight.

The function of lead stocks is constant, but there are subtle variations in the way they were made. Some have a core of wood inside the arms. All stocks have a box-like opening in the middle to take the wooden stem of the anchor, but occasionally there is a bar of lead across the middle of this box. These bars suggested that on certain anchors the wooden stem must have been made in two pieces which were pushed through the stock on either side of the bar, then lashed together below and at the crown. The idea was not entirely convincing, for two bits of wood would obviously be weaker than one. However, no other explanation sprang to mind, and reconstructions of anchors were drawn in this way until Barnier solved the problem by examining the lead stock found at Anthéor.

The crown of the Anthéor anchor was made of a single piece of wood, but its stock did have a lead bar across the stem-hole. Barnier observed the lead and decided it must have been sand-cast. 'Sand' is a slightly misleading term when we visualize what actually happened. The wooden stem of the anchor with a hole pierced through it at the level of the stock must have been up-ended in clay soil. A mould of the stock was then scooped out of the clay around the level of the stock-hole. When molten lead was poured into this mould it flowed through the hole in the wood. Thus, the stock was cast directly on to the stem.

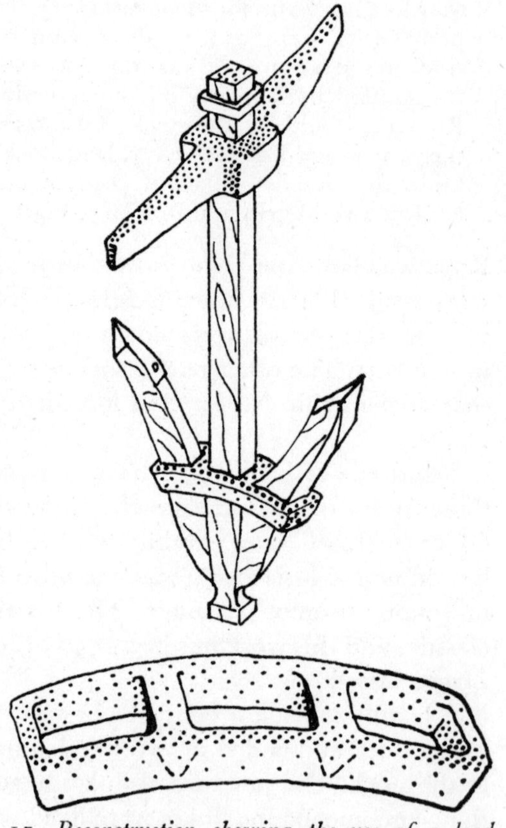

15. Reconstruction showing the use of a lead assembly-piece.

This analysis of Barnier's was quoted

by M. Benoît in an address to the First International Congress of Underwater Archaeology, organized by the *Club Alpin Sous-marin* at Cannes in 1956. The excellent printed report of these proceedings makes sad reading today, for it laid a rational plan for underwater research which, unfortunately, was never followed. The right questions were posed and many of their solutions suggested, but all was forgotten: amateur experiment and pillage dignified by the name of archaeology continues.

In the sea the wooden stem and flukes of anchors are nearly always missing, because they were exposed on deck when the ship sank. Only the wood which was sometimes put inside the leaden arms when the stock was cast is always preserved. In the early days these wooden cores intrigued free-divers, who had been told about the following passage from Diodorus Siculus:

> So far indeed did the [Phoenician] merchants go in their greed that, when on occasion their boats were fully laden and there remained a great amount of silver still to be shipped, they would hammer the stock off the anchors and have the silver perform the purpose of the lead.[1]

The passage was misconstrued and taken to mean that the Phoenicians filled their lead stocks with silver. This would have meant cutting them from their stems, extracting the armature and removing the tenon. Then, after the hollow had been filled with silver, replacing the stock, which could have been held by a rivet passing through both lead and stem. A further insurance against loss of the stock would have been to crown the stem with a ring for rope which had a diameter larger than the hole of the stock. Be this as it may, even when there was no question of smuggling, we do find variations of attachment at the crown. The mistaken translation of Siculus' remarks gave western divers an added incentive to lift all lead stocks in the hope of finding silver; had there been any, it would, of course, have been too corroded to have commercial value.

Detachable stocks seem to be in the minority. This is surprising when we consider the amount of anchors ships had to carry and the space they took when assembled. Documents and the wrecks themselves both prove that anchors were kept on deck. As to numbers, on St Paul's wreck four anchors were cast out from the stern; the crew never got round to the others in the forepart of the ship, not to mention the 'sacred' or spare anchor. From this, one can assume a minimum of eight anchors, and Roman historians mention twelve to a ship, while

[1] Diodorus Siculus, Loeb Ed., Bk. V, 35, 4.

more reliable medieval records (of Mediterranean ships) list as many as twenty. One variant of the lead stock has a curved arm which possibly made it easier to lever the anchor overboard. They must have been difficult to cast, as both St Paul and wrecks attest; it was not always possible to dispose of anchors before the ship sank. So far we do not know the answer, but in the eighth-century illustration (Plate 7) it looks as though the stone anchor is being dropped by means of some kind of boom.

Without imaginative effort, descriptions of detail are unrewarding. The problem must be visualized: a stock, or cross bar at the top of an anchor, is small in proportion to stem and flukes. If we dismiss as exceptional the 6-foot stocks of Nemi, Mahdia and Anthéor and imagine a group of anchors which have only 4-foot or 1·22-metre stocks, each complete anchor would still be much larger than a man. Next, we visualize four such anchors lying on the fore-deck of the *Cutty Sark*, the 60-metre windjammer at Greenwich. They would take up a considerable amount of space, indeed it would be difficult to imagine them on a smaller ship. No definite conclusion can be drawn from these imaginings, but they illustrate the sort of practical background which a diver builds up for himself. Compare this with a scholar's literary and pictorial sources and his capacity to interpret them.

Pictorial representations are necessarily formalized: on Trajan's column human figures are as large as the boats. Moreover, sculptors were unlikely to have specialized knowledge of ships; they did the best they could. The same goes for classical authors and their modern translators. A Byzantinologist once read me a list of ship's equipment; he would pause and remark: 'I think this could be translated as "rings" and the metal might perhaps be "lead".' Shipbuilding tradition was unbroken from Roman to Byzantine times, and anyone who has worked on a Roman wreck will have come across lead rings. These were sewn on to the sails to keep the ropes in place as they were furled and unfurled, but the text had not been clear without this archaeological corroboration. If divers were trained to make records and send them to an appropriate seat of learning they could already have made a valuable contribution to the interpretation of texts. This is apparent long before we reach the point when an assessment has to be made of the information which can reasonably be expected to result from examination of wrecked hulls.

Pliny says that lead stocks were an Etruscan invention. So far this has not been substantiated by divers, perhaps because anchors from Etruscan wrecks have been lifted at different times and by different people from the associated pottery and no one has kept a record. It is therefore impossible to date the invention of lead stocks, but there are indications as to the period of, and the reason for, their disappearance.

Iron anchors with small, relatively light and, incidentally, movable stocks came in Roman times, and I would suggest that their use depended on the availability of chains, since, as Cousteau has explained, they would never have held without chains. As usual, there is a certain number of misleading texts. Philo of Byzantium[1] states that chains were introduced as early as 332 B.C., as a result of divers cutting the mooring-ropes of Alexander's fleet during his siege of Tyre. Philo was writing several hundred years after the event, and though his deduction was logical, in the absence of proof it smacks of wishful thinking. A much more persuasive mention of chains occurs in Caesar's *de Bello Gallico*.[2]

Caesar found himself at a disadvantage during an engagement with the fleet of the Veneti, a tribe from Southern Brittany. He records the circumstances and compares the performance of the Veneti with the Roman warships. Now Caesar was not a sailor, and to us the comparison between two unknown kinds of ship is not very enlightening, but these drawbacks are inherent in most texts. He gives sufficient detail for many interesting inferences to have been drawn about the ships themselves,[3] and one definite and precious statement about anchors: 'The Veneti anchors were secured fast by iron chains instead of cables.' Presumably the Roman fleet in the year 56 B.C. was still using ropes. From this statement the Veneti were credited with the invention of the anchor chain; the tribe had relations with the Wessex coast, where they plied a trade in sling stones and eventually emigrated. In 1881 an anchor and chain [Fig. 16 (2)] were found in a Veneti hill fort, Bulberry Camp, east of Bere Regis; they are now in the Dorchester Museum. The anchor is iron, no stock is visible, but it may not have been in place. Another which closely resembles the Dorchester anchor is at Pompeii, and a fourth came from the Roman wreck off La Ciotat [Fig. 16 (1), (2) & (3)] and is now in the Boreli Museum. In the latter instance only the flukes, part of the shank and bits of the rings were preserved. It was the ghost of an anchor; being in salt water, the iron had disappeared, like Barnier's implements at

[1] Phylo of Byzantium. *Veterum Mathematicorum Opera*, compiled: Théviot, 1693.

[2] *De Bello Gallico*, III, 13.

[3] R. Y. Creston, *Structure des Navires Venètes*, and P. Emmanuelle, *César et les Venètes*, Annales de Bretagne, Rennes, 1955–58, pp. 88 and 85.

Anthéor, leaving its shape within a mould of concretion. Concretions are fragile; hence the missing portions. An iron anchor encased in wood was found at Nemi (Fig. 14); it was contemporary with the lead stocked anchor, of the first century A.D.

Julius Caesar considered anchor chains worth recording, which is not surprising, as any landsman notices the important manoeuvre of dropping anchor. So we can infer that chains and iron anchors were not used in the Mediterranean before Caesar's time and that the innovation came from the north. One thing certainly emerges from his comparison between Veneti and Roman ships: they were different. So are the navigational requirements of the Atlantic and the tideless Mediterranean. If northern ports were as shallow as those in the Mediterranean, ships would be left sitting on the mud when the tide went out. An illustration to Bernard von Bradenbach's *Pilgrimage to Jerusalem* in 1483 shows two distinct types of craft side by side in the harbour at Rhodes. One is 'round' and low, with two masts, oars and a deck-house built aft and to starboard, like certain Roman or Byzantine ships. Behind it is a single-masted vessel with a high poop and stern; lines which one associates with northern ships.

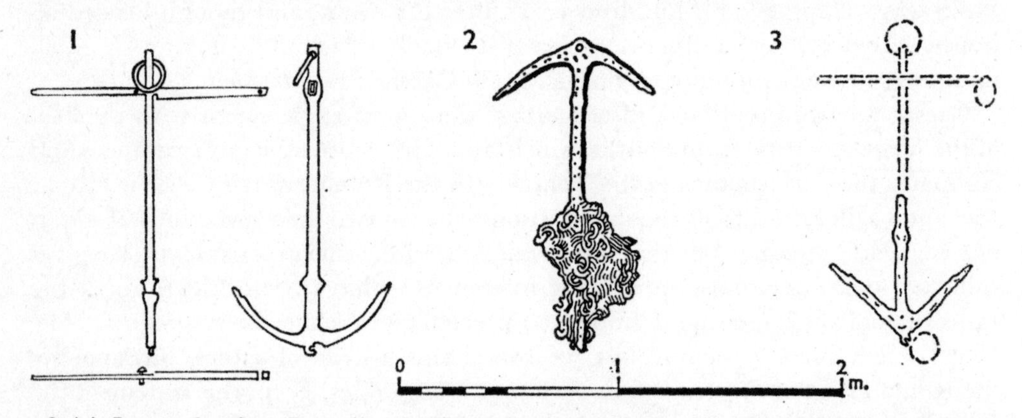

16. (1) Iron anchor from Pompeii. (2) The anchor and chain found at Bere Regis in a hill camp probably used by the Veneti (Dorchester Museum). (3) Cast taken from a natural, concretion-mould of an iron anchor found in the sea at La Ciotat (Boreli Museum).

Interchanges and counter-claims between northern and Mediterranean traditions extend even to anchor stocks. Until recently the movable stock was attributed to Capt. Rodger, R.N., who showed his prototype in the Exhibition of 1851. When the Italians discovered a movable stock on the iron anchor at Nemi they claimed it as a Roman invention. Admiral Siriani presented reproductions of the Nemi anchor[1] to Mr Alexander in 1931 as an

> appropriate souvenir of the Naval Agreement. To landsmen the anchor is the symbol of hope, the sentiment naturally felt about the event that smooths the path for the Disarmament Conference next year.[2]

It would be an added irony if we accept Julius Caesar's evidence and infer that the chain and its accompanying iron anchor with a movable stock was a Gallo-British invention after all.

When anchors were kept on deck the movable stock may have been designed as a convenient space-saver. On the other hand, stocks had always been made separately, because they used to be of a different material from the stem. At the outset it may not have occurred to designers that the stock could now become a rigid part of the stem. After the invention of the chain, heavy stocks were unnecessary; their only remaining function was to ensure that the anchor fell in such a position that a fluke could engage itself on the bottom.

[1] The iron anchor at Nemi (which, of course, postdates Caesar's observations) had no chain; this explains its casing of wood. Without the wood, an anchor of this design would have sunk into a muddy bottom and could not have been extricated without a chain and winch. Similar anchors have been found recently at Agde. Without the wooden casing, the iron structure is much the same as Fig. 16 (1) from Pompeii.

[2] *Birmingham Post*, March 13, 1931.

PART III

PORTS

What city is like Tyrus, like the destroyed in the midst of the seas? [1]

[1] Ezekiel, 27 v. 32.

PLANS OF TYRE AND SIDON

The plans and drawings of the ports of Tyre and Sidon are based on the reports and surveys published by Père Poidebard; see Bibliography.

CHAPTER 5

The Existence of Early Harbours – Structural Classification – Silt and Silting – Changing Sea Levels – Buried Cities – Tyre in History – Geological Position – As Seen Today – Poidebard's Aims in Excavating – His Methods – Findings – Outstanding Questions – The General Picture

THE variety of stone anchors first struck me at the bottom of the antique port of Tyre. An individual can co-ordinate and understand such isolated objects, but ruined harbour-works themselves are baffling. What, one wonders, are the principles that dictate the design of a port or area of water that has to remain calm in all circumstances? That it is difficult to create this condition is proved by many short-lived harbours, both ancient and modern. On the spot one tends to assume that moles and quays are put there so that ships can come alongside and unload, but this is incidental to their real purpose. Neither swell nor silt must enter a harbour; the latter is the more difficult to deflect, coming as it does from the most unexpected directions. Both swell and silt are governed by changes in the weather. This, too, makes it hard for a foreigner, seeing a harbour in spring or summer, to grasp the reason for its design. Further, if he comes from the north he inevitably thinks in terms of tide.

As with the structure of Roman ships, a diver who has acquired a first-hand, comparative knowledge of ancient ports from the remains he has been able to examine is bound to formulate questions and make inferences. However, with ports it is even more difficult for him to substantiate his beliefs than it is in the case of ships. Until effective methods of excavation are developed and used, and a corpus of reliable evidence is published, there is nothing definite for him to quote. On the other hand, if problems are not posed there will be little incentive for this difficult kind of research. The excellent work started on two Phoenician ports, which I describe in the following chapters, has raised questions applicable to other early harbour sites in the Mediterranean.

Anyone who lives, year in, year out, in the Mediterranean becomes accustomed to the behaviour of the sea. Familiarity with various kinds of rock pool, for instance, acquired subconsciously in childhood, leads one to expect a certain type of phenomenon on one coast and not on another. I had seen ancient ports and even dived thereon, but always observing details rather than the whole; a natural tendency in such large structures. My stays in Lebanon spread over every season, and this, coupled with the Jericho experience, aroused my interest in Tyre and Sidon, which flourished over a longer period than most ancient harbours. But it was the work of three men, Poidebard, Lauffray and Mouterde, that made their structures comprehensible; their conclusions illuminate, and the way their work was conducted sets a standard for future excavation of this nature. Unfortunately, the methods used were so elaborate that no individual or small expedition can hope to emulate them; nevertheless, certain principles were established.

Sizeable harbours must have existed to accommodate Egyptian, Minoan and Phoenician fleets. Boreux, in his *Etudes de Nautique Egyptienne*, says that river boats of the Old Empire attained 30 metres. Others of 20 and 25 were common, while the Palermo stone records the construction of three ships, 52 metres long, under Snefrou. Homeric references to beaching pertain to certain kinds of boats in specific conditions; moreover, Homer does mention the existence of anchors and at least one harbour: 'There is an island in the surging sea, which they call Pharos, lying off Egypt. It has a harbour with good anchorage, and hence they put out to sea after drawing water.'[1] Of course, little bays in Aegean coasts are not comparable with Pharos or Alexandria, the flat stretches of North Africa, Lebanon and parts of Crete. It is impossible to date the earliest rock cuttings in these parts, but everything points to the existence of artificial anchorages for merchant ships in the Bronze Ages.

For convenience, early ports can be divided into three groups according to their structural pattern. The earliest are rock cut; that is to say, natural features are adapted by man to give shelter to craft riding at anchor. In the second group vertical walls are built on convenient shallows. Harbours of this type are in protected places such as bays and their installations connect with the defences of a walled town. Third and last come the harbours which were imposed on even

[1] Homer, *Odyssey*, Book IV.

unpromising coastlines as a result of Roman innovations such as the arch and a perfected form of hydraulic concrete. Unfortunately for archaeologists, things are not so simple in practice. Greek and Roman engineers knew a good thing when they saw one, and have often obscured the evidence we now see, by repairing and over-building serviceable Phoenician harbours.

All early ports had one thing in common: they had to be kept clear of silt at a time when dredging was unknown.[1] This was done variously: by designing the outer parts so that they deflected silt-bearing currents, by careful adaptation of depth in relation to the layout of the docks on the overall plan, by allowing a controlled current to sweep through the port or by flushing it out when necessary by means of channels. Diagnosis of the particular solution adopted is essential to the understanding of any port. The solution may even have a bearing on the date of the original structure.

To understand harbour-works and why they have a certain orientation, one must know the prevailing winds and currents. As it is impossible to assess these in one short visit, a good deal of preliminary research is required. It is certain that every diver, whether he is investigating shallow harbours, deep wrecks or just chasing fish, is affected by sedimentation and must understand how it forms. The bottom of the sea would have the same structure of hills and valleys as the land were it not for a continual levelling caused by sedimentation which is, in turn, due to land erosion.

Rains and winds carry earth and other matter into the sea. Rivers bring rock which becomes pebbly beaches. These pebbles are washed about by the swell, but remain in shallow water, being too heavy to go farther. The distribution of sediments is in fact governed by the size of the individual units, whether pebbles, or grains of sand, or mud. Any Mediterranean diver knows that if he swims out from a pebbly beach he will reach sand. Sand will give place to mud according to the force of local winds and currents and the weight of particles which they can carry over a given distance before depositing them in calm water where they can-

[1] The history of dredging is obscure; probably various methods were used contemporaneously in different localities. Marseille provides an interesting case history, since the Lacydon, now called the 'Vieux Port', has been in constant use from at least the sixth century B.C. Documents in the town's archives attest early dredging operations. According to Auguste Bouchayer, *Marseille, ou la Mer qui Monte*, Paris, 1931, the rate of flow of two torrents into the natural port diminished by 1323; a text records the invention of a 'machine to clean the port'. A sixteenth-century engraving, *Le vray portraict de Marseille dessiné en 1575 par Belleforest*, shows a dredger consisting of a windlass between two pontoons.

not move. He will also notice that there are two main kinds of sand: the sort found on 'a good beach for children' (which is usually quartzy) and another near, or where there have been, fields of seaweed. The latter is calcareous, being the broken shells of small animals that lived in the weed. It is also important for him to realize that in the sea, contrary to land, rocks are fertile and attract both fish and plant life, while sand and mud tend to be barren. Over wrecks, which like fields of weed were at one time also pasture for marine life, there will be a similar deposit of calcareous sand. Mud, the finest particles of all, starts at roughly 50 metres in the Mediterranean, and even at lesser depths there is an admixture of mud with sand. The process need be followed no further.

The silting of ports depends on winds and currents and the geography of the hinterland. Nesteroff puts it very clearly:

> It is the movement of water that keeps tiny particles in suspension until sooner or later, by the agency of currents, they leave the troubled zone. In ports, constructed expressly to reduce rough seas (at least such is the hope of their builders), one often finds mud. Whereas at the same depth outside the jetties there is sand.[1]

Once a harbour is abandoned, it falls into disrepair, or if in the first place its design was faulty, it fills with silt. Nearly all old harbour-works, whether they are now on dry land or whether they are still under a certain depth of water, are, at least partially, covered with silt.

Apart from silt, two other factors make harbours difficult to examine. The first is a change of sea-level due to earth movements, and the second, sea erosion. In the latter case, where swell and the greed of lithophagous animals have lowered moles and breakwaters, their lines can still be traced under water. It is possible to tell whether the sea-level has fallen by examining rocks for signs of an earlier water-line. If, on the other hand, the land has sunk it is useless to attempt a survey until geologists have analysed exactly what took place and when. One does occasionally come across submerged rocks which are undercut, indicating an earlier sea-level, but I do not think that observation alone will give a satisfactory answer on questions of subsidence. Greek and Roman harbours, even when partially buried, may be sufficiently like our own to be comprehensible. Courses of masonry are recognizable as moles and quays, but this is not the case with earlier and more interesting rock-cut works. In some Minoan harbours,

[1] W. Nesteroff, 'Géologie Sous-marine', *Bulletin Officiel de la Fédération Française d'Etudes et de Sports Sous-Marins*, Oct. 1960, no. 10.

such as Mallia in Crete, it is impossible to tell what part it is of the structure that emerges from the sand. We may be looking at the top of a fortification, part of a mole, a water channel or the wall at the bottom of a dock. Here there must either be a preliminary geological investigation or archaeologists themselves will have to devise methods of discovering the ancient level. Drilling, for instance, could produce a core sample through rock and sand.

Harbours are difficult to sound or excavate, because so far no instruments have been designed to dig in shallow water. Existing dredgers would be out of the question, while the air lift, so dear to underwater archaeologists, works only in depth, as it is powered by the rate at which air expands in relation to decreasing water pressure between bottom and surface. These problems are not insoluble, but they have never been given much consideration; hence our small comparative knowledge of ports. On shore digs the archaeologist tends to break off with a note to the effect that 'remains of harbour works can be distinguished under water'. At many early settlements known for their export trade the whereabouts, let alone the character of their harbours has never been queried. Divers have surveyed one or two classical ports, but land and underwater work have not run concurrently. When new techniques are devised they will, in turn, pose a fresh series of questions. Some have occurred to me in swimming over antique harbours; being without professional inhibitions, I can set them down, for it would give me as much satisfaction to be proved wrong as right, providing research were stimulated. To begin with: what other cities are like Tyre 'destroyed in the midst of the seas'?

I hasten to add that Tyre was built on an island, for readers of diving books have come to expect 'sunken cities'. These places are omitted for partly subjective reasons. Were I asked to dive on one, I might be too weak-minded to refuse, if the site were in a pleasant part of the Mediterranean. I can, however, imagine with distaste what the work would be like. A demon archaeologist would drive us out at dawn into turbid water with our measuring-rods, compasses and marker buoys. In a maximum depth of 3 metres some rubble would emerge from the sand, and if one were lucky there might be paving-stones, tumbled columns and part of a drain. What a horror of boredom! The earth itself must have heaved a sigh of ennui engulfing the whole squalid community. Let us have no illusions about cities sinking upright and undisturbed to a respectable depth. In any case, why should archaeologists, at vast expense, examine submerged towns when so many land sites cry out for excavation? In Turkey alone there are countless cities to dig. Aspendos is marked by a Roman theatre, standing with its booking offices open, a monumental question mark in the middle of rolling fields (Plate 12). Where did the 10,000 spectators that filled its seats come from? Was it once surrounded by a town now buried or by farms rich as Texas ranches, whence the owners in Cadillac-litters converged when the Antioch players were on? These valid questions could be answered on land with a fraction of the effort and expenditure required to excavate the dullest submerged ruins. And yet . . . there are always exceptions: I remember rock-cut tombs and a Minoan settlement submerged . . . places where I long to dive again.

Tyre and Sidon were not the first ports I saw through a mask, but as I have said, they were the first to interest me. The marvellous associations of their names might seem reason enough, but, in addition, careful (and underestimated) research made them intelligible. Here, at last, port survey had been tackled on a grand scale: 'On land, from the air and underwater', to quote the sub-title of the Tyre report. When the work started, Lebanon was under French administration and Père Poidebard had at his disposal Air Force planes, standard apparatus divers, and boats from the Navy, also various specialists from the Department of Public Works. Curiously enough, it was the rapid silting of the modern ports that occasioned this high-powered research. The *Survey of Tyre* started in 1935, before free diving had been invented. What is more, Père Poidebard published his report by 1939 with a promptitude that amounts to archaeological heroism.[1]

Lebanon today, though surrounded by the changing Arab countries, has the gaiety of Monaco and some of the political character and prosperity of Switzerland. The commercial instincts of the Phoenicians, which still persist, give the tiny state a certain stability and resilience in the midst of external turmoil and the delicate internal balance between the Christian, Moslem and Druse communities. Tyre and Sidon are old Moslem towns near the Israeli border. They do not now compare with their predecessors, nor even with other modern Lebanese ports such as Beirut and Tripoli. There is an oil refinery near Sidon, but it does not employ much local labour. Orchards and gardens still cover the fertile hinterland and evoke biblical descriptions, though the ports themselves are used only by small craft.

Things have not changed since Père Poidebard was called in before the war.

[1] A. Poidebard, *Tyr*, Librairie Orientaliste Paul Geuthner, Paris, 1939; A. Poidebard, J. Lauffray and R. Mouterde, *Sidon*, Imprimerie Catholique, Beyrouth, 1951.

Having made an aerial survey of Roman remains in the Syrian desert,[1] he was asked to apply the same methods to discover silt-bearing currents. Since he was an archaeologist, he would also survey the ancient harbour-works at Tyre. Their exact position was unknown; moreover, the secret of their construction had practical importance, since it might solve present silting problems. He took full advantage of the opportunity, photographing not only Tyre but also Sidon and other Phoenician ports along the coast. Meanwhile, as though to justify him, a jetty was being constructed at Sidon, and within a few months this new port also filled with silt. War intervened, so nothing was done about it until 1945, when Poidebard was again consulted over the post-mortem, and started his second survey of the ancient installations at Sidon.

There was ample documentary and archaeological proof that Tyre and Sidon had been flourishing ports from Bronze Age to Roman times and must therefore have been kept free of silt for over a thousand years. How had this been done? How big were the ports and how were they subdivided?

According to Herodotus, Tyre was founded in 2550 B.C. at the time of the Caananite invasions. However this may be, by the ninth century B.C. its mercantile expansion led to the establishment of overseas trading posts, on the lines of the East India Company, throughout the Aegean Islands and the Mediterranean in general. The Phoenicians were too sensible to settle in cold climates, but their trade extended to the tin mines of Cornwall. The *zeitgeist* of the island town is better savoured by skimming Ezekiel's, albeit biased, account. He regards its prosperity with the severity one would expect from a Wahabi viewing America through a Hollywood film. After foretelling the destruction of its 'pleasant houses', this seventh-century B.C. account continues:

> Shall not the isles shake at the sound of thy fall. . . . Then all the princes of the sea shall come down from their thrones, . . . and put off their broidered garments. . . . And they shall take up a lamentation for thee . . . thou that art situate at the entry of the sea which art a merchant of the people for many isles. . . . Thy borders are in the midst of the seas, thy builders have perfected thy beauty. . . . They have made all thy ship-boards of fir trees of Senir: they have taken cedars from Lebanon to make masts for thee. Of the oaks of Bashan have they made thine oars; the company of the Ashurites have made thy benches of ivory, brought out of the isles of Chittim. Fine linen with broidered work from Egypt was that which thou spreadest forth to be thy sail: blue and purple from the isles of Elishah was that which covered thee. The inhabitants of Sidon and Arvad were thy mariners: their wise men . . .

[1] A. Poidebard, *La Trace de Rome dans le Désert de Syrie*, Geuthner, Paris, 1934.

> were thy pilots. The ancients of Gebail and the wise men thereof were . . . thy calkers: all the ships of the sea with their mariners were in thee to occupy thy merchandise.
>
> Tarshish was thy merchant by reason of . . . all kind of riches; with silver, iron, tin and lead, they traded in thy fairs. Javan, Tubal, and Meshech . . . traded the persons of men and vessels of brass in thy market. They of the house of Togarmah traded in thy fairs with horses and horsemen. . . . Syria was thy merchant by reason of the multitude of the wares of thy making: they occupied in thy fairs with emeralds, purple and broidered work, and fine linen, and coral and agate. Judah and the land of Israel . . . traded in thy market wheat of Minnith, and Pannang, and honey, and oil, and balm. Damascus was thy merchant in the multitude of the wares of thy making, . . . the wine of Helbon, and white wool . . . Arabia, and all the princes of Kedar, they occupied with thee in lambs and rams, and goats: . . . The merchants of Sheba and Raamah with chief of all spices . . . precious stones and gold . . . the merchants of Sheba Asshur and Chalmad . . . in blue cloths, and broidered work . . . chests of rich apparel bound with cords, and made of cedar . . . and thou wast replenished, and made very glorious in the midst of the seas.[1]

This description makes it clear that Tyre was at the apex of the great land routes. Like other Phoenician towns, her policy was to trade with the current Imperialist power, even providing it with ships when necessary. Tyre, Sidon and Ugarit paid tribute to Egypt in the 18th Dynasty, and during Tyre's greatest prosperity she had similar relations with Assyrians, Neo-Babylonians and Persians. However, she was not without local rulers, and some of their names are very familiar; Abibal governed in the tenth century when David was King in Hebron. Hiram, his son, sent craftsmen and cedar trees to David and later to Solomon to build the temple in Jerusalem. Another Abibal, a priest who succeeded Hiram, married his daughter Jezebel to Ahab of Israel. Miss Kenyon has remarked that 'research in Palestine is beginning to show how strong Phoenician influence was in the process which began under David, which was in fact the civilisation of Israel'.[2]

The much sung Dido, daughter of Belos, King of Tyre, and sister of Pygmalion (who killed her husband Sychaeus), led a local faction of aristocrats in a *coup d'état* which failed and then seized a fleet, conveniently lying in port, sailed off to found Carthage and met her destiny in the person of Aeneas. All this is the general picture we have of Tyre, but it is a hard fact that Alexander the Great considered it to be the key of the East and had to interrupt his conquest by a long

[1] Ezekiel, Chapters 26 and 27.

[2] Kathleen Kenyon, *Archaeology in the Holy Land*, Benn, 1960, p. 244.

siege. The city fell to him in 332 B.C. and he resumed his pursuit of Darius. After Alexander's death, Tyre with Syria passed to one of his generals and continued under Seleucid rule until it fell to the Romans in 64 B.C.

Although Tyre became an early Christian bishopric, its Byzantine and Crusader history are of no direct interest, for its great prosperity ended with the Romans. After that, the harbour shrank and took on the easily recognizable and dull characteristics of a Crusader strongpoint.

Tsor in Hebrew means rock. The derivation is significant, not only with regard to the original island of Tyre but also to the surrounding docks and anchorages. Other Phoenician ports—Arados (Ruad), Byblos and Sidon—were also built on rocky islands or promontories. At certain parts of the flat Lebanese coastal strip reefs run parallel to the shore in a north-to-south direction. The strongest prevailing wind comes from the south-west. The island of Tyre was in the middle of one such rock cordon (Fig. 17). In times of peace it was joined to the shore by a causeway which could be destroyed when there was danger of attack. When Tyre fell to Alexander he built a permanent causeway out of the ruins of the town itself and almost fulfilled the prophecy: 'they shall destroy the walls and break down her towers: I will also scrape her dust from her and make her like the top of a rock. It shall be a place for the spreading of nets in the midst of the sea . . . it shall become a spoil to the nations.' But the town was rebuilt and the ports continued to function.

To anyone motoring from Beirut, Tyre now appears, at least from the north, to be on the mainland. One turns right, off the coast road, into the old Arab town, and I have to admit with regret that when I was there one had to continue through it at top speed. On three consecutive years my visits to Lebanon coincided with external, and then internal, political upsets, and Tyre was a notorious trouble spot. At best its strict citizens took exception to women in bathing-suits. There was talk of ugly incidents. Certainly, boys threw stones and insults at foreign cars. A picnic at Tyre was *mal vu* by Lebanese friends and officials. Even

---

17. (over) *Tyre: the outer Egyptian and Sidonian ports and the closed port within the city's fortifications. Remains of the ancient harbour-works are shown in solid black. Depth contours indicate the now almost submerged line of dunary reef. Note the area of water (depth over 10 metres) which, before the construction of a solid causeway, would have encircled the island town. This depth of water, the breaks at the base of the reef and the direction of the prevailing winds would together have allowed sufficient through-current to prevent the formation of silt in the ports.*

20 m.
reinforcing moles
EGYPTIAN
HARBOUR
10 m.
5 m.
0
500
1000 m.

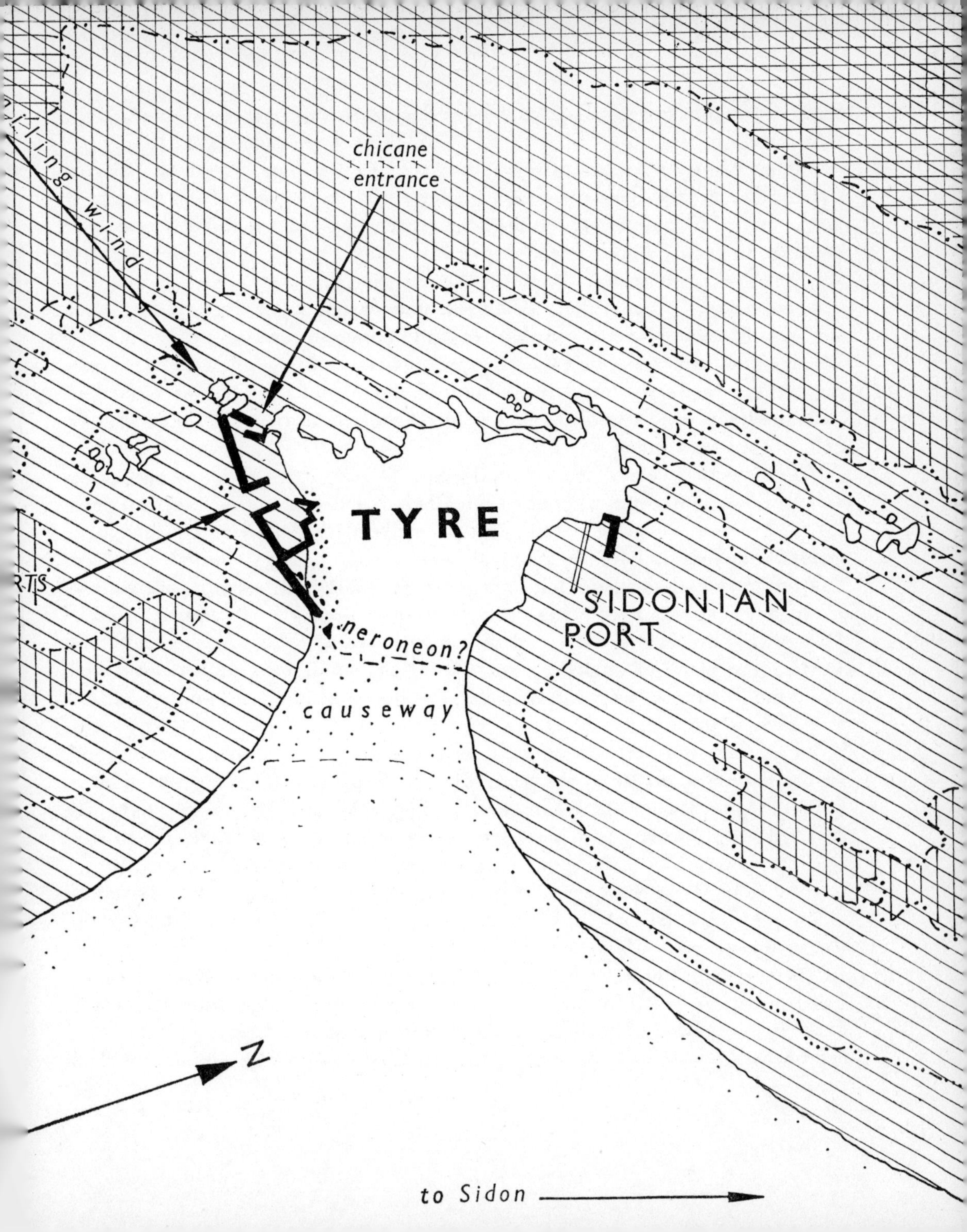

chicane
entrance
TYRE
SIDONIAN
PORT
neroneon?
causeway
to Sidon

a devoted maid from Beirut refused to accompany her employers on an outing in that direction.

I think it was as a result of this refusal that I once found myself standing on the high waste land, past the modern cemetery at the far side of the town, with an American acquaintance, his untended, three-year-old son and a twelve-year-old Arab boy who, more enterprising than the rest of his gang, had jumped on to the car as we sped through the town. We regarded this boy with embarrassment until it became apparent that he had not only learned a few words of English at the local Missionary School so that we could communicate but he was also devoted to small children. Since the father was bent on shooting fish and I on examining harbour-works, the boy delivered us from the dilemma of what was to be done with the baby, who could not be left in the middle of rock-cut tanks with his elders submerged, some way off.

This incident occurred before I realized the full extent of the taboos on bathing at Tyre. Two years later, when the Emir Chehab, Director of the Beirut Archaeological Museum, suggested that I went officially, with full diving equipment, to examine the foundations of a mole, all sorts of complications ensued. I realized how lucky we had been, and felt some pangs of remorse at the embarrassment we might have caused. Tyre being near the frontier, passes were required from its Port Authorities before one could dive in the bay. On this occasion, however, we had the place to ourselves, apart from the small boys and a one-armed dynamite fisherman, whose presence was as illegal as our own, and who therefore gave no trouble.

To revert to the harbour-works: from the high open ground where we stood, on the southernmost tip of the peninsula, the limits of the ancient city with its ports were just discernible. Facing south, with our backs to the modern town, the rock fell steeply seawards to the right and ended in a narrow shelf strewn with columns, pierced by mysterious cuttings and awash. In front of us, down a gradual slope, both masonry and rock-cut installations were visible above and below the water. Beyond was a huge bay about 4 kilometres long by 2 wide; the cordon of reefs which once enclosed it is now only visible from the air, except at certain times, when they are indicated by the movement of the waves. Landwards, to our left, in an area still reserved for excavation, the recognizable harbour works become buried under sand dunes. One could see how Nature had encroached, where once an arm of the sea had separated the island from the coast.

It must be stressed again that neither a diver nor an archaeologist could have made head or tail of that view without Père Poidebard's report. As a result of his research and a certain experience of similar sites, I think I can see a pattern emerge and a connection between this and other contemporary ports. If I am right, it would amount to a point of departure, to the possibility of posing valid questions on similar rock cuttings. The answers on, say, a Minoan port could be obtained only by repeating the processes Poidebard evolved, and many others as well.

Before starting his survey, Poidebard knew that there had been two kinds of port at Tyre. Strabo describes them in his *Geography* (XVI, 11):

> Tyre is wholly an island built up in nearly the same way as Arados; and it is connected to the mainland by a mole which was constructed when Alexander was besieging it; and it has two harbours, one that can be closed and the other open; the latter is called the Egyptian port. They say that the houses have several storeys and are higher than those of Rome, and on this account, when an earthquake took place, it lacked but little of destroying the whole City.

Closed, in this sense, means a port within the city's fortifications. The open ports used by foreign ships might be described as anchorages (Fig. 17). The extent and design of the inner, closed port had never been fully established, while the position of the Egyptian port, except that as its name implies it must have been to the south, was completely unknown. Some thought, like Renan, that it was below the sand dunes. Local sponge divers, on the other hand, told Poidebard that there were anchorages in the bay and that they had seen traces of masonry on the bottom.

Aerial photographs also showed a line of shallows that turned out to be the submerged reef which ran along the coast from either side of the island. The oldest fishermen said that two specific points on the southern part of this reef had been lowered by 1 metre within living memory, worn away by the famous local swell. This tallied with Maundrell's description of Tyre, which he visited in 1698 on his pilgrimage to Jerusalem. From a vantage point in the town he had seen two enormous bays, one on either side of him. They were protected from the sea by a terrace-like mole, tangential to the tip of the peninsula. He was too far away, he said, to see whether the phenomenon was natural or man-made. Actually, it was a bit of both.

To Poidebard, these clues warranted investigation, but a glance at the map (Fig. 17) will show how absurd the theory of a port in the bay must have appeared to archaeologists accustomed to logical compact structures built on land. The line of shallows was over 2 kilometres long. Besides, fishermen's tales are always suspect. Poidebard did in fact find the foundations of two moles, reinforcing the inner face of the southern reef. They were cunningly orientated to deflect the silt-bearing currents which had shown on some of his aerial photographs. He concluded that this was the site of the outer, Egyptian harbour, the anchorage for foreign ships. Its colossal size is explained by the fact that the design, depending, as it did, on the natural reefs, was consequently dictated by their dimensions. When we compare Tyre with the survey made by Gaston Jondet of the ancient harbour works at Pharos[1] and with Poidebard's own survey of Sidon (not to mention any unsurveyed ports of that period) we see that the areas covered are similar and justify his conclusions on Tyre.

The method of work which Poidebard evolved, long before the invention of free-diving apparatus, was exemplary: but like Pitt Rivers' innovations, it fell into oblivion. First comes his use of aerial photography. For archaeological records, under-water photography tends to be overrated: in depth, even if an overlay is achieved, it is difficult to interpret. On the other hand, in shallow water aerial photographs of ports seem to me an indispensable preliminary to any serious work. The earlier the port, the more essential the air survey. In areas of several square kilometres a slow-moving diver, even if he is lucky enough to chance on masonry, will be unable to orientate it and follow its course. It will be interrupted by breaks or covered in places by sand and weed. Subtle changes in depth, so important to the function of early ports, will not be apparent on the bottom. Divers move three-dimensionally, with no horizon to guide them. Relief is not noticeable in diffused submarine light where there are no cast shadows. Once aerial photographs have established the salient features of a port and the questions that arise therefrom, then significant features can be buoyed so that divers start work within well-defined limits. There is a school of thought which recommends submarine Vespas, bubble cars, torpedoes or subaqua-planes for general survey. It is doubtful whether these machines are much good for detailed prospection in deep water, but they are certainly not practical in shallows, where their driver is too busy avoiding obstacles to be able to observe.

After the air survey it took Commandant Gizard (Poidebard's chief diver) and his assistant thirty-three diving hours to buoy, plot and measure the moles in the

[1] Gaston Jondet, 'Les Ports Submergés de l'Ancienne Ile de Pharos', *Institut Egyptien*, Tome IX, Cairo, 1916.

Egyptian harbour. These consisted of one and sometimes two courses of colossal blocks laid on the rocky shallows at depths ranging from 7 to 13 metres. In some places the stones were scattered, in others lines of headers each measuring $3 \times 1 \times 0{\cdot}75$ metres were faced by blocks of $3 \times 3 \times 0{\cdot}75$ metres.

On clear days Père Poidebard, ever resourceful, took vertical photographs of these stones from the surface, by simply putting his camera into a *calefat* (a bucket with a glass bottom used by all Mediterranean fishermen) and shooting over the side of the boat. The plans were drawn from the divers' measurements afterwards sited on the surface from buoys.[1] Even more remarkable, in the year 1935, Poidebard made the first archaeological record photographs underwater. His diver was given a camera in a watertight case and photographed the elevation of the masonry at the bottom. Curiously enough, this same camera case was used by Commandant Tailliez at Mahdia during one of the first wreck excavations by free divers. Again we must recognize the distinction between aerial photographs of ruins in shallow water which, providing the water is clear, are in every sense similar to aerial photographs of land remains, and the completely different visual problems that occur the moment the camera lens is submerged. Poidebard realized this and saw that he could not make a satisfactory overlay-plan of architectural remains by shooting photographs in the water; the limitations of underwater photography will be discussed later when we come to wreck survey.

Reading the Tyre Report today, after so many amateur attempts at submarine archaeology, one is constantly impressed by Poidebard's foresight and understanding. Most striking is his grasp of the psychological effects of diving. When men surfaced he would take down signed and witnessed statements. A professional diver dives to do a specific job and comes back with the facts; only then does he start to rationalize. His interpretations are not necessarily useless, depending on his skill, knowledge and intelligence, but the unvarnished data that a scientist requires remain with him for only a few moments of truth. The practice of taking statements has never, to my knowledge, been repeated,

[1] Buoying: generally speaking, a line between a buoy and its anchor should not be tight; if it is, the slightest current will displace the mooring or force the buoy below the surface. The greater the depth, the less precise will be the surface mark made by the buoy. At about 10–15 metres even a large buoy with a very thin line attaching it to its anchor is unlikely to be vertically above its mooring. At 40 metres such marking would be impossible, but at 5 metres (which is an average depth in port work) the degree of accuracy in buoying is not incompatible with surveying from land by means of a theodolite.

though it becomes essential when archaeologists use amateur divers who imagine that their minds are quite unimpaired by depth.

The final evidence on the constructions in the Egyptian port was geological. Samples of bedrock, the reef and the blocks themselves were submitted to M. Lucien Cayeux, geologist and author of a work on sea-levels in the Mediterranean in historical times. The bedrock was a fine, hard limestone, the reef a common Mediterranean rock of coarser but also calcareous nature, known as 'poros'. The blocks were a conglomerate in which flint pebbles predominated. In Cayeux's opinion the conglomerate was not local, and even had there been a chance deposit of this sort of stone, it would not have fractured in regular blocks. M. André Godard, an authority on comparative architecture and Director of Antiquities in Iran, inspected the remains and confirmed that they were masonry. Finally, André Watier, a specialist in harbour construction, commented:

> There is no reason to doubt the antiquity of this structure. Even heavier units were used in the temple at Baalbek. The ancients had both divers and adequate means of lifting. Divers could easily position blocks which weighed 9 tons (6 tons under water) and were lowered on ropes.

All agreed that the reef had been eroded and the moles partially destroyed by the powerful swell. There was no evidence that the sea-level had risen.

Land archaeologists confronted with underwater reports naturally tend to disbelief or over-credulity; some still doubt that Poidebard found the Egyptian harbour, on the grounds that the blocks he photographed might have been a natural formation. It is true that rocks often look artificial under water, and one must be very careful. There is also the problem of camouflage: weed in the Mediterranean is comparatively sparse, but what there is, is mostly in shallow water. Poidebard says that on his second season, in spring, when the sea burgeons like the land, his divers could not find the masonry they had measured the previous autumn because it was overgrown. These were the reasons why I, as an outsider, was asked to dive on the moles in 1958, but the Lebanese troubles intervened and I never got there. However, unlike Poidebard's critics, I have some underwater experience. I think that he proved his point, but in the case of these two moles I can judge only from the report and photographs.

If we accept that the now submerged reef was reinforced by moles in ancient times, then it is, beyond reasonable doubt, the site of the lost Egyptian harbour. Everything else falls into place, and the relationship of the island to the other ports, which encircled it except to the seaward side, becomes comprehensible. Remains of the two closed ports (that is to say the ports that came within the cities' fortifications) are visible not only on the south, as described, but also to the north outside the jetty of the modern port. The town's landward docks are lost below the dunes, but the masonry shows that they were still in use in Roman times. When Tyre was an island the northern and southern closed ports connected with each other and encircled the town. Current from the open or Egyptian anchorage would have flowed through this sea channel and kept the now-buried docks clear of silt. When the causeway was built artificial channels may have served the same purpose, but only land excavation can prove their existence. Poidebard does not, explicitly, suggest that there were channels, but then he does not claim his survey was complete.

On his plan the reef moles in the Egyptian harbour measured respectively 550 and 280 metres by 30 metres wide. The individual foundation stones, as we have seen, were colossal. What was their date? In a narrow sense the question is almost irrelevant to the aims which Poidebard set himself. Ezekiel had been quite categorical: 'Though thou be sought for, yet shalt thou never be found again, saith the Lord God.' There might have been a certain irony in the priest disproving the Prophet. However, judging from the size of the blocks, the southern moles are likely to be Roman; why, then, should their presence indicate the lost Phoenician anchorage? The argument is that these moles, even if they were Roman, were reinforcing the reef, which must already have been in use; that this reef is an integral part of the general layout of the harbour and that this layout is not Roman. When the reefs were above water level they were probably cut like those at Sidon and Ruad and even certain parts of the inner ports of Tyre itself. In all these places a wall of rock is left to seaward and built up where necessary with stones quarried from inside, where the reef had been levelled to make landing quays (Fig. 18). It seems probable to me that the reefs at Tyre did not last, because they had been intrinsically frail, with narrow bases. Tyrian engineers greedy of space, like Dust Bowl farmers, weakened the sea-wall. Once the notorious swell reached and in certain seasons pounded the installations, they started to disintegrate. Roman reinforcements probably date from this period. Maundrell, in the seventeenth century, saw 'terraces', a description which makes one suspect that the sea defences had been so lowered that the structure was doomed.

Unvarnished conclusions fall flat: after all this fuss, what had been found?

only broken courses of foundations inside an eroded line of rocks. Yet, if these were quays which, taken together with part of the reef, extended well over a kilometre, complementing the closed ports round the town, then we can imagine the 30-metre ships from Egypt drawing alongside, unloading on to lighters, picking up a return cargo of cedar or taking rafts in tow if, as has been suggested, the wood was floated and not carried in the ships. It cannot be overstressed that the method of research Poidebard developed was as important as the archaeological results. No future excavators can afford to disregard them.

As on all good excavations, something has been left for posterity. When

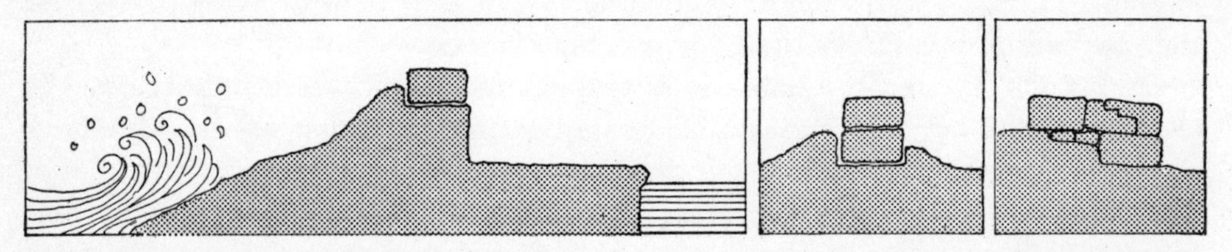

18. Section showing the Phoenician method of adapting rock to make a mole. Swell breaks on to a natural slope of rock, which is then cut to make a sea-wall and levelled on the sheltered side to form a landing quay. When necessary these walls are built of large blocks laid in rock-cut trenches. Alternatively, the blocks may be cut in steps and keyed together.

methods improve, further research will be profitable at Tyre, both on land and underwater. Poidebard himself formulates questions for future generations. He does not claim to have surveyed the entire area of the bays and reefs: there may be more traces of construction. Judging from similar anchorages, it would be worthwhile looking for landing quays on shore, under the dunes, opposite the reef-moles. At Sidon there is part of a Roman quay where lighters could unload the cargo taken on from ships alongside a similar, outer anchorage; there may be another at Tyre. Alternatively, in Phoenician times the lighters may have beached; this is another question. Thirdly, it should eventually be possible to date at least some of the submarine remains. To do this, considerable thought would have to be given to problems of shallow-water excavation, moving sand, coring or blasting trenches through seemingly natural formations with small, controlled charges of dynamite. Even the samples of conglomerate, taken by Poidebard's divers from the reef, were disguised beneath a thick deposit of concretion. Traces of hydraulic concrete containing datable sherds, or rubble-fill, might well remain in crevices of reef, while anchor stocks or jetsam would be buried in the surrounding sand.

I spent some time in the closed port or the naval docks within the fortifications of ancient Tyre. Before completing the picture of the overall mechanism of this port, I cannot resist a digression which concerns a quite different aspect of marine research. By the seaward entrance of the closed port, in only 3 metres of water, a tile and a heap of shells caught my eye, so I dived. Sure enough, there was an octopus in a tolerable, stone-built house with a one-tiled roof. After seeing tile-carrying wrecks, I became interested in this common but undocumented trade, and reproach myself for missing any clue to the type and provenance of ancient tiles. However, at that time I was more interested in the octopus: a little beast, about 18 inches long from tentacle tip to tip, who looked up reproachfully until I replaced his roof. Some minutes later, the one-armed dynamiter went in. This illegal and destructive method of fishing is all too common in Lebanon. As a result, there are few adult fish along its coasts, only the young and foolish venture near rocks, where a charge of dynamite not only kills them but also the organisms on which they feed. Dynamiters swim with the charge grasped firmly in one hand. The arm sticks straight up, so that from a distance the swimmer looks like the snorkel of a submarine. When he sees even the tiniest fish below, he lets fly. In the bay where I lived the bona fide professional fisherman implored me not to venture outside, as I would most certainly share the fate of the fish. Once a charge went off about 20 yards away, slightly winding me. A less-fortunate diver told me he had been a closer target, and subsequently revenged himself by ducking the dynamiter. The one-armed man had obviously blown himself up when inexperienced. His loss of limb probably occurred on land; victims of underwater explosion die from internal haemorrhage.

On that occasion our man let off his charge directly above the octopus, and was rewarded by a meagre catch of tiddlers. Silver corpses floated to the surface, others he had to dive for. The twelve-year-old boy who was with us retrieved a minute fish which he presented to the baby, who carried it back to Beirut, where it got confused in the kitchen with his father's harvest. Octopus is a great delicacy, worth twice its weight in fish, so I waited to see whether the man would return with the corpse. When he left I went back and found the animal in the ruins of its house, which I helped to repair. Jet propelled and exuding ink, the octopus shot backwards when I touched it, quite unharmed. One would suppose a virtually boneless creature to be immune, but it is more likely that the tile roof took the shock. Blast injury has its strongest effect on parts of the body where there is gas; in men it is the guts and lungs that are damaged, and in fish the air bladder. Sharks do not seem to mind dynamite and lobsters stand it very well, but of course if the explosion is near enough the animal is destroyed.

Let us now return to the waste land, whence I first saw the port of Tyre, and which dominates its closed ports. To seaward, directly below the tip of this high ground, partly submerged and apparently formless constructions turn out to be the first of three docks, all bounded by the same long wall or mole parallel to the land. Taken together, they constitute the closed port. The westernmost dock juts out to sea, cleaving and deflecting the swell like the prow of a ship. Its tip is on a line with, and indeed founded on, an extremity of the submerged reef of the Egyptian harbour (see Fig. 17).

The seaward entrance to these docks is a narrow affair, only 20 metres wide and built in a *chicane*, or a break between the inner wall and the outer parallel mole. This design would not only be easy to shut by chain but it was also dominated by a watch tower on land. The orientation of one side of this *chicane* entrance deflects streams of silt, which might otherwise get into the docks. What construction remains on the rock-based, prow-shaped entrance is comparable to the sea-walls of Mahdia, Sidon and Ruad. The rock having been flattened at water-level, a trench was cut to hold the foundations of a wall; some of the blocks are still *in situ*. The mole which bounds all three docks, as it continues landwards from this entrance, is founded underwater on prismatic headers held by concrete and divided into caissons by transverse lines of blocks placed end to end. Most of the surface masonry from these docks has disappeared because, according to Poidebard, they were used as quarries for buildings in places as far away as Beirut, Acre and Jaffa.

The westernmost dock was divided from the eastern by another and larger entrance, some 40 metres across, known as the *Bab el Mina* or Lighthouse Gate. Just outside the docks at this point the bottom is littered with concreted lumps of masonry labelled on the plan (made by the *Bureau Topographique des Armées du Levant*) as 'remains of exterior organization'. There is something touchingly human in the studied vagueness. One can imagine a soldier suggesting that the stuff might have some connection with a lighthouse, while the archaeologist, reluctant to jump to conclusions, devised a less-positive term. The lumps were certainly shapeless rubble.

This Lighthouse Gate opened on to the protected waters of the Egyptian harbour. From either side of the gate lines of fill, or moles which had lost their facing of blocks, ran inwards, separating the docks. The last, landward division of the closed port, known as the repair dock, is now mostly buried in sand. The wall common to all three docks, and separating them from the harbour, also ends on land at the remains of a defence tower. Here Poidebard put down a trench in 1936. The tower was the junction of the mole bounding the docks and the landward, city wall. Poidebard found that the two lower courses of the mole corresponded with the foundations of the tower at a pre-Roman level. There was an adjacent and buried Roman quay; this too may have been on earlier foundations; this is a question that might now be answered, but Poidebard had not the machinery to dig in watery sand below sea-level. In the future, he concluded, some method will have to be found to enable archaeologists to go down to bedrock in such places.

In these circumstances excavation, if it is to be reasonably efficient, is a job for engineers. It is, however, apparent that the machinery they use in port construction is neither suitable nor within the budget of an archaeological expedition; dredgers, for instance, would be quite impracticable. I am not competent to solve these problems, but certain instruments which are often used by divers do spring to mind. A water jet, working on essentially the same principles as a fireman's hose, could be adapted to clear sand from masonry that was awash. There are even ways of adapting air-lifts for certain kinds of shallow water work.[1]

The watch tower at the extremity of the closed port, where Poidebard made his sounding, brings us to the causeway that now joins Tyre to the mainland. The general opinion from Renan onwards is that the Emporion or commercial warehouses are now below this causeway, the encroaching sand dunes and the modern town. This part has not been excavated. The Emporion probably stretched along the landward side of the island by the channel connecting the Egyptian harbour with the Sidonian harbour north of the town.

The last part of the jig-saw puzzle is this northern Sidonian harbour, which almost corresponds with the present port (Fig. 17). Remains of an ancient mole can still be seen on the seaward side of the present jetty; it is more curved and closed to the north than its modern counterpart. The structure was pierced by channels (to allow through current and prevent silt from settling) which show it

[1] W. Haag, 'La Recherche Archéologique dans nos Lacs Suisses offre-t-elle le moindre Intérêt?' *Informations sous-marines*, No. 6, 1958.

to be of Roman origin. This design makes it unlikely that the mole was built on earlier, Phoenician foundations. We should look for the remains of Tyre's earliest 'Sidonian' harbour on the northern extension of the now submerged dunary reef. Poidebard's survey does not cover this area, so this is another of the questions he had to leave for posterity.

Connecting as it did with modern Tyre, the 'Sidonian' port was out of bounds for me. Nor was I sorry, as any diver will understand; a port in use has about as much attraction as a cesspool. I once had the doubtful privilege of diving for a Venetian ship in the old port of Heraclion (which is still in use); afterwards I had to beg a double water ration and scrub myself from top to toe with detergent.

To sum up: when the city of Tyre was on an island the basic design of its ports depended on the line of reefs running parallel with the shore and tangential to its seaward tip. In some places they emerged as islands, in others they can have been no more than shallows, but the breaks between, coupled with the formation of the bottom, which sloped towards the south, prevented silting. These natural features were adapted and improved. There was no need for special flushing channels, as the current from the south circulated in a controlled way throughout all the harbour-works.

No clear archaeological evidence as to dating emerged, but in the circumstances the type of cement or dressed stones is of secondary importance to the overall layout. We can imagine the military, commercial and shipbuilding yards in the closed ports and the large foreign ships lying off the reefs. Perhaps their cargoes were transhipped at the anchorages and taken to the opposite shore, or to the now buried Emporion, whence, in turn, the city's exports were loaded.

Tyre has a place in the history of diving; Quintus Curtius and Thucydides say that the Tyrians used divers during the siege to destroy Alexander's blockade made of wooden posts and also to cut the anchor ropes of his ships. Philo of Byzantium, as we have seen, asserts that, as a result, anchor chains were substituted for ropes. He also advocates sentinels with tridents as a defence against divers. Again, Alexander's general, Seleucus Nicator, who ruled Tyre, had descendants who retained an anchor as their emblem (though it has never been suggested that this had to do with the Tyrian divers during Alexander's siege).

Medieval legends attribute the first diving bell to Alexander, though there is no contemporary account of this. The most amusing stories are to be found first, in the twelfth-century *Alexandriade*, secondly, a Coptic legend, and thirdly, in

Masudi's *Golden Fields*.[1] In the first Alexander is shocked by the things he saw through his glass bell:

> *Seignieurs, Barons, fait-il, bien me suis aperçu*
> *Que le monde en entier est damné et perdu*
> *Les violents grands poissons devorent les menus.*

In the Ethiopian legend Alexander prays to God that he may be allowed to explore the wonders of His submarine creation in order to glorify them. Divine agreement, supplemented by self-help in the form of another glass bell, allows him to see weird monsters.

Masudi's story brings us back to our subject, for it has to do with the construction of a port at Alexandria. Each day's work disappeared in the course of the night. At last Alexander made a wooden box with glass windows and went down in it, accompanied by two draughtsmen, my first recorded predecessors. They saw demons with human bodies busy destroying the harbour-works with saws, hammers and crowbars. Life-size replicas of these demons were made from the underwater drawings and placed around the construction. The following night, when the monsters were confronted by their doppelgängers, they took fright and never returned.

[1] 'Alexandriade', published by Paul Mayer in *Alexandre le Grand au Moyen Age*, Vol. I, Paris, 1886; E. A. W. Budge, *The Alexander Book in Ethiopia*, Oxford, 1933; Mas' oudi, *Les Prairies d'Or*, XXXII.

CHAPTER 6

The Layout of Sidon – Island Anchorage – The Closed Ports – The Hidden Mole – Fortifications – The Sluices – Structural Comparisons – Natural Rock-Pools – Tabarja Interlude – The Port of Byblos

WHAT other ports are there like Tyre? Sidon for one; on paper it looks different, but for the very good reason that its layout was also dictated by natural features (Fig. 19). Otherwise, the principles are similar, with one important exception: the desilting arrangements in Sidon's closed port. Poidebard's pioneer work at Tyre would lose most of its value if we could not compare the way this Phoenician port worked with another, contemporary mechanism.

Like Tyre, Sidon had an outer anchorage for foreign ships. Here, the strong, wide-based reefs are still above sea-level, so the ancient installations remain for all to see. Nevertheless, before Poidebard's survey there were doubts about the situation of the outer harbour. Two bays to the south of the town misled Renan[1] and subsequent archaeologists, who took them for natural anchorages. The Southern bay, called Minet er Ruman (the bay of the Pomegranates, not the Romans), is too small, while the larger is not sufficiently protected. Nor have ancient remains been discovered in either place. On the other hand, the long, rocky island at the extremity of the reef cordon, to the North of the town, has everything (Plate 11).

The seaward slopes of the reef-island break the swell more effectively than a vertical wall. A decent interval is left to complete this deterrent, before the rock is cut vertically and then levelled on the shore side to make landing quays. The resulting sea-wall, partially cut and partially built, runs the length of the island. In one rock-cut section there are sockets for beams, which would have carried an upper storey of, perhaps, a quayside warehouse. A chamber 12 × 15 metres

[1] E. Renan, *Mission en Phénicie*, Paris, 1864.

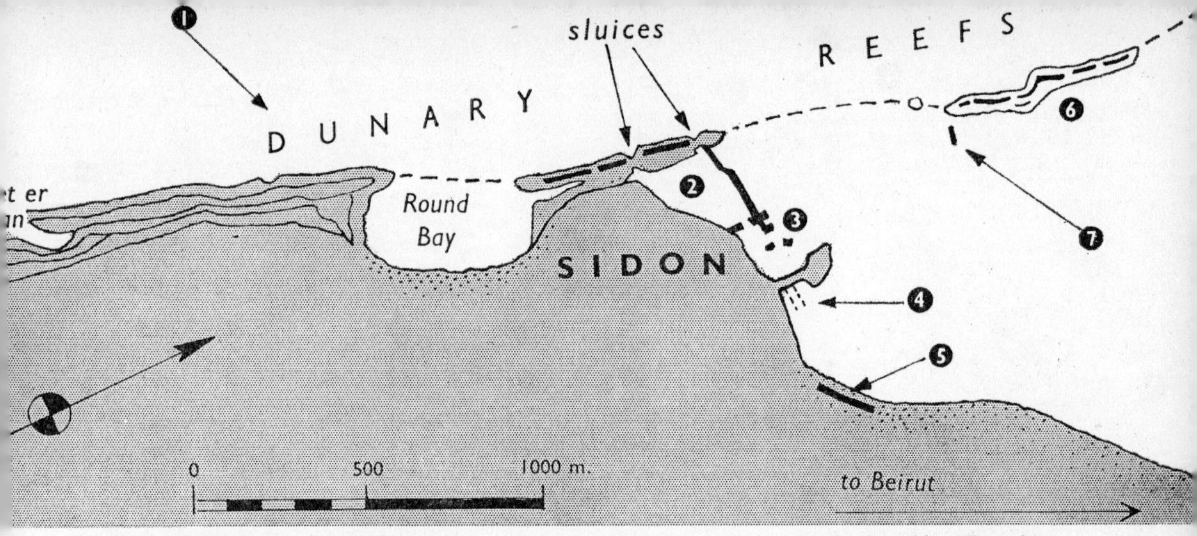

19. Sidon: the closed port within the city walls, and the island anchorage for foreign ships. Remains of ancient harbour-works are shown in solid black. Key: (*1*) *Direction of prevailing wind and swell.* (*2*) *The closed ports.* (*3*) *Blockships sunk in 1634.* (*4*) *Artificially deepened channel connecting the closed ports with the landing quay that served the outer anchorage.* (*5*) *This landing quay.* (*6*) *The island anchorage for foreign ships.* (*7*) *Jetty, probably Roman. Compare Fig. 21 and Plate 11.*

connects with the quay by a tunnel in the rock. The room, once paved, has drainage channels running to seawards. Lauffray, who was Poidebard's surveyor on this expedition, suggests it might have been used as a fish tank. Mooring bitts pierced in the rock still stand on the northern end of the island and may have been distributed along its entire length, but it is tempting to assume that in Phoenician times, before a jetty was built to the south, the safest anchorages were at the other northern end, where the old mooring bitts still stand (Fig. 20).

20. One of the rock-cut mooring bitts from the north-eastern quays of Sidon's island anchorage.

This jetty, running landwards from the southern tip of the quays, prevents swell from swirling round the reef-island (see Plate 11). It is 50 metres long by 15 wide. A gap

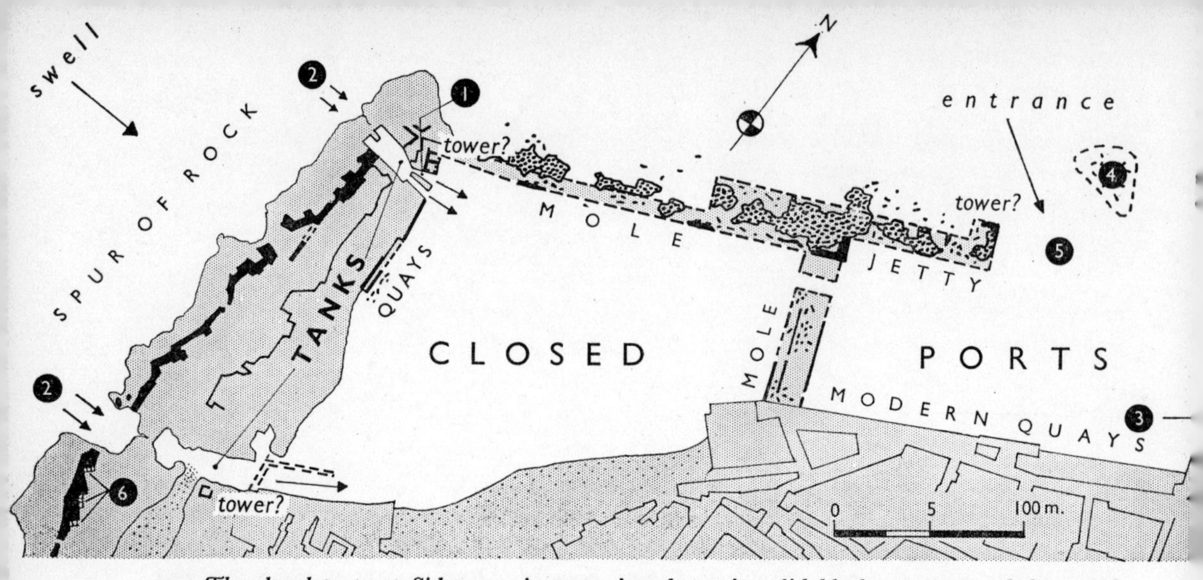

21. The closed ports at Sidon: ancient remains shown in solid black, reconstructed features in broken line. Key: *(1) The remaining sluice gate (compare Fig. 23, p. 88); the corresponding sluices on the southern tank have disappeared. (2) Gaps in the sea-wall which allowed swell to filter over sloping rock and fill the tanks. (3) The artificially deepened channel which, before a causeway was built between the Crusader castle on the island and the mainland, linked the closed ports to the town's landing quays, which served the outer anchorage. (4) Submerged and unidentified masonry. (5) Blockships sunk in 1634; the original silting of the port may have been caused by this obstruction, which upset the balance of the current-deflecting moles. (6) Rock-cut steps leading to the top of the sea-wall.*

of 8 metres separates it from the island; small craft still use this as an entrance to the anchorage, though its original purpose must have been to let in current and prevent a sandbank from forming north of the mole. The masonry differs on the outer and the inner faces of this structure. To windward, cubic blocks alternate with headers 4 or 5 metres long, laid on bedrock, whereas the blocks are smaller on the protected side. In between is rubble-fill embedded in concrete; similar concrete is found on the Hellenistic portions of the closed port. Concrete in the interstices of the large blocks contains Roman sherds, one of the few clues to date. On the shore opposite, beyond the town, are the remains of a Roman quay for disembarking the cargoes transhipped at the island anchorage [Fig. 19 (5)].

The actual town of Sidon, unlike Tyre, has always been on a peninsula. The layout of the closed ports depends on a spur of rock which points north-west, like the index finger of a hand (the peninsula itself being the fist) emerging from the shore. Geologically, the spur is part of the same dunary cordon as the island anchorage. Again, the swell breaks its force on the inclined, seaward face of the spur, and landing quays are carved out of the rock on the other side. From the tip, a mole built on shallows encloses the port within the city's fortifications. The area is roughly triangular, but the seaward mole has a subtle change in direction at the extremity, where it turns inwards to deter the swirling silt (Fig. 21).

Survey techniques and results are very similar at Tyre and Sidon; however, on method there is one new point worth noting at the latter. The enclosed port at Sidon had been divided into two docks by a jetty running from the present shoreline towards the seaward mole. It stopped short of this mole, so that the ships could pass from one dock to the other. When Poidebard started his survey no traces of the dividing wall were visible. In Renan's time one or two blocks of masonry could be seen under water in the middle of the harbour. By 1945 the mole was buried in mud and showed only on aerial photographs; without these it would have escaped both divers and archaeologists. Even if they had found it, under several feet of mud and in water too shallow for an ordinary air-lift, they could not have excavated the blocks. As it was, the remains had to be moved by heavy dredging machinery in order to deepen the modern port. During the year 1947–48 hundreds of colossal blocks were raised and left on the quay. Lauffray could not see what was happening below the surface, but by careful calculations and deductions he managed to analyse and plot the structure.

The entrance to the closed port is dominated by the Crusader *Château de la Mer*, built on a rocky, inshore island where there are traces of the usual Phoenician rock cuttings and masonry (Figs. 19 and 21). The causeway, which now joins the castle to the land, cannot have been built on earlier foundations, for it runs across a submerged channel linking the enclosed port with the landing quays that served the island anchorage. Again, the silted remains of this channel were only visible on aerial photographs. The existence of an artificial cutting is explained by its proximity to the shore and consequently to the shallow and sandy bottom.

22. Sidonian coin of 385 B.C. *showing a war galley in front of the city's fortifications.*

This completes the pattern of the inner ports. The design is Phoenician, though most of the remaining overbuilding is Greek, Roman or Byzantine. At the extremities of its triangular layout, the foundations of towers indicate that the port was fortified. A Sidonian coin in the British Museum (Fig. 22), struck between 400 and 385 B.C., shows a war galley in front of a battlemented wall with towers. Formalized motives are difficult to interpret, so it is not certain whether these defences belong to the city or the harbour. Ezekiel says: 'And he shall set engines of war against thy walls, and with his axes he shall break down thy towers. He shall enter thy gates as into a city wherein is made a breach.' He completes the picture of seventh-century fortifications by mentioning sentries. The city proper is now below the modern town; only the aforementioned port towers remain at the base and tip of the rocky spur and the extremity of the mole. Of greater interest in reconstructing the port defences are steps cut in the solid rock of the spur, which, presumably, lead to a sentry walk running the length of the wall and may well have belonged to the earliest structure [Fig. 21 (6)].

23. The remaining rock-cut sluice gate on the seaward tank of Sidon's closed port [see Fig. 21, Key (1)] viewed from inside the tank. The wooden frame supporting the gate would have been implanted in the holes on top of the rock, while the gate itself slid in vertical grooves. The groove shown above was about 2 metres high and 40 centimetres in depth and breadth. The mortise slots to the right (respectively 40 and 20 centimetres square) carried the butt ends of reinforcing timbers. The arrows indicate traces of Roman cement.

Sidon's dramatic revelation is the device for flushing out the closed port, whose single entrance would otherwise have spelled doom. As we have seen, the fortified city docks at Tyre had many openings, through which judiciously controlled currents could circulate and prevent silt from settling. Deterrents did exist at Sidon, indeed every scrap of masonry was designed to deflect silt-bearing streams, as modern engineers were to find to their cost when they altered the line of the outer mole. Prevention was not enough; in the long run, some silt was bound to get in, and there was nothing to stop it from settling in the enclosure, so the ports had to be flushed out mechanically. That this mechanism has been preserved and recorded makes Sidon the most important example of a principle which, though its application may vary, has to be understood before attempting to examine any ancient port.

The rocky spur broke the swell on the west of the closed ports; a wall, probably topped by a sentry walk, ran along the seaward side, and at either end of it there were gaps. The natural reef was indented at these places, and the indentations corresponded, on the inside, with large tanks like swimming-baths whose floors sloped towards the port (see Fig. 21). Sea swell filtered through the gaps in the wall, filling the tanks, which on the inside were separated from the port by sluices. Rock-cut sockets and grooves held what must have been their wooden gates. The sluice in the northernmost tank is intact (Fig. 23).

The tanks filled with clear water; not only did it come from depth, but what particles of sand there were, filtered downwards and back over the sloping rocks of the seaward gaps. Thus, when the gates were opened, currents of siltless water could be created to oppose the entrance of what small quantities of deposit did manage to get past the deflecting mole at the opposite end of the port. It is impossible to date the rock-cut grooves of the sluice, but the port was known to exist in the tenth century B.C., and could not have lasted until Roman times without some such system.

The classification of ports according to their construction—rock-cut; vertical submarine walls; and lastly arches and concrete constructions at any depth and bottom—is chronological. From the de-silting arrangements at Tyre and Sidon, we see the possibility of alternative groupings, but these are less easy to categorize by date, as pre-dredging devices depend for their design on local geography. Indeed, there is a modern example of a flushed port at Bridport West Bay in Dorset: at low-water spring tides a sluice gate is occasionally opened to clear the entrance channel of silt. In northern waters tide can be harnessed in such a way that when a port is emptied, then a flow of water is released to flush out the mud. Despite the difficulty of doing this in a non-tidal sea, there seems to have been a similar arrangement at the first port of Seleucia, built when Alexander's general founded his capital. This man-made harbour is now underwater, but when it was in use a channel ran into it from the coast. Chesney saw traces of a sluice and concluded that there had been a lock whereby the dock could be drained and then flushed out. Père René Mouterde compares it to Sidon,[1] but the system did not work for long at Seleucia, where torrents soon silted the port. The Flavian Emperors diverted these streams into a channel 1,300 metres long and 8 metres

[1] A. Poidebard, *Sidon*, p. 31.

wide, sometimes passing into a tunnel 8 metres high. Port work continued under Diocletian and Constantine, but later records do not refer to de-silting measures.[1]

Judging from a map,[2] the Roman port of Taposiris Magna on Lake Mareotis may have been kept clear in a similar way. A wall was built across the lake, there was a deepened channel within the port, whose only outlet was through a narrow bridge. There the ruins unfortunately were never examined from the point of view of de-silting. The earliest port in Alexandria, used in Phoenician times, was on the Pharos island, and so depended on current for its de-silting.

Before Poidebard's work on Tyre, nothing comparable had been known. Originally the ports at Delos and Mytilene were based on offshore islands, and their construction and later adaptations also depended on through currents. Carthage, Mahdia, Motya and Apollonia were Phoenician colonies. The three first mentioned had *cothons*, or rock-cut docks, but no work has been done on local winds and currents or the de-silting measures adopted in these places. With the exception of Poidebard's excavations, research on ancient ports has been concentrated on the size and shape of their visible masonry. Reefs that are now submerged, ancient river beds, prevailing winds and local currents are omitted from published plans. The mechanism of individual ports has never been questioned before their detailed archaeological survey began.

If one takes the view that early ports were machines which functioned without dredging, then they can only be understood through a study of their mechanism. If motor cars were unknown it would be impossible to reconstruct an example from the parts without admitting the possible existence of internal combustion. From an archaeological point of view, towns and the ports that go with them are distinct problems. Town excavation makes more or less sense according to the ability of the archaeologist. Markets, temples and private houses build up a picture, but the omission of one temple or a few houses is not necessarily fatal to the understanding of the whole. They were organisms which grew, subject to political, cultural and economic conditions.

The same is not true of harbours: the few plans that exist are frustrating when they do not give compass points, scales, and the direction of prevailing winds. In no cases do they show sources of silt, and they are usually cut out of the con-

[1] Lehmann-Hartleben, *Die Antiken Hafenanlangen des Mittelmeers*, Klio, Beiheft XIV; V. Chapot, 'Seleucie', *Mémoires des Antiquaires de France*, 7ème s., Vol. VI, 1907, p. 207.

[2] Anthony de Cosson, 'Mareotis', *Country Life*, 1955, p. 110.

text of local geography, which makes it impossible even to guess at the relevant factors. Sometimes a plan shows traces of canalization or tanks, but these are meaningless when they stand alone; they are often labelled 'Piscina' or 'slipways' (even if a wall blocks their launching end!); indeed, the amount of slipways on a reef to the seaward side of a perfectly good harbour can be astonishing. The text which goes with such documents is also depressing: there is no reference to geology, or one so remote that it offends common sense. As a result, the traveller who has observed an ancient port is unable to substantiate his inferences by any recorded data, but must go back himself with an amphibious research team and an aeroplane.

Poidebard's conclusions were so revolutionary that, though they would be comprehensible to harbour engineers, they are doubted by archaeologists and even by seafaring men who do not know the Lebanese coast. In general, the southern and eastern shores of the Mediterranean are flat and sandy, with dunary reefs and the strong swell, natural to unprotected coastlines; the same conditions apply in parts of Crete. On the other hand, the North Mediterranean and the Greek islands tend to be mountainous, with a steep, rocky coastline and natural anchorages. I have heard an experienced sailor query the sluicing system at Sidon, because he could not believe, on paper, that artificial current released from a couple of 'swimming-baths' would be sufficient to prevent silting. Nor did he think that the swell, in the absence of tides, would fill the tanks, but in fact it enters them to this day. Knowing the Lebanese coastline, this doubt never occurred to me; moreover, the artificial current at Sidon was only supplementary to elaborately designed deflecting moles which prevented the main silt streams from entering the mouth of the closed ports.

History explains the sailor's contention, for later harbours at Sidon, built by foreigners, whether Crusaders, Moslems or French, were all failures. The *coup de grâce* to the early harbour was given by Fakr ed Din, who sank blockships in 1634 near the mouth of the closed ports; creating havoc among the silt streams. It could not be that all foreign engineers were less intelligent than the natives; their failures were due to the fact that they did not have an intimate knowledge of local conditions.

That an artificial current was sufficient to preserve the closed ports and that the swell at Sidon was sufficient to fill the tanks seems, to me, no more than a repetition of the natural process whereby clear rock-pools are filled, all along the Lebanese coast. This can be seen at Tabarja, where shelves of rock extend for miles to either side of the creek. These shelves are just above sea-level; the rock falls abruptly to a sandy bottom at a depth of about 6 metres. Waves break furiously over the rocks and filter back, leaving clear, sandless pools. Another feature of this shelf would puzzle a visitor: the rocks are covered with shallow, rectangular cuttings which look very like the remains of ancient quarries. At Tabarja they are unlikely ever to have served this purpose; in fact, they are salt pans. They fill with spray, which dries out in the sun, leaving crystals which the villagers scoop up for their kitchens, as I did myself.

During the Lebanese troubles in 1958, when the shops were shut for months on end, I took up spear fishing and spent most of my time on the rocks. One day, accompanied by a villager, I was fishing in one of the larger rock-pools, as the sea was rough. Suddenly I saw an exquisite creature, like a pink dragonfly spread out on the bottom. I am ashamed to say that I shot it. '*Une poule de mer!*' screamed my companion, when I brought it up. The beautiful wings shrivelled and drooped, while it shrank visibly. I took it to be a flying fish, but am told it was probably a winged gurnard, though these latter are deep-sea fish. The edible parts were no more than a small whiting, though the flesh was better. As we walked back to the village, the boy pointed down at some completely circular rock-pools, about 2 metres in diameter, near the church. 'You know who made those? It was the horse of Holy George (my informant was a Maronite Christian), the monster and the maiden were there on the rocks, at the mouth of the bay and he came down past the church. When his horse saw the monster it stamped on the rock there and there. Then George rode up to the monster and killed it.'

St George is claimed by the Lebanese; indeed, we share him with them as a Patron Saint. The site of his encounter is claimed by at least two other communities: the people of Ein el Mreissi in the centre of Beirut and those living at Junieh, a little town to the north. Another village tradition is that St Paul once sailed from Tabarja. It would have been a likely enough port in his time, but I have never found out on which voyage he was supposed to have used it. 'That,' say the villagers, 'is why the church is out on the rocks and not on the hill with our homes.'

During this period it was prudent, indeed inevitable, that one should stay on Christian territory. Byblos made a good outing, being only twenty minutes up the road by bus. There, the ancient harbour works are very puzzling and have never been examined with the same care as the land-remains. A rumour current in archaeological circles had it that there was a wreck somewhere outside the port in deep water. This I never saw, which is not surprising, as the chances of finding a wreck in open sea without a boat to drag, or to tow the searcher are remote. In any case the existence of this wreck was not known to my sponge-diver friends.

Whether the creek at Byblos, used by fishing-boats today, is natural or man-made is not quite clear. Lauffray notes Byblos[1] as an example of 'the round port so common in antiquity and comparable to Latakia and Gebele'. On the other hand, it could be a natural, geological formation resulting from the action of a torrent which hollows out a circular basin in coastal rock, and then finds an outlet-channel at some weak point to seaward.[2] Depending on the depth of this channel, the steepness of its walls and its orientation in relation to the local sources of silt, it is possible for this type of creek to keep itself clear. It has been suggested, on archaeological evidence, that the round port at Byblos was improved by man at an early date because pebble stones were found in the defence wall encircling one of the lower settlements in the *tell*. These came from the port, but from shallow water, as sand starts near the shore; their removal, however, would not have been sufficient to deepen the port.

My own observation at the bottom of the entrance channel confirmed that its rocky walls were vertical, about 10 metres deep and that this submarine cutting could not have been man-made. The bottom was sandy and scattered with ancient columns from the *tell*, probably dropped by Crusaders, who quarried them to strengthen the walls they built. The pebbles would, of course, have come from inside the round harbour, where they had been deposited by the same erosive torrent responsible for piercing the channel through the cordon of rock. Comparing this harbour with other early sites, the round port at Byblos is not entirely convincing; one is tempted to look for supplementary anchorages.

South of the *tell* is a long beach now exposed to the prevailing winds. However, it is interspersed with rock outcroppings, some cut with flights of steps, as at Sidon and other Phoenician harbours. Since this rock cordon in the sea has a narrow base and is exposed to the full force of the swell, it may, like the reefs at Tyre, have been eroded by the sea. If this had indeed been so, the conjunction of rocks and beach may have provided a seasonal anchorage in ancient times. Byblos was a religious centre, and pilgrim transport in the Mediterranean, even

[1] A. Poidebard, *Sidon*, p. 54.

[2] M. A. de Rouville, *Le Régime des Côtes. Eléments Hydrophiques des Accès des Ports*, Paris, Dunod, 1934, pp. 79 and 396.

in medieval times, was less solid than commercial shipping. The town had exports, but if large trading ships could not get into the round port they may have lain offshore and had their cargoes transhipped to a lighter. This unsatisfactory expedient persisted in my day; I am told that my baby-clothes went down between steamer and lighter at Jaffa, farther down that coast, together with a grand piano and more important bits of cargo. As a child, I remember standing on deck watching clusters of cows, tied together by their horns, being lowered from the ship to the lighter, which rose and fell in such a way that it seemed touch and go whether the cattle would drop into the boat or the sea.

Cedar wood was, and is to this day, worked at Byblos, but the port never seems to have had shipyards. Ezekiel, as we have seen, mentions that the 'skilled men and caulkers' left Byblos and went to work in the yards at Tyre. To prove any of these hypotheses about Byblos would be a long and expensive job; however, one day it may be possible, that is if the evidence is still there. If, for instance, there were outer anchorages and cargoes were transhipped, then the things that had fallen overboard in the course of centuries would by now be stratified in the sand of the sea-bed. By the time machines like electronic detectors and core-samplers of large diameter have been adapted to the needs of this kind of excavation the magpie instincts of well-meaning amateur divers may have cleared the surface of the sea-bed of all recognizably ancient artifacts.

CHAPTER 7

Asine – Mochlos – Mallia – A Rock-cut Tank at Nirou Khani – Komo and Matala – Greek and Roman Harbour Construction

PHOENICIAN, Minoan and Mycenaean ports are worth a visit even if the traveller is not in a position to survey their buried and submerged remains. There is always some tantalizing bit of evidence that should stimulate research. I have made a point of never passing one of these places without walking or swimming over it. Of course, this whetted instead of satisfying my curiosity, and led to some odd excursions, among which quite the most absurd took place at Asine. I was a guest in a chauffeur-driven car which my host had hired to take him to Mycenae. This citadel looks over the sea, dominating the Corinth and Phlius roads as they descend into the plain of Argos. It crowns a hill where on one side cliffs rise out of a ravine, while on the other a road mounts to fortifications of colossal masonry pierced by the Lion Gate. We arrived at sunset after the last charabanc had left; Helen, Agamemnon, Clytemnestra, Orestes, Iphigeneia and Electra seemed to rise with the evening mists. Even the whining of the wind took on the cadence of Aeschylus. Looking over the plain to Argos, Nauplia and Tiryns, and beyond to the sea and Crete, one could imagine Pelops with more ancient and monstrous ancestors flocking to join their tragic spawn. In this day-dream Schliemann fell into place as a kind of Parsifal looking for his Holy Grail.

In the more realistic light of the following morning we returned as dutiful sightseers, with a babbling guide. He braved and withstood my host, whose classical education prompted him in anglicized Greek to correct and cap the man's quotations. My own eyes and thoughts strayed back to the sea which had carried the peoples of this plain on their legendary journeys and, indeed, into history. Time being limited, it would have been useless for me to look for the harbours they used on that flat and silted coastline. Later in the day, Mr Verdelis, curator of the Nauplia Museum, and our chauffeur (who had driven archaeologists all his life) provided the information I wanted: they said that on the rockier coast to the east there had been a Mycenaean port. Having established the existence of a *taverna* at this place, which was called Asine, my host agreed to lunch there (he was given neither to sea-bathing nor long walks). I laid my plans accordingly, and when we arrived at Asine was relieved to see that they were geographically practicable.

We drew up at a small, sheltered bay with headlands to either side. The *Blue Guide* explained: 'to the E. an acropolis fortified in a pre-historic era, with very impressive polygonal walls'—this was on the headland. 'In the middle of the enclosure, a primitive town. Very fine view.' Ships could certainly have anchored in the bay, but what lay beyond the promontory? A beach, or an alternative anchorage which they used when the wind changed? The farther point, to the west, being a long way from the ruins, seemed less interesting. I estimated that if the car were to drive me round the eastern headland I would be able to swim back over the most significant part of the site in the time it would take my companions to drink their *apéritifs*; so off we went.

As I expected, there was a long, flat coast on the far side where ships could have beached; I had no desire to explore that shallow water. The western face of the headland, however, was steep cliff, and the water below had a depth of 15 metres. I left my clothes in the car, which drove back to the café, and stood irresolute holding mask and fins. It seemed stupid to get into the clear water without first looking down into it from the top of the cliff, to see whether there were signs of masonry or rock cuttings round the base of the headland. From the vantage point at the top it would also be possible to see beyond the western headland in case the next bay was a Mycenaean harbour, after all. Two things made me hesitate: the first was time, and the second the propensity of Pan-like shepherds to misinterpret the motives of women who climb hills alone in their bathing-suits; however, I decided to risk it.

The sight that met my eyes when I reached the summit was so unnerving that it was all I could do to get myself down again into the comforting sea. Beyond the western headland, five high-prowed Mycenaean warships were drawn up on the beach, while warriors, each sheltering behind a Cretan double-shield (like those painted on the walls of the Palace at Knossos), seemed to be defending the ships against other groups of men with Argolid shields who were hurling torches. One boat was already so burned that it revealed a stout skeleton like a caïque. I was in no mood to question matters of construction.

Safely back in the water, I spent most of my time during the long swim round the promontory avoiding shoals of jellyfish, in the circumstances a welcome diversion which allowed me to pull myself together. Apart from the jellyfish, the visibility was good, and I was able to see that there were no man-made remains until I got back to the bay under the western side of the citadel. Here there must have been a landing quay; however, the rubble-fill, now under a metre or so of water, was not reminiscent of Mycenaean masonry. There were Byzantine sherds among the stones; all this tallied with the one Byzantine building I had been able to notice among the prehistoric remains on top of the citadel. In early times the bay appeared to have been an unembellished, natural anchorage.

After lunch we drove along the coast to the west, past the headland, where, to my relief, the warlike vision was explained. Fighting still raged, but not fiercely enough to satisfy a man with a loud-speaker who, in a mixture of American and Greek, was directing the assault for the benefit of a battery of film cameras. We had noticed a platinum film-star, some latter-day Helen of Troy, signing autographs in an Athenian restaurant a few nights before, but beyond these encounters I have no idea what the film was about or whether it was ever finished. No nagging doubts draw me back to Asine, or to the majority of natural harbours found among rocky coasts. There are harbours that leave one with a faint regret and others in a ferment of suspicion.

Mochlos in north-eastern Crete was a faint regret. It had been an early Minoan settlement,[1] which was destroyed by earthquake and left uninhabited until Roman times. There, I had come on the sand-anchor mentioned earlier, lying inside a rock-cut 'fish-tank'. The modern population is dying out; those who remain in the village live in half-derelict houses built out on a point, and are, I think, the poorest people I have seen. When the underwater expedition of 1955 (organized by the British School of Archaeology in Athens) arrived the only eatables we could buy at Mochlos were dried peas and the only drink *arak*. Water was carried in small containers from a well half a mile away. On the first evening we produced our own tins of food and settled under the oil-lamp in the large deserted café. It was not long before every remaining man, woman and child in the village gathered and stood silently watching, amazed at the quantity and variety of our fare, though all we had was bread, Spam and cheese.

Half a mile of sea separated the point on which their houses were built from a cone-shaped island. East of this point and island was a bay whose rocky shores

[1] J. D. S. Pendlebury, *The Archaeology of Crete*, pp. 47 and 186.

ANCIENT PORTS AND BUILDINGS

VI (opposite). *The moon rises over a Bodrum mosque while the last rays of the sun light up the Crusader castle across the bay; the dark mass of Kara Ada, the 'Black Island', is seen in the distance.*

VII (centre, top left). *The same castle seen from a hill which was probably the site of Mausolus tomb. The modern part of Bodrum, in the central bay, corresponds with the ancient port of Halicarnassos. The Crusader castle and the early citadel that preceded it were on an island, but this is now joined to the mainland by a causeway built in the nineteenth century. The small bay of Salmacis is on the extreme right and the Greek island of Cos on the horizon behind Kara Ada.*

VIII (below). *Ancient, submerged harbour-works, possibly the remains of Artemisia's secret port, viewed from one of the castle towers. In the foreground the tower belonging to the Italian Knights.*

IX (top right). *An Ionic capital from Halicarnassos, which like many ancient marbles was re-used by Crusader architects; it now displays the armorial bearings of the Italian Knights.*

X (below). *A Minoan rock-cutting on the site of the harbour of Mallia in Crete. In the middle distance the present course of the stream can be seen (see p. 104).*

XI (verso). *One of the neo-Minoan houses in a remote village on the Carian coast (see p. 141).*

VI. F. Dumas

VII. F. Dumas

VIII. F. Dumas

IX. F. Dumas

X. F. Dumas

XI. F. Dumas

were cut with the aforementioned fish-tanks, while behind mountains rose abruptly. As far as I can remember, the two things the expedition had been asked to investigate were: the existence of a submerged causeway linking the island to the point, and the possibility that votive offerings had been thrown over the cliff of the necropolis-island into the sea below. It did not take long to discover the submerged line of rubble running from the island to the land, but it was not until the last day, when the main body of the expedition had left, that the prevailing north-westerly wind allowed a swimmer to get to the cliff-side of the island to look for the votive offerings. It fell to me to do this. My efforts were abortive, for the cliffs being vertical and the water at least 40 metres deep, search without an aqualung (and none was available) was impossible.

The general impression I carried away from Mochlos was of a 2-kilometre stretch of shallow but unsilted water protected on the west by the point, the causeway (which served as a breakwater) and the island. I saw this place before my 'conversion' in the aeroplane above Damascus, so that, unlike even the short search I had made at Asine, I had at that time no clear idea of what constituted a port; were I to go back to Mochlos now, I would pay far more attention to that stretch of calm water, to the masonry around its eastern shores and to possible entrance channels out to sea. Without aerial photographs no expedition could find out how this large stretch of water had been used, but they might pick up one or two clues. With luck more anchors, Minoan and Roman, remains of docks or shipyards might be found, and possibly the sacrificial amphorae that were thrown overboard in Roman times as ships left the harbour mouth.

A short sail from Mochlos, to the west, lay the island of Pseira (literally translated 'the Louse', an insect which it resembled in shape). Here, too, a series of Minoan settlements had been destroyed by earthquakes. There was no difficulty in placing the ancient port, as it was the only creek where now, as then, a boat could drop anchor when the westerly wind blew. On one side of the creek Minoan houses had covered the steep promontory. In the water round this settlement was a phenomenon which reconciled me, temporarily, to the dreary task of prospecting 'sunken cities'. Various earthquakes have toppled land and at times houses down different parts of the headland into the sea, with the result that the submarine landscape changed every few metres with each landslide. The bottom, round the point, had a slope of about 30°.

Inside the creek, the rocks at water-level gave way to sand, but farther out at the first landslide one met masonry in what appeared to be small terraces. At first glance the terraces looked like the result of subsidence *in situ*, but in fact they were more likely to have been caused by buildings sliding downwards and fortuitously regaining a shape. At the top of the slope the stones were mixed with sherds; farther down, at a depth of about 20 metres, there were unbroken pots, two of which we raised.[1] The temptation to lift more than the minimum of samples was great; one had to remember that prospection was not a treasure hunt. Continuing round the point, landscapes changed abruptly with each distinct landslide: moss gave place to sand and rocks to veritable forests of Neptune's Cup sponges, until at the far side of the point the water became shallower and the normal sand and grass began again.

It is accepted that Minoans and Mycenaeans made use of islands when they wanted to establish a port. Mr R. W. Hutchinson recently pointed out and translated a passage by Dr N. Platon, curator of the Heraclion Museum, discussing a Minoan site on the island of Skopelos:

> They [the Minoans] also founded settlements on islands divided by a narrow strait from the mainland, or on peninsulas connected by a narrow neck which afforded double harbours so that their boats would be protected whichever way the wind blew. Pseira, Mochlos and Palaicastro in Crete are characteristic examples. The part of the mainland colonized by the Cretans affords analogous examples such as Asine, Nauplia and the Minoan Nisea of Megara.

Islands and headlands always give some natural shelter and facilitate defence where this was necessary, but Cretan towns were not fortified in early times.

Islands, however, were not a *sine qua non* to Minoan port builders. At many of the larger settlements in Crete we find traces of harbour-works on relatively unprotected shores. These complex and incomplete remains have not been explained. Five years after seeing Mochlos and Pseira, I visited the great Minoan town of Mallia, where unexcavated ruins still cover several kilometres. The main palace (dug by the French) is on high ground, which runs seawards and becomes a promontory whose extremity is covered by tombs. Out to sea, rock outcroppings take an easterly turn and do link this promontory with a small island; a geographical coincidence which, in this case, is misleading. Rivers, on either side of the high ground, debouch into bays. The larger stream, to the east, runs through a deepish valley, and is therefore unlikely to have changed its course. It flows into the creek protected by the rock outcroppings and the island. The

[1] M. S. F. Hood and John Boardman, 'Archaeology in Greece', *Archaeological Reports*, 1955 (supplement to the *Journal of Hellenic Studies*, Vol. 76, 1956), Fig. 8, p. 34.

western stream, on the other side of the promontory, loses itself on a wide, flat sandy shore. Here a hump-backed Turkish bridge, almost buried in sand, is a hundred yards from the present course of the river and separated from it by a flat spur of rock which runs out to sea.

When I asked the guardian of the antiquities, who lived at the Mallia 'dig house', the whereabouts of the Minoan port, he said without hesitation that it was in the eastern creek to the lee of the island. He indicated a path which led to it through the burial ground and down the steep slopes of the promontory. No Minoan would have carried cargo up that path; it was hard walking downhill with only mask and fins. I assumed that there must have been another easier road to the palace, along the valley. The sheltered bay appeared the obvious site for the port, but once in the water things looked different. Though deep in places, the bottom was so irregular that anchors would have got stuck and there was hardly room for a ship to swing without hitting a submerged rock. Dumas, who was there, took a look at the rock outcroppings, and with a seaman's eye for entrance channels struck out in that direction. He returned with the verdict that no ship could have got through between the rocks. On the other side of the bay the island was joined to the mainland by a causeway similar to, but narrower than, the one at Mochlos. Thus, the so-called harbour area turned out to be entirely enclosed. Furthermore, there were no signs of quays or even a propitious landing-place on the shore, though this in itself would not have been sufficient to rule out the possibility of an anchorage. We climbed the headland again and examined the coast on the other side, to the west.

The port of Mallia, which we found in the end, is one that gives rise to the wildest surmise. At the foot of the western slope of the headland we reached some large excavated buildings; these were separated from the beach by a boundary wall of oblong and typically Minoan blocks. About 200 metres across the sand to the west the area was bounded by the spur of rock. Had this been higher, it would have given adequate protection from the prevailing wind. Here without a doubt was the site of the harbour. The stream having changed its course (not to mention earthquakes and subsidence), the harbour-works were probably buried under sand and silt.

The only visible remains of Minoan installations was a rock-cut trench which continued for about 30 metres (parallel with the near side of the spur) and ended in the sea (Plate X). At right angles to the landward extremity of this cutting a line of Minoan masonry protruded above the sand. If a relatively modern bridge was now buried, what had been the height of this wall and cutting in ancient times? and what the purpose of this channel? Lastly, what had been the course of the river which, in the nineteenth century, must have passed under the now buried bridge? That the flow of freshwater streams was controlled by tanks and put to use in the de-silting of early harbours is a suspicion that frequently recurs to me. The rock-cut channel might have been part of such a system, but this could only be shown by land excavation once the geological question of subsidence had been answered. Until this was settled it was impossible to guess whether the cutting represented the top of a parapetted mole or the bottom of a dock. Moreover, the bay itself may, in ancient times, have extended inland to the cultivated fields, where there are now traces of unexcavated ruins.

In Crete the generally accepted explanation of subsidence is that the island pivoted like a see-saw at some period; the eastern half, excluding Knossos and Mallia, sinking for a metre or so while the extreme west rose out of the sea. This assumption is too vague a basis for harbour excavation, and it does not explain many of the phenomena we can see along the eastern shores. The system by which a port, or area of calm water, had been maintained at Mallia as at other places along the north coast can only be examined archaeologically after localized geological *expertise*.

The rock-cut channel at Mallia, with its pronounced seaward slope, cannot be confused with Minoan quarries. Westwards from Mallia, at every point I have visited right up to Knossos, the beach-rock is riddled with these quarries. In some places the rock still rises to a height of 2 or 3 metres above water-level. This is the case at some fishermen's cottages 3 kilometres west of Mallia. Here there is another strange structure which has nothing to do with quarries, but which may be a clue to Minoan harbour installations. The rocks are cut vertically and dead trees firmly implanted on top. Boats hang from their branches above the water (Plate 10). This local alternative to beaching may have been used in Minoan times. The hanging boats remind one, incidentally, of a motive found on seal-stones wherein a female figure sits beside a tree which appears to grow out of the middle of a boat. A religious interpretation has been given for these designs, but in view of the boats which hang from trees there may be a more practical explanation.[1]

[1] Sir Arthur Evans, *The Palace of Minos at Knossos*, Vol. II, p. 251: 'The advent of the goddess from the sea, which recalls so much in later lore, is the more interesting from the fact that her arboreal form accompanies her on her voyage.'

Still farther along the coast, 20 kilometres east of Knossos and Heraclion, the harbour remains at Nirou Khani have been discussed by archaeologists. About 2 kilometres from the sea a Late Minoan I building was excavated and described by Sir Arthur Evans as a 'Propagandist Depot'. It consisted of storerooms containing such things as ceremonial double-axes and about fifty portable clay altars. The port from which these objects bearing the Minoan religious 'message' were diffused is of particular importance, because Evans himself, Dr Marinatos and other archaeologists recognized the remains as being part of a harbour. Quoted as the first Minoan port to be discovered, it was at one time thought to have served Knossos; this cannot be so, for remains of much larger harbour-works have been found where one would expect them to be, at the end of the valley which leads from the Palace of Knossos to the sea.

During my first visits to Nirou Khani in the late summer of 1955 the north-west wind blew over a period of three months, churning up water and sand and covering the low rock-cuttings with surf. In addition to the immediate inconvenience of weather on sites like this, winter storms can alter their aspect so that walls and columns visible one year are covered with sand the next or vice versa. Returning in the spring of 1960, when the sea was calm, I was able to see many things that had escaped me earlier. The reverse was true of the fields behind the beach. They had not been easy to examine in 1955 when they still contained mines laid during the war; however, I do remember a bank where sand and fields met, where buildings excavated by Dr Marinatos in 1926 were still visible and where one could always spend a happy half hour pulling sherds out of the loose soil. In 1960 the whole area was covered by a rubbish dump from the nearby American base.

The part of this large sandy bay which has been discussed and referred to as 'the port' is bounded to the east by the usual rocky promontory and a river bed. The promontory is larger than, but otherwise comparable to, the spur at Mallia. However, there is no surface indication that the river has ever changed its course at Nirou Khani, though this too ought to be checked by a geologist. The promontory was overbuilt in Minoan times; it rises in parts to a height of 10 metres and still provides a certain amount of shelter. Since no plans of this much-discussed area have been published, I am forced in the interests of clarity to illustrate it by a page of notes from my 1960 diary (Fig. 24). The sketch was a personal *aide mémoire*, the various features were drawn relative to each other but without being measured. I have since added the buildings mentioned by Dr Marinatos.

The windward or north-westward slopes of the promontory are cut at water level and below by quarries. From this Sir Arthur Evans estimated that there must have been a subsidence of 3 or 4 metres, since stone could not have been quarried underwater. This degree of subsidence would conflict with Dr Marinatos' interpretation of a certain rock-cut tank which is the most important feature of the site. Despite the evident common sense of Evans's deduction, expert geological survey remains, as usual, an essential preliminary to future

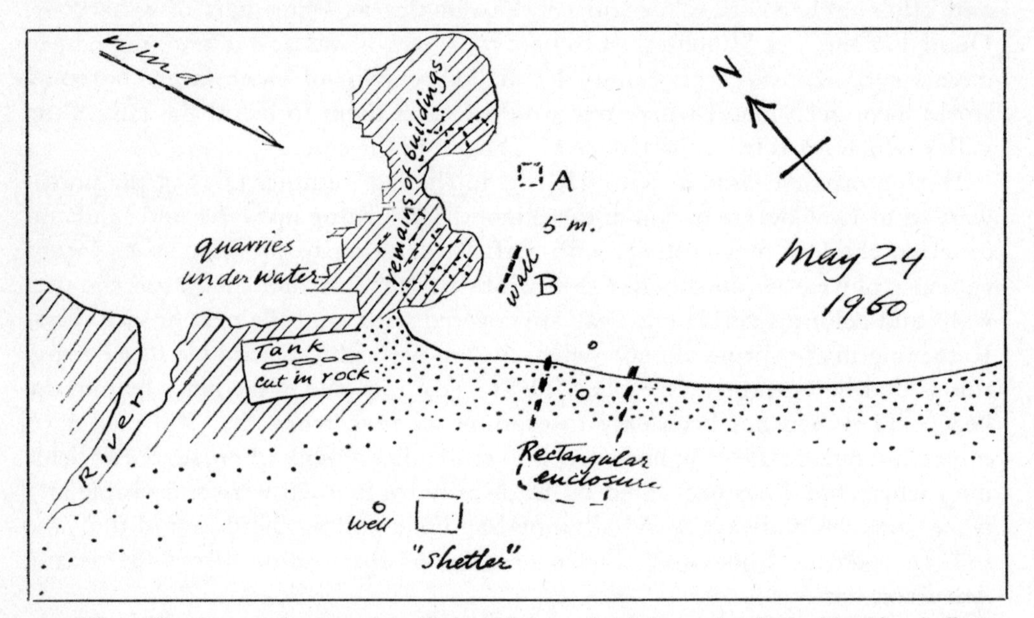

24. Nirou Khani; some harbour installations from a sketch in my log book. Hatching indicates rock, and stippling sand.

excavation or interpretation. This seam of rock may have been tipped to one side as a result of tilting, dislocation or faulting.

In the report describing Dr Marinatos' excavations of 1926[1] two structures, 'a flagged shelter of poros stone containing quantities of late Minoan jars and perforated ceramic spheres', and also a water well, were excavated in the field now covered by the rubbish dump. 'A large rectangular space with walls of big limestone blocks, one metre across' started in the field, to the east of the well and

[1] *Bulletin de Correspondence Hellénique*, Vol. I, 1926, pp. 573–4.

'shelter', ran across the beach and ended in the sea. The *clou* of the whole area was the tank-like cutting at the junction of the rocky promontory and the beach. This cutting—

> 40 metres wide by 42 metres long is divided into two unequal compartments by a wall; the whole is now about 1·80 metres below sea level. The use of the construction will only be explicable if it is possible to determine the degree of subsidence of the land. In any case it was either a mooring for boats or a Minoan shipyard. The port, which was the first Minoan example to be discovered, must have had connections with Knossos.

I have translated this passage from the original report on Nirou Khani, but I suspect that there must have been a misprint where distances are concerned. The tank in question is nearer 10 × 12 metres than 40 × 42.

From this report of Dr Marinatos' findings, Père René Mouterde associates the Minoan tank with Phoenician *cothons* at Carthage and Motya.[1] Tempting though this comparison may be on paper, it brings us back to the question of subsidence. If the level at Nirou Khani has sunk by 3 or 4 metres, then the tank which is at present barely awash would have been 3 or 4 metres above sea-level and was more likely to be a store than a shipyard or dock. As already mentioned, it is just possible that a form of faulting tipped this side of the rock-mass out of the water while submerging the quarries on the other side. I, personally, do not think that this could have happened, for my own observations made in 1960 in the sea on the same side of the promontory as the tank showed that there were also submerged remains to the east. These corroborate Evans's view on subsidence and add a metre or so to his estimate. In 5 metres of water there is a rectangular construction of stones which are not natural to that bottom, but resemble the building stones on the adjacent promontory ('A' on Fig. 24). Farther inland, parallel to the promontory, is a wall of large, oblong blocks ('B' on Fig. 24). In 1926 marine excavation was unknown, but now by judicious use of up-to-date methods this mysterious harbour could be explained.

Poidebard demonstrated that the tanks at Sidon flushed silt out of the closed ports, but the tank at Nirou Khani and the *cothon* at Motya still need explaining. Motya was a Phoenician trading post, built on a small island at the western extremity of Sicily. There are reefs and other little islands to the seaward of this settlement, which is separated from the land by a shallow lagoon. Traces of construction are said to have been found on the reefs. Though there has been a

[1] R. Mouterde in A. Poidebard's *Sidon*, pp. 16 and 17.

certain amount of excavation at Motya, the island reefs and lagoon have not as yet been examined as a functional whole: the raw material for a flushed or 'self-de-silting' Phoenician port. The *cothon* has been cleaned up and trenches dug in the town site, but whether Motya, like other Phoenician towns, had closed ports within its fortifications and anchorages for foreign ships by its reefs, and if so, how these were kept clear of silt, has never been asked. There may be difficult problems to explain. Sicily was not home ground for Phoenician settlers, consequently they may not have been sufficiently familiar with local tides and currents to build harbour-works that stood the test of time. Were this the case, the harbour-works would now be under deep silt. Only long-term marine survey and excavation under expert direction could settle the general layout of the port, but until this is done the specific function of the *cothon* will remain a mystery.

Comparison of single functional components of ancient harbours is unrewarding unless the civic organization, such as fortifications, and the geographic and geological structure of the site are also taken into consideration. If isolated features, such as tanks, are to be compared we might with equal justification point to similarities of construction between Bronze Age harbour-works in the Mediterranean and, for instance, the large tanks with sluice gates recently excavated by Mr S. R. Rao at Lothal north of Bombay.[1] The Lothal tanks were mostly built of brick (stone being scarce locally), though they too had some rock-cut channels. They were probably docks, but however this may be, their function was governed by the tidal river estuary on which they were built. In date they could be contemporary with the Sidonian tanks, which also had sluice gates (as we have seen it is impossible to give a precise date to the latter). I mention the Indian tanks not only because of their similarities of construction but also because certain findings elsewhere on the site, such as seals and copper bun-ingots, have either a Middle Eastern provenance or connection and point to a sea route to India in the Early Bronze Ages.

At Nirou Khani one unquestionable fact remains: it has all the characteristics we have come to expect of a port on that northern part of the Cretan coast. On the opposite side of the island, south of the great Minoan towns of Phaestos and Hagia Triada and the Roman capital of Gortyna, the structure of the coast is utterly different and the ports vary accordingly. No spurs of rock stretch out to

[1] Siri S. R. Rao, 'New light on the Indus Valley Civilization: Seals, Drains and a Dockyard', *Illustrated London News*, February 25, 1961.

sea like breakwaters punctuating mile after mile of sand. Instead pebbly beaches near river mouths give place to rolling dunes and then to cliffs.

The southern Ports in Crete have a particular historical significance because they were the natural outlet for Minoan trade with Egypt, and for Roman dealings with North Africa. It may not be fashionable to venerate archaeological opinion when this antedates the practice of 'scientific method', however, Sir Arthur Evans's *Palace of Minos* remains the only coherent source of information about marine matters in Crete. When one has the means, which Evans had not, to examine the underwater aspects of sites that he discussed one discovers that his inferences can be justified and his suggestions are always worth pursuing. He had the ability to set the right question, which is the hallmark of genius. Were he alive today, he would probably be the first to put on a mask and get into the water to see for himself. He might have seen farther than the few metres required to settle immediate questions, such as the measurements of specific submerged structures; questions which are but an extension of land work and have little to do with marine problems.

Various objects of Egyptian manufacture were found at Knossos. In Sir Arthur Evans's time a Minoan road was traced from the Palace across the plain until it ended on the southern coast of the island at Komo, the obvious place for a port serving Egypt. The bay of Komo is guarded by an island and protected from the weather by a promontory to the south. To the north a partly submerged reef even now breaks the force of the strong westerly wind that blows during the summer months. This reef may have subsided or, like the reefs at Tyre, been eroded by the heavy swell. Erosion is more likely, because there are traces of harbour-works on land under the sand dunes, which suggest either a lowering of the sea-level or silting. West of this reef is the mouth of a much larger river than any mentioned hitherto on the northern coast. In its natural state it serves as a refuge for ships in rough weather. Sponge boats which leave from this district to fish off North Africa take a southerly course to Derna, 180 miles away, then turn east and sail along the coast towards the Nile Delta. Their Minoan forbears probably took the same course. The harbour at Komo is larger than those on the north of Crete. The presence of a reef makes its topography more comparable to Phoenician ports. A good part of it seems to be on land; otherwise it raises much the same questions of survey and geology. Archaeological evidence on land shows that Komo was one of the most important commercial ports on the island and that this persisted throughout all the phases of Minoan civilization. A 'customs house' full of oval oil-containing jars called *pithoi* gives, for instance, one hint of the island's exports at that date.

Farther east, the port of Matala is in complete contrast with Komo: a natural, land-locked harbour, it is enclosed by steep cliffs. The Romans made it into a military port and linked it by road to their administrative centre at Gortyna. Relative to Komo, Matala raises two questions: why did the Minoans not make use of this natural harbour (for there is not a sherd or trace of the early civilization in the vicinity)? and secondly, why is there indisputable evidence of subsidence at Matala, while at Komo only a few miles to the east there are signs that the land has emerged from the sea? In the absence of geological survey, the traveller is left to conclude that Matala is a case where earthquake caused an entire rock mass to slip downwards, over some softer stratum, leaving the rest of the coast unchanged. As to the Minoans' choice of site, one is tempted to assume that in their time port design was conservative; they preferred to adapt reefs and islands in the traditional way, rather than to construct a long road over difficult country to a less conveniently situated natural harbour.

When I saw it, Matala could not be reached by car; the Roman road (which must once have linked it with Gortyna) had disappeared. By sea, our *caïque* was hurled eastwards by the *Gharbis* that was blowing, then it suddenly swung into what had appeared a few moments before to be a solid face of rock. Inside the bay the cliffs around us were honeycombed with tombs. Still containing coffins and rock-cut couches, they gaped all down one side, but opposite they had been enlarged and now sheltered the village. The rising sea curtailed our visit, but I do remember troglodytes trooping down to the *caïque* and one old woman holding out her hand and insistently demanding penicillin. I do not doubt that it was needed. As though ashamed of her importunities, a young matron gripped my arm, led me to her cave (seedy geraniums growing in a tin outside) and offered coffee. All this must now be changed, for a motor road has been begun which will link Matala to Phaestos. This means that day trippers who leave Heraclion in the morning to visit 'the other Minoan towns' will be able to bathe after their sightseeing before they are borne away to catch their cruise ships. Cafés advertising Coca-Cola will spring up, and for the villagers' sake one can only be thankful.

Sir Arthur Evans put the subsidence of these tomb-cut cliffs at 1·80 metres; again, I would suggest that it is even greater. I estimate that with a good kick and three strokes of the arms I can get down to a depth of 6 metres. Having done this under the tombs, I remember holding on to the top of a chamber entrance and, upside down, peering in. The swell being great that day, the visibility even inside the land-locked harbour was only about a metre, so beyond seeing that tombs did continue underwater, and that in the centre of the bay there was some kind of large structure with columns scattered around it, detailed observation was impossible. Natural ports raise few problems, but at Matala it would be interesting architecturally to reconstruct what must have been a colonnaded jetty.

Matala has brought us abruptly to Roman times, omitting the intervening Greek period. Nor does Matala, as it is a natural port, illustrate the contrast between the Bronze Age sites already described and Roman harbours. The Romans, as a result of their technical innovations, could impose a harbour on any coast that was convenient from the point of view of land communications; natural shelter was no longer essential. By Roman times the building of underwater walls had become common practice, but even more important were their own innovations, notably the use made of the arch and of concrete.

A stone-built arch consists of wedge-shaped blocks or voussoirs, the central one at the apex being known as the key-stone. This construction exerts an outward thrust; to compensate the arch has to be strengthened or buttressed at either side; this would be too complicated to build underwater. Arches, however, are extremely useful in harbour construction, and in some cases indispensable. Openings at the base of sea-walls allow engineers to control a through current while preserving surface calm in an enclosed area of water. The current prevents silt from settling within the area.

As can be seen in hundreds of aqueducts, buildings and monuments, the Romans could build arches by using thrustless concrete. When these principles were applied underwater they resulted in an entirely new conception of harbour design. Hydraulic concrete had, of course, been used earlier by the Greeks, but not for arched constructions. Greek harbours fall between the extremes of Bronze Age and Roman design. Deep bays abound along the rocky shores of Greece, Southern Turkey and the Greek islands; bays which need no more than landing-quays and a couple of jetties (extending the town fortifications) to turn them into harbours. This type of coast is utterly different from the long windswept stretches of North Africa, Syria and parts of Crete where the early seafarers or the Roman colonists had to accommodate their ships.

Greek and Roman harbours are relatively easy to elucidate, because their parts are sufficiently like modern structures for us to be able to follow the intention of their designers. Later harbours are entirely man made, so the most important clues as to dating, and also to the function of their parts, are found in the actual building materials. The way stones are cut and joined can be compared with dated masonry on land. The same is true of concrete; in addition certain admixtures of pumice, rubble or sherds indicate the builder's intention and point to the function of a structure. Here the archaeologist (to mix metaphors) is on home ground, even if he is working in the sea. Moreover, ports like Ostia and the Lechaion at Corinth, which were built in defiance of Nature, became silted as soon as their installations were allowed to fall into decay; they thus come literally within the field of land archaeology. An early Christian basilica is, for instance, being dug on the site of the Lechaion.

Poidebard's elucidation of Tyre and Sidon has led me to speculate on similar unknown harbours, where reefs were put to use as quays, where rock-cut channels suggested the possibility of artificial currents being created, or where currents may ingeniously have been deflected. In conception these Bronze Age ports are like sophisticated Japanese gardens which look natural only because they are designed by men who have a deep understanding of natural laws. Until other early rock-cut harbours have been studied it is only possible to formulate certain questions and then, alas, delicately to grade the negative replies. If these questions prompt future excavators to reassess their aims, both in survey and excavation, they will have served a useful purpose.

PART IV

WRECKS

God made me behold the sea, and I saw the ships sinking and the planks floating; then the planks too were submerged. And God said to me, 'those who voyage are not saved'. And he said to me, 'those who, instead of voyaging, cast themselves into the sea, take a risk'. And he said to me, 'those who voyage and take no risk shall perish'. And he said to me, 'the surface of the sea is a gleam that cannot be reached. And the bottom is a darkness impenetrable. And between the two are great fishes, which are to be feared.' [1]

[1] Niffari the Egyptian, a tenth-century Moslem Saint quoted by Aldous Huxley; *The Perennial Philosophy*, Chatto and Windus, 1946, p. 240.

CHAPTER 8

Wreckless Lebanon – Variations on a Submarine Landscape – A Conversation: Halicarnassos, Seals and a Magic Spring – What Are Ancient Wrecks? – Their Formation not Continuous in Time – Wreck-formation and Geology – Their Appearance – Antique Cargoes: Mahdia, Anticythera, Artemesion – Modern Wrecks – On Travel – Beirut to Ankara – Afyon

INCURSIONS into harbour construction, inspired by what I saw at Tyre and Sidon, have made me digress geographically, though not in the dimension of peculiar time that governs ideas. After my return from Jericho I became interested in both anchors and Phoenician ports; the change of domicile also affected my life in other ways. Compared with Jordan, Lebanon was a lotus land; a land where one could not only ski and dive on the same day but where the mind was entertained. People wrote and painted, the cosmopolitan community was fertilized by visitors of all kinds, using Beirut as their base for travel in the Arab world. Every luxury from Europe and America was available, and frustrations were few. Diehard Arabists disapprove of the Lebanese because they are not of Bedu stock; 'Phoenician' is so vague as to be considered meaningless, yet for want of better, it is a term I would accept. The society, with its well-assimilated French influence, is not quite the same as those almost forgotten Levantine communities like Smyrna, where foreign traders lost their own language and culture after one generation while still holding themselves apart from the country of their adoption. This state of affairs is unsatisfactory only in appearance, for Levantines are as essential a part of the Middle East as the indigenous peasantry.

In Lebanon the traveller's curiosity is easily satisfied: public transport is good, remote places can be visited, there are libraries, and the Beirut archaeological museum is a model of both scholarship and display. However, the one thing I could not do there was to look at wrecks. The urge that came over me at Jericho, to reassess my ideas on anchors and ports, had been partially satisfied. For entirely subjective reasons, these were not the aspects of underwater archaeology that most interested me. Relative to marine research as a whole, wreck excavation is not of first importance, but I started my diving life on a wreck and the subject never ceased to fascinate me. Though I did some surface recording of tomb sites, I am not a surveyor, and plotting trenches or drawing finds in an office is not my line. On the other hand, tomb and wreck work is comparable. Wreck-formations are, of course, much more complex than tombs, but both are closed groups with analogous technical problems. Getting back to a wreck to see whether even the surface layer could be recorded became an obsession with me. As far as I know, it had never been attempted.

I asked Lebanese divers whether they had seen wrecks along the coast; a vain question in a part where the preservation of wrecks was a geological improbability. A flat, sandy bottom extended for miles out to sea under relatively shallow water. Ships must have gone down during storms, but they would either have been broken up or covered by silt. There were no precipitous cliffs or dangerous rocks continuing underwater to the requisite depth, at whose base one might, logically, expect to find a sunken ship. Nor were there trawlermen, as in other parts of the Mediterranean, who brought up amphorae from offshore waters in their drag-nets. I must also admit that this flat submarine landscape was beginning to pall. Though weird, its monotony made me realize how much the bottom varies from one part of the Mediterranean to another. If I were blindfolded in a plane and dropped into the sea with diving-gear I think I could tell where I was, providing I had already visited the region. I could certainly tell whether I was in the Mediterranean or the Atlantic; weeds in the ocean grow like veritable forests in comparison with the scrub-sized varieties in the enclosed sea (compare Plates I to V).

In Lebanon the sea-bed bears no relation to the mountainous and beautiful land. Surprisingly, the water is not clear, containing at most seasons a white, mucus-like matter held in suspension. In depth, this storm of rather disgusting snowflakes persists, instead of being confined, as one might expect, to the top layers. The bottom is flat rock or sand covered with slimy mud on which grow 'dead men's fingers'. Blackish-green, these sponges stick up as from a corpse buried in the act of surrender. There are also huge, round, black sponges, shiny and 'bad', that can never be cleaned of their skin; bath sponges are almost indistinguishable to the layman. A diver like Edouard could tell the good ones from afar by the shape of their holes and their brownish bloom. On the bottom he would push himself unerringly from sponge to sponge while I swam around, with all the mobility of my fins, feeling duds. Heavily weighted at the end of their narghiles, Lebanese sponge divers have to protect their feet from sting-fish and urchins. Edouard wore tennis shoes, which annoyed his captain and crew, it being a tradition among Arab divers that white is to a shark as a red rag to a bull. Sad to say, not only nature but also man contributes to the desolation of these waters. Even in depth, the bottom is littered with indestructible plastic garbage as well as ephemera like tins and orange peel. Cleaning a freshly picked sponge, we found it had grown round an olive stone. The sea's power of assimilation is locally reduced, for reasons I do not understand. Perhaps Lebanon with its prevailing onshore winds, being at the extremity of an enclosed and tideless sea, is a kind of terminus where matter accumulates from both sea and land.

In the clear, cold waters of the Bosphorus and Sea of Marmara there are armies of white jellyfish, reminiscent of a parachute descent. They are carried along by currents over rocks covered by pretty, calcareous violets and an abundance of mussels and crabs. In some parts of Greece Poseidon cup sponges preponderate, and where rock and stone end Pina shells grow upright from the bright sand. All must know by now that orange and red gorgonia, baroque saffron sponges, coral, and purple lichens abound in the South of France. Images implanted in the mind by photography force one to describe them in terms of colour. Similarly, so many underwater photographs have been published that anyone can conjure up the Barrier reef, Red Sea corals or Bermudan fish. These photographs taken by light from a flash bulb bear no relation to the monochrome scenery which we know at 40 metres. The ability to reveal a hidden, apparently useless riot of colour by pressing a button went to people's heads, and dazzling pictures became universal. The transition of opalescence to monochrome seen in the normal way, is no less lovely (see Plates IV, XVIII and XXII taken without flash). Attempts to apprehend even earthly surroundings through reason are so unsettling that in everyday life they are left to philosophers. Pragmatism becomes an impossibility when, bereft of weight, man breaks through the gleam which is the surface and passes into regions where he can no longer rely on his senses. If colour be reality it is transformed; in addition, the diver is aware that continuing downwards to inevitable narcosis he will lose even the frail functioning of his conscious mind.

Herein lies the challenge which drives people to break records or justify their life below by some exacting task.

After nine months in the Arab world I had an Easter holiday at Istanbul. When dining with Turkish friends an art critic started talking about Bodrum, or Halicarnassos. He used to go there for holidays on a sailing-boat and described the wild rocky coast, classical remains and Crusader castle. Kalymnos, the Greek divers' island, was not far off, and Bodrum was the centre for sponge fishing on the Turkish mainland. Then, too, seals lived on an uninhabited island outside the port, where there was also a hot mineral spring known for its rejuvenating properties. After bathing in it the critic and his companions had shed twenty years and, like Edward Lear characters, danced hand in hand along the deserted strand.

The very name Halicarnassos took me back to my student days when the Mausoleum was, to me, an architectural exercise. Furthermore, the first gallery in the British Museum contains statues of King Mausolus and his wife, taken from this tomb, besides many other sculptures, which combined with its commanding position and architecture to make it one of the seven wonders of the world. The Mausoleum gripped our national imagination; St George's Church, Bloomsbury, the Masonic Hall in Great Queen Street and many other buildings have versions of its pyramidal spire. Paris is epitomized by the Eiffel Tower, but I never had to assimilate its details during endless sessions of architectural drawing; Halicarnassos, on the other hand, became part of my mental baggage, like those irrelevant poems, learned at school, which travel with one for the rest of one's days. Of course, I knew the building had been destroyed and nothing remained except an underground chamber. Curiously enough, *bodrum* means cellar in Turkish and is a fairly common name for villages where there are ruins.

Then there were the seals; in Lebanon I twice dived with these animals and fell in love with the species. When I first met them I was swimming up a tunnel leading to a sea-cave, with a pencil torch held above my head. Exploration was momentarily interrupted by two large bodies gliding below in the opposite direction. The passage ended in a circular, vaulted chamber where the water was shallow and the seals had made their home on a narrow, pebbly beach. A few months later I found an enchanting baby seal, about the same size as myself, in the next-door cave, where there was sufficient natural light for us to be able to see each other (Plate 14). We played catch for almost half an hour, he darted from rock to rock, pausing to rest on the bottom, his body horizontal, looking levitated, but in fact balancing on one flipper. Opposite him, in a similar position, I gazed back into his eyes. We also played peep-bo, upside down around rocks. It was charming, but I tore myself away, knowing that if he learned to trust human beings he would get blown up by dynamiters. Indeed, one of them was fishing outside the cave when I left. This family of seals owed their survival to the fact that they kept indoors during the day, hunting after dark. On a desert island I need have no scruples and could play with them to my heart's content.

All this made me want to visit Bodrum, but when I checked the critic's descriptions against books and charts I found more serious reasons for deciding it was the place I was looking for. Geographically and historically the coast was bound to have wrecks, while the presence of sponge divers meant that their position would be known. The next thing to find out was how to get my bottle filled with compressed air once I got there, for Turks use helmet suits. I could, of course, carry one bottle of air from Lebanon; this would mean saving my dive until such time as I could be certain that there was a good wreck. Alternatively, local divers might lend me their suit, but apart from the fact that I had never used standard apparatus, it would have been an abuse of Eastern hospitality to borrow working equipment. I made enquiries in Istanbul and discovered that Bodrum came within the territory of the very active Izmir divers. They, I was told, possessed a home-made *narghilé* which would obviate the necessity of having my bottle filled. Armed with introductions to this '*Kurbağa Adamlar Külübu*', or 'frogman's club', and the sponge men's '*Sünger Kooperatifi*', I flew off to Lebanon to finish the work I was doing.

What, the reader may wonder, were these wrecks I was after? It is a question of cardinal importance, for among all the vagaries of verbal communication, it would be difficult to find a word as imprecise. Undefined, it is liable to lead to misunderstandings among archaeologists. It would be interesting to know what kind of picture forms in the mind: perhaps a Roman ship, lying mast and all on the bottom. Our knowledge is at present so small that in depths as yet inaccessible to divers we are not in a position to deny this possibility. Those interested in the structure of ancient ships need to know, first, whether they can expect to find a significant amount of wood in the wreck of, for instance, a Roman ship; second, if a good part of the ship is preserved, whether its excavation is a practicable proposition underwater. Before attempting to define wreck-formations, from the hundreds of sites which are known in the Mediterranean, we should examine some of the published accounts of ancient wrecks in other waters. Tide, the salinity of the water, the rates of growth of both plants and concretions vary in different seas and have a direct effect on the preservation of wrecks.

Ships of all shapes and sizes sank throughout the centuries on to every type of bottom and in every sea and lake. The layman who reads Anders Franzén's account of raising the *Vasa*, a sixteenth-century warship, from Baltic waters may conclude that the same is theoretically possible with hulks in the Mediterranean.[1] The differences between the two seas are sufficient to preclude this. There is relatively little salt in the Baltic, no teredos and, finally, the *Vasa* was buried in mud. As a result, the hull was complete and kept its shape; when the ship was raised preservation problems would not be insoluble. There can be no comparison between excavation techniques in these two seas. According to press accounts of treasure found by free-divers on Spanish galleons, Pacific wrecks must differ from those in either the Baltic or the Mediterranean. There is no mention of ships' structure in these stories, but whether this is due to the divers' lust for gain or the quick growth of coraline concretions in Pacific waters I cannot say. There is certainly no hint of sand burial, which is perhaps the commonest characteristic of Mediterranean wreck-formations.

Reports of wreck-prospection also seem to be a misleading blend of science fiction and treasure hunting. The aims of most serious forms of submarine survey differ so much from archaeological requirements that standard techniques are almost useless for finding ancient wrecks. Oceanographers have means of taking samples of the bottom or of locating submarine mountains and valleys in really deep water. All navies spend their time looking for lost mines, torpedoes and other expensive gadgets, but their methods and equipment show a glorious disregard for economy. They can experiment where commerce or scientific research cannot. Though there is a universal willingness to spend money for military reasons, it is ironical that when an object really does have to be found, even naval men often have to resort to such primitive techniques as dragging, or towing a diver over the bottom. Commercial surveys are usually a practical attempt to discover the relief of the bottom so that pipelines and cables can be laid on the flat, where they will not be damaged by sharp obstacles, whether rock or wreck.

The only wrecks capable of damaging pipelines would be modern metal ships. In Mediterranean waters even jagged metal undergoes a sea change within twenty or thirty years; there would be little difference between a nineteenth-century and a classical wreck, and neither would damage a pipeline. On the

[1] Anders Franzén, *The Warship Vasa*, Norstedt and Bonnier, Stockholm, 1960.

whole, surveyors are interested in sizeable objects and pronounced relief. It follows, and this is important to archaeologists, that methods normally used to chart the sea-bed, whether they be echo soundings or professional diver-surveyors, neither register nor recognize ancient wrecks. An echo sounder would show a modern hull, or rather a solid of that size, but it might pick up the feeble relief of an ancient wreck only if the sea were absolutely calm and the surrounding bottom completely flat. Even a professional diver on survey would be unlikely to notice the tumulus which may mark an ancient wreck, or be able to interpret odd jetsam on the surface of the sand, unless he had a comparative knowledge of wreck-formation. Different methods of prospection have to be devised for finding ancient wrecks; this is a subject to which we must return later.

One of the most surprising facts that emerges from a study of wrecks is that their formative process is not continuous in time. When the ship has settled on the bottom its degree of decay will be arrested at a certain point. This stabilization will occur at different times on different wrecks in accordance with local submarine conditions. The fact that decay is arrested after a relatively short period accounts for the quite astonishingly good preservation of some antique ships.

Members of the Cannes Club used to dive on the *Robuste II*, a salvage ship which sank, unaccountably, one night in 1943 in Golfe Juan. The *Robuste* is not going to make a 'good wreck', but I mention it because it has been possible to time its disintegration. Rebikoff first visited the wreck in 1950 and reported that, though the decks had been damaged by teredos, the hull was intact, and he went down into the engine-room, where he came face to face with a giant moray eel. The next year the mud was higher in the engine-room; the eel was still there. In 1961, eleven years later, I asked after this wreck: the eel, so they told me, was now in the collapsed remains of the funnel, but the hull had disintegrated; sand had piled up and jagged bits of metal were strewn around. Dumas has described a paddle frigate 100 years old and a Russian warship 200 years old, both made of wood. They are now marked by gentle tumuli. In the case of the Russian ship the tips of its cannons protrude from the sand, like amphora necks from a Roman wreck; in both cases the ships themselves and their fitments are buried. Once a wreck is assimilated by its surroundings, the remains do not alter for centuries. The process of assimilation may vary between the entire disintegration of a wreck and its almost entire preservation. Burial usually connotes preservation.

Dumas was the first to analyse the process and classify Mediterranean wreck-formations according to their geological environment.[1] The examples he gives are drawn from personal log books covering a period of twenty years. His thesis has permanent value, but archaeologically it remains theoretical. Like a newly discovered drug, its clinical application must be based on a series of practical tests. A corpus of archaeological information will have to be built up; a task which is as colossal as it is inevitable.

Wrecks are extremely varied in appearance. For the moment we may accept that in Mediterranean waters sand accumulates simultaneously with a certain structural collapse in most, but not all, wooden ships. Distance from the coast, the type of bottom and local variations in sedimentation also affect these formations. How and why sand collects will be treated later with the question of digging into a wreck and recording its contents. The first thing we must realize is that sand is a pre-requisite of any site worth digging and the archaeologist's friend (though he may not appreciate this until he learns to understand its behaviour).

With few exceptions, a ship sinks as a result of what must remain for us an unaccountable accident. If we wish to excavate a wreck we do not need to know what caused the ship to sink, because it will in no way affect our choice of excavation method. Comparative experience of wrecks teaches us that it is important to analyse the events that occurred after the ship submerged, because these events will have combined to produce the particular type of formation that confronts us on the bottom. Excavation, if it is to be successful, that is to say if it allows us to reconstruct the ship as well as salvage its cargo, must be based on a preliminary analysis of the wreck-formation. After the initial accident a ship may either nose dive or plane down to the bottom. This, the change of element, the complicated effects of submarine gravity or buoyancy and the final impact and list of the hull on the sea-bed, will all have contributed to a certain kind of redistribution in the cargo and other parts of the ship. After the wreck has settled, biological and geological processes continue the metamorphosis of what was once a mobile, functional mechanism.

Within apparent disorder, there is a logic in wrecks; they conform to submarine laws which, once understood, make it possible to reconstruct the series of events and then, by excavation, the original mechanism which was a ship. As we have seen, the accident followed by a sea change makes these sites utterly different in kind from land remains. Buildings, whether they are made of bricks or blocks of stone, are imposed on a certain bit of ground; even in ruin they maintain

[1] Frédéric Dumas, *Deep Water Archaeology*, Routledge and Kegan Paul, London, 1961.

this same relationship with their environment and, furthermore, their collapse would be dictated by the familiar law of gravity. Whereas both towns and houses are structural growths, ships and harbours are essentially self-contained mechanisms.

A ship which falls on to a rocky bottom will never make a well-preserved wreck, because only certain imperishable parts of its cargo will survive, and that in indecipherable disorder. If a fragmentary cargo were of exceptional value or interest it would justify excavation, but from an archaeological point of view this would amount to specialized salvage. The hypothetical ship could never be reconstructed from remains scattered on rock.

Wreck sites are not necessarily marked by artifacts. A slight geological anomaly, visible only to the trained eye, betrays the presence of many wrecks. It follows that only certain kinds of wreck-formations can be explained to non-divers by drawings; most sites are better explained in a written report. Some of the best-known wrecks, such as the Congloué, were marked on the surface by only one or two bits of pottery; antique jetsam is common in the Mediterranean, and does not necessarily mean a wreck. Even when cargo is visible on the bottom it is not always worth drawing. In some cases when it is free standing, above the level of the sand, it may be covered by a 'pie-crust' of concretion, or individual artifacts may be encased in separate, baroque lumps. Alternatively, even on a 'good wreck', the surface layer or cargo may be dispersed, or little may show through a field of weed.

It would not only be meaningless but also misleading to draw two amphorae, in order to explain to a land archaeologist what one knows to be a large, buried ship. Only an expert with his comparative knowledge can evaluate the importance of a site. A damaged or disordered surface does not mean that a wreck is worthless, though a drawing of it would certainly convey this impression. As to concretions, free standing or otherwise, they are the draughtsman's nightmare. He knows that they contain cargo, and if he is experienced he can have a good guess at its nature, but the tortured shapes he sees do not correspond to their contents. Photographs and drawings of this sort of thing are not intelligible. Concretions sometimes show as an oval mass the shape of an entire ship, in which case the whole can be measured and explained in a written report. If a concreted wreck is going to be excavated, then the surface layer has to be surveyed; the method used is described later, together with other recording techniques.

The wrecks which I started to look for when I became interested in making underwater plans were those with drawable top layers which would make sense on paper. It follows that all the sketches reproduced herein represent very exceptional virgin sites, because on the average wreck recording can start only after the first layer of sand, weed or concretion has been removed.

Through Dumas' analysis of wreck-formations and the ever-increasing possibilities of visiting these sites, archaeologists and free-divers are gradually reaching a stage when they can begin to apprehend the subject as a whole, and even interpret such existing records as there are of submarine excavations. The holes that have been dug up to now on the sites of Greek and Roman wrecks are technically errors made by pioneers. The time has come when we should begin to learn from these mistakes. So far no ancient ship has been reconstructed as a result of submarine research. Coherent and consecutive plans have never been made underwater. Nor have analyses of the formation and axes of a wreck (the essential preliminaries to methodical excavation) been attempted before digging began. Judged on the level of salvage rather than archaeology, no complete cargo has ever been raised.

The nearest approximation to complete salvage took place at Anticythera off the southern tip of the Peloponnesus in 1901,[1] but even there not all the cargo was lifted. Today the hull of this ship still lies on the bottom under 50 centimetres of sand. Unless diving techniques improve it will remain unrecorded, for it is in 60 metres of water, where a depth-drunk draughtsman would have only a few minutes working time per day. Moreover, the Anticythera finds were so exceptional that their salvage did not help to answer the basic archaeological question: what and how big was the cargo of the average Roman merchantman? Indeed, in the past all wrecks which attracted the attention of archaeologists and enjoyed professional salvage were atypical, because, like this one, they contained works of art. The Anticythera, Artemision and Mahdia wrecks of Roman loot ships, that had been carrying art treasures away from Greece, were all found by Greek sponge divers.

At Mahdia sufficient *objets d'art* were raised to fill the museum at Bardo.[2] Marble columns and other prefabricated architectural components were left on the bottom above the wood of the hull; the latter is so well preserved in the mud

[1] *Anticythera*, Archaeologiki Ephemeris, Athens, 1902; George Karo, *Archaeology* (*U.S.*), winter, 1948.

[2] A. Merlin, 'Submarine Discoveries in the Mediterranean', *Antiquity*, Vol. IV, 1930, pp. 405–14.

that it still bears traces of paint.[1] Many years later Cousteau and then the diving club of Tunis went back to the wreck to see what remained.[2] Reports made by the original Greek divers seem wildly imaginative. They gave the impression that the hull had not collapsed and that they got inside it. The reports also suggested that the heavy marble columns had been loaded on deck, above the lighter and more fragile cargo of bronzes. Taking all three accounts together, we can now see that the Mahdia ship, as an example of wreck-formation, was fairly unusual; this may explain some of the original misunderstandings. It sank in open sea off a flat coastline to a depth of 40 metres. Free-divers would never have come across the site, only trawler or sponge men had reason to visit such parts. Flat like the coast, the bottom was hard, consisting of closely packed pebbles covered by only 60 centimetres of mud. When the ship came to rest the hull could not settle into this bottom; waterlogged, it opened out over the resistant shingle. Being far from the coast, sedimentation was minimal. The cargo of heavy, imperishable objects must have held together and remained a high, unburied tumulus. The Greek divers pulled bronzes and marbles from this pile, working by touch in a cloud of mud. In that visibility they could not know where they were. Any odd plank, coupled with a desire to impress, would have convinced them that they were inside a hulk.

Reports taken from the sponge divers who salvaged the Anticythera wreck make much more convincing reading. Perhaps they were more observant men, or perhaps they scrupled about hoodwinking archaeologists who were their compatriots. The site itself was archetypical, being partly on rockfall at the base of a submarine cliff and partly on the adjoining sand. Sand had piled up, and in the normal course of erosion large rocks also fell from the cliff on to the cargo. Technically, the excavation reports are very similar to those on the Grand Congloué. The cargo lifted, though incomplete, was staggering. At Mahdia the Roman looter's taste had been doubtful and the statues rather debased. Anticythera produced masterpieces which are now the pride of the Athens Archaeological Museum. The over-life-size, bronze Ephebe had been broken, but sponge men carefully collected bits out of the sand so that the figure could be put

[1] I am indebted to Frédéric Dumas for the information that he also saw paint on the wood at Anticythera; I do not think that this has been recorded in print.

[2] Gui de Frondeville, 'Les Visiteurs de la Mer', *Centurion*, 1956; Gui de Frondeville, *L'Epave de Mahdia, Le Plongeur et l'Archéologue*, Confédération Mondiale des Activités Subaquatiques, Marseille, 1960; J.-Y. Cousteau and Frédéric Dumas, *Le Monde du Silence*, Editions de Paris, 1954, p. 114; Philippe Tailliez, *Nouvelles Plongées sans Câble*, Arthaud, 1960, p. 80.

together again. The fifth-century Zeus and second-century Jockey in the same museum come from yet another wreck off Cape Artemision. It is interesting to note that all the major bronzes in the Athens Museum are from the sea and to examine them from this point of view. The number of breaks give one a healthy respect for the intelligent craftsmanship of those divers who must have gone down again and again to search the sand for a finger, a toe, a few centimetres of torso or a scrap of drapery. One can also see how the statues lay on the bottom: 'the Jockey', from Cape Artemision, must have had one foot sticking out of the sand, for it is eroded, whereas the details of sandal straps and toe-nails are so sharp on the other that it might have come straight from the foundry.

The relatively careful salvage at Anticythera produced quantities of ceramics which, as a closed group, are after more than half a century being studied by the American School of Archaeology in Athens. Bronze ornaments off furniture were found, also an ear-ring and, surprisingly, nearly all the parts of a time-calculating machine.[1] Ingots, lead weights, anchors and tackle were so abundant as to remain almost an embarrassment to the busy museum staff, in the crowded cellars where they await specialists who will one day come to study them.

To me, the most awe-inspiring memorial to this wreck is in a museum courtyard and consists of twenty or thirty life-size marbles of horses and men (Plates 17, 18 and 19). Nor is this vast gallery complete, for lifting machinery being inadequate, many statues fell back and rolled down to a depth from which even such intrepid and expert divers could not retrieve them. During the war I heard a London fireman describe the night Mme Tussaud's burned; familiar faces of sportsmen and politicians leered at him in a semi-liquid state. Historical figures swayed in weird distortions, while melting criminals in the chamber of horrors seemed to be meeting a retribution as macabre as in any medieval hell. Here something similar was happening in lucid, Greek sunlight. These strange beings, crowded into the space of a good-sized deck, were more assertive than their counterparts in the exhibition halls. Pock-marked by burrowing molluscs and gnawed by the sea into Giacometti forms, the movement of each figure was accentuated not only by surface distortions but also by the balance which many had lost together with their legs and plinths. Their gnarled condition contrasted with patches of suave surface where part had lain in the sand and been preserved. Polished buttocks merged into decaying backs and shoulders. Here and there a carefully set and formalized hair-style backed the leprous distortion of

[1] *Scientific American*, June 1959.

face and neck (Plates 18 and 19). It is a pity they are not on view to the public; they would look well in the garden in front of the Museum.

I have never dived on a treasure ship. Partly from 'sour grapes,' partly because sporting divers talk of nothing else, I have dismissed them as 'archaeologically irrelevant'. Nevertheless, like anyone else, I long to see one. The courtyard statuary would have looked even better underwater, magnified by a quarter and festooned with sea-growths. An amphora-carrying wreck, on the other hand, is no more frightening than a prehistoric tomb, age being an emotional antiseptic. At Jericho we used to pick brown matter from between bones, put it into a thermos flask and label it 'human flesh'. It was all in a day's work. A modern wreck, on the other hand, is, to me, like stumbling on a week-old corpse in a forest. Usually the position of a wreck is known, so one can steel oneself with reason and proceed. This was impossible on one occasion when I was alone, swimming out of a bay on an uninhabited part of the Cretan coast. The water was very clear, with a visibility of at least 25 metres, that is to say, to the bottom. Suddenly a dark mass loomed up; I realized what it was, turned tail and swam furiously for about 50 metres in the opposite direction. Gasping for breath, I pulled myself together, then returned in a resigned frame of mind, as to a cemetery. She must have been a small tramp. No name was visible. I went down the mast, and a big grouper came out of the funnel. The chain was out and the anchor some distance away, almost inside the bay. Closer inshore I came across coarse ship's china. A broken cup with a blue line round it seemed familiar and British, but had no mark. I never understood this wreck, and there was no one to ask. The place was not on a sea lane and there were no dangerous rocks. The only explanation seems enemy action, yet it was eight years after hostilities, and the ship was well preserved in comparison with other wartime wrecks round Crete. Why had she not been salvaged? The worst thing about her was that she was sitting bolt upright, instead of having a decently dead list. Pleasant or unpleasant, wrecks draw one like a magnet: back in Lebanon, I fretted for the complicated journey to Bodrum, whose wrecks, though I did not know it, were going to occupy me for three years.

What, one wonders, are the attractions of travel? A thrill, depending neither on destination nor transport sets in before departure. On waking one might have swallowed a couple of pep pills. Then there is the satisfaction of pressing down a bursting suitcase and relaxing inside the taxi. Familiar streets take on a freshness, as though seen for the first time. Once the traveller's cables are cut he becomes an interesting stranger, even to himself. So great is the benefit of doubt accorded to him in a primitive community that good clothes, fair hair, an ability to read, write and tell the time will, at least to begin with, command respect. The smallest knowledge of a language, or local customs, are received as a sign of brotherhood. Satisfaction derived from this form of flattery lasts for a longer or shorter time, depending on the individual. Like a child who cries, 'Look, no hands!' the traveller learns about himself through a form of exhibitionism, but he must have something to test, or the experiments pall. Missionaries make good travellers, because their spiritual luggage is portable. Like a transformer, convictions connect them with improbable currents, explaining other peoples' taboos. Similarly, specialization of interest is a key to unknown lands. It can also be turned in the lock, preserving its owner from outside interference. In either case he is better off than the open-minded, who, paradoxically, are circumscribed.

Some enjoy the act of travel and dream of a corner seat in the Orient Express. To me it is claustrophobic torture to pass places where I would like to get out and have a walk. Only aeroplanes, which are so fast and remote that the journey is unnoticeable, or transport so frail that it is likely to break down and do the unexpected, have any attraction. As to destinations, blends of flavour or known delights draw me: Paris is strawberries and cream, Beirut cucumber and taragon and Lake Van, possibly, walnut sauce. I do not yearn for bird's-nest soups when roots, and therefore limitations, lie within Europe and the Levant. Reactions to anything beyond are bound to be artificial.

At last the time came to leave Beirut, to fly to Ankara, across the Anatolian plain to Izmir and then, by less-reliable transport, down to Bodrum. John Carswell, the painter, was also travelling back to England by this devious route. He had been teaching in the American University in Beirut, and before that worked for seven years as archaeological draughtsman with English, French and American expeditions all over the Middle East. His interest in Bodrum lay in the land sites. We left Lebanon with relative decorum, despite Kemal Jumblat, the Druse leader, who was trying to take the airport. The rate of his advance, denoted by puffs of cannon fire slowly descending the foothills, had to be calculated against the speed of our taxi. We were both in a bad temper: I, because I had shot the tip of a finger with a harpoon gun the night before and had not had a chance to get it treated, while John was resenting his promise to wear my belt of diving leads under his jacket; they would have looked odd on my summer dress. Nor was his mood improved when the guard at the airport frisked him for a gun and was puzzled by what he found.

This was nothing to the arrival next day at Ankara. Trouble started when the Customs discovered my bottle inside a suitcase. An Anatolian official could hardly be familiar with diving equipment. In any case, the Turkish *gümrük* have a traditional hostility to gadgets which may date back to Byzantium, when, I suppose, I would have been suspected of carrying Greek Fire. My mother, as a girl, was accused of having explosives, and they confiscated her glass-sided travelling clock on the frontier at Nish. My grandfather, who worked in the Arsenal at Scutari, stated with some authority that the thing was not a bomb. I was not in such a happy position as my mother. '*Yok*', the official remarked, but one of the things one learns in Turkey is not to take '*yok*' for an answer.

'*Balik spor!*' I cried, 'fishing sport' (sport being much encouraged). I showed the man photographs of myself wearing the apparatus and demonstrated the harpoon gun. He was mildly interested, but unmoved. His duty was clear: the thing had to be impounded until I returned to the airport to catch the plane for Afyon. Unfortunately the plane left at 6 a.m. and the Customs opened an hour or so later. I demanded to see his superior, who was out, then invoked the British Embassy. What really saved the situation was a group of Jamaican cabaret artists waiting behind, who had an engagement at the local *Gasinosu*. Our discussion, conducted in a mixture of English, French and Turkish, convulsed them. Their unbridled mirth so discountenanced the official that he was willing to do almost anything to rid himself of the embarrassment and waved me towards the taxi.

Once I had a sticky time getting the bottle off the Orient Express at Istanbul, but apart from these incidents the equipment always passed the frontier with surprising ease. Next year I armed myself with Turkish club membership papers, but even in the military zone, between Syria and Turkey, they hardly glanced at the documents. Of course, they said, they knew all about free-diving, it was the most natural thing in the world. This was probably due to the showing of the film *The Silent World* and the fact that the book had been serialized in the principal newspaper.

But to return to the Customs at Ankara; a fleet of taxis stood by to take passengers into town after their luggage had been cleared. My one anxiety was to see that the case containing my bottle was firmly tied to the boot of the car with the inadequate lengths of knotted string available. Finally, John and I squeezed into the front seat of the crowded taxi. At the terminal, released from our cramped position, we almost fell out. In a scuffle with the door my handbag opened and its contents, passport and money, slipped into a sewer. Our tempers had not improved. I blamed John, and in a gallant attempt to make amends he retrieved the things. By this time the luggage was sitting on the pavement, or rather my cases were there, but not his. It must have dropped off on the way. The Lebanese Airways were informed and, gathering up the remainder, we made for the most comfortable hotel in town, longing for a bath. It was not until we arrived that we realized what we must look like. John had come out of a sewer and had no luggage; my own was not particularly presentable, and by this time I was wearing my lead belt, disguised beneath a smock which I carried for such eventualities. We stopped for consultation and decided that, though there was not much to choose between us, I was perhaps the more presentable, so I took both passports and went to ask for rooms with baths. The receptionist looked doubtful, while the chasseur, who had seen John, whispered a few words. Would we wait; we did, in the bar, which was crowded with American service families. The receptionist returned with a verdict that the hotel was full up.

The scene was re-enacted elsewhere; but to cut a long story short, we ended in the most central but least salubrious hotel in town, where baths were out of the question. Before I could start the patter I had by now perfected about lost cases, the Levantine porter said: 'I think you are coming from Lebanon. One man who is with truck has been passing and saying that he is finding one valise dropped from Lebanese aeroplane.' We got the rooms and we got the case. This degree of honesty would be a wonderful thing by any standards, but in a poverty-stricken eastern country, where there was such a shortage of consumer goods, the return of an unlocked case full of new clothes was overwhelming. It makes travel in Turkey a joy, despite material inconveniences.

Next day we were asked to the Seton Lloyds. Mr Michael Gough (who succeeded Mr Lloyd as director of the British School of Archaeology at Ankara) was there with his wife and Miss Freya Stark. They all knew Turkey well, but with the exception of Miss Stark, had not visited Bodrum in Caria. She listened to my wreck projects and suggested that I might look for the warships that sank as a result of Alexander's naval engagement. She had not visited the miraculous spring on Kara Ada, but I understood her to say that in classical times it had been known as the Hermaphroditus cave and that those who bathed in its waters underwent a change not to be confused with rejuvenation.

Various fascinating junctions on trans-Anatolian journeys, such as Ankara itself, Edirne, Adana and Afyon, are strictly outside my terms of reference, having nothing to do with the sea. Nevertheless, Afyon has such character and surprising associations that I cannot resist a digression. Travelling by plane from Ankara or Antalya to Izmir, connection is made at Afyon. The first time I passed with only a short wait at the airport, but on the second occasion I was delighted to be forced to spend a day and a night there. From the airport the attraction had been two-fold: travellers rushed to the buffet to buy a *lucoum* stuffed with fresh, clotted cream, also plates of this cream or *kaimak*, which they consumed on the spot. Secondly, it looked an astonishing town from the air. On the western extremity of the great plateau, near its boundary of mountains, Afyon lay on flat agricultural land round two sugar-loaf rocks. The modern town, built by Mustafa Kemal in the 'twenties and 'thirties, had Germanic public buildings along rectilinear boulevards, a park, and beterraced war memorial to his victory over the Greeks. Behind, like an incongruous drop curtain, rose the stalagmitic shapes, one of them crowned by a citadel overbuilt in the Middle Ages by an Armenian fortress, though defence walls seemed superfluous on sides so steep. The rock was orange-pink, covered by yellow lichens, and the whole reminiscent of an oleographed illustration of some elaborate dessert from an early edition of Mrs Beeton. The old town huddled round this rock; there, houses were built in the traditional combination of herringbone brickwork within a wooden frame; they were not unlike Elizabethan houses, except that the overhanging first floor was entirely wood and the windows screened by lattice. Streets were cobbled, and in the modern quarters paved, which in itself distinguished the town from others in the plain and made it the more surprising to be pushed aside at every turn by a sultry cow, or a *gamuş*, the Turkish water buffalo, drifting around alone.

These animals explained the variety of meat and dairy produce in the eating shops. Afyon was the Bourg en Bresse of the Anatolian Plateau. Personally, I am very fond of Turkish food, but in small country places it is monotonous. Transport being bad, variety is governed by local water supplies. The staple diet consists of bread and olives, yoghourt, baked beans, tomatoes, onions, peppers and fruit, usually melons, grapes and peaches, according to place and season. Grilled mutton kebabs, meat balls, a dish of eggs scrambled in tomatoes and oil called *menemen* are universal. Meat, whether goat or mutton, is not always available; in some villages they slaughter only once a week. Archaeologists are accustomed to live on a shoe-string and off the land; the more dedicated Anglo-Saxons hardly notice what they eat. One such expedition lost its cook. These men, who are employed from year to year and sometimes from father to son on successive digs, pick up a knowledge of field routine and one or two foreign dishes like Irish stew.

WRECKS AND DIVING BOATS.

15 (opposite, left). *A ship of the time of Augustus sunk off the French coast near the Ile du Levant. This picture of the* Titan *wreck was taken before excavation, when untouched amphorae gaped like* 'blind mouthes'. *Compare Plates 13 and 27 of the same site.*

16 (right). *A German cargo ship wrecked near Cannes during the 1945 war; notice the anti-aircraft gun still in place.*

17 (below). *View of the courtyard in the Athens Archaeological Museum showing the quantity of marbles taken from a single wreck at Anticythera (the entire cargo was not salvaged). The headless horses to the left, and indeed the human figures, are all life-sized.*

18 and 19 (centre pages left and right). *Marble figures from the wreck at Anticythera; those that were not buried in sand have been eroded, but the undamaged torso must have been lying on its back.*

20 (verso, left). *Bags of sponges, each one the harvest of a single diver, are hung over the side of the* caïque *so that their black skins can decay before cleaning. White 'milk' drains off, clouding the sea.*

21 (right). *A* congoa *or diverless sponge boat. A net attached to an axle and wheels is dragged across the bottom. These trawls are used on sponge beds at a depth inaccessible to divers; they often bring up parts of ancient wrecks, indeed the* Izmir Demeter *was found in this way. Being non-selective, the method is destructive to marine life.*

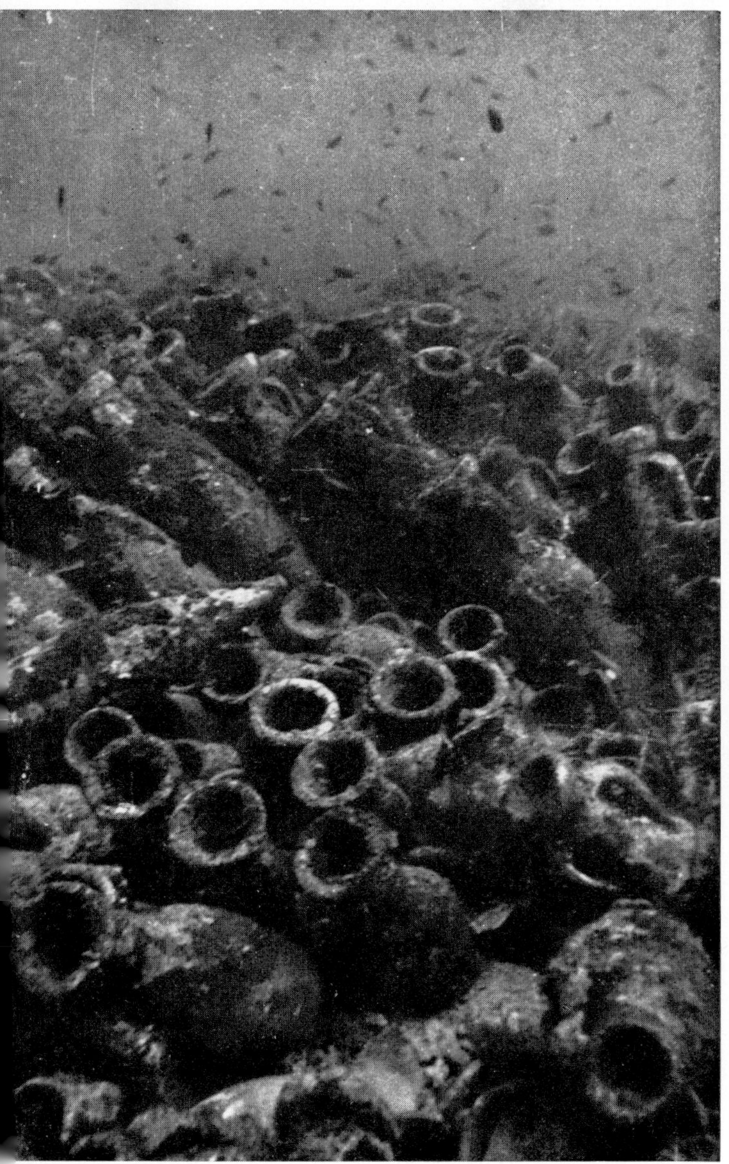

15. Bulletin F.F.S.M., photo Y. de Rolland

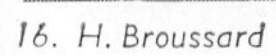

16. H. Broussard

17. F. Dumas

18 & 19. F. Du

20 & 21. M. Kapkin

They also stew fruit and call it 'composta'. In this case the British-trained cook was replaced by one who had worked for the French. He served prunes and custard, which were much enjoyed. Afterwards a lady remarked that the custard was strange, though nice; he was asked how he made it. His terms baffled the assembly until they caught the word 'mayonnaise'. 'Dear me, had I known I would have taken a second helping,' one gentleman remarked.

When Frédéric Dumas came to Turkey with the American expedition on the Bronze Age wreck his every Gallic fibre rebelled at the fare. Gastronomically, the site was badly situated; we were lucky to see one skinny goat a week, among eighteen people. Loud were his laments at the cement-like cheese, hard bread and inevitable salad. Most of us were broken to 'dig' food and surprised that a traveller, who had spent long periods on desert islands, should be so demanding; but, of course, he had always been on the *Calypso*, and the *Calypso* had a French cook. Against this background of archaeological *pis aller* and traveller's pot luck, the restaurant at Afyon was Lucullan. There were various soups: rice, chicken and lemon and cold mixtures of yoghourt and sorrel, also hot yoghourt soups; an especially rich *mussaka* of meat and *aubergines*, assorted kebabs, a summer pudding of bread covered with preserved cherries soaked in syrup and served with clotted cream, and last, and most unexpected, strawberries like Royal Sovereigns; their Turkish name deriving from the Italian, *fragole*. Many excellent wines come from Ankara, but here at Afyon they had a sweet and heavy, local variety like Madeira. In a country where water is the subject of more serious connoisseurship, Afyon could also boast of *Maden Su*, an equivalent of Evian water, famous throughout Turkey.

Its real fame rests on a more exotic product, for the full name is Afyon-Kara-Hisar or the 'black castle of opium'; the hotel is called the Sağlam Palas or 'Palace of recovered health'. Here was the link with my past. In a distant part of the Arab world I developed a curious relationship with a man who sold *filaffils*, a form of deep-fried rissoles made of beans. At that time I was suffering from a complaint that restricted my diet to boiled rice. Every day he would come out and offer *filaffils*. Our mutual Arabic and English were insufficient for me to explain my reasons for repeated and seemingly churlish refusals. Finally, some healthier colleagues turned up, accepted his hospitality and learned his story. Money-changers abound in the East, not even tourists need visit a bank; in the unsettled post-war conditions there were bargain currencies. Our man saw a way to ensure his future security: he bought cheap Turkish money, then, by bus and *dolmuş* taxi, set off across the intervening countries for Afyon, a journey which must have taken him at least two weeks. There he bought opium and returned to the best drug market of the Levant, where he sold it at great profit. Having converted a few pounds into a few hundred, he set himself up in his native town with the shop of his dreams. During the period that I knew him, years later, the exploit was discovered and retribution meted out by the police in his country, but I hope his sentence was light.

CHAPTER 9

Izmir; Demeter and Divers – The Meander Valley – Bodrum – The Castle – The Ancient Harbour – Project for a Maritime Museum

BEFORE the first war and the Turkish revolution, life for foreigners in Smyrna must have been as in Beirut today. My parents were married there, and photographs in the family album show *fêtes champêtres*, where elaborately dressed women with flower-bedecked and veiled Edwardian hats reclined on cushions while servants unpacked picnic hampers in the background. This carefree affluence was to end; the Greek quarter in the centre of the town was burned to the ground. It is replaced today by a very beautiful park with lakes, for the Turks are wonderful gardeners. The Archaeological Museum and the Pavilions which house the Izmir Fair come within this area. In the old days a flourishing British colony lived in villas beyond the town on the other side of the bay. When I got to know the place better I discovered some properties were still inhabited. A vintage Rolls-Royce was sometimes to be seen, taking its octogenarian owner to his weekly round of golf. I heard of a house built in 'Scottish Baronial', whose stately stairs were guarded by an upright, stuffed bear. In the garden of another villa two elderly English ladies collected maimed and starving animals which they nursed. However, my immediate interests being of another order, I never penetrated this social preserve.

My first concern was to contact the *Kurbağa Kulübü* and visit the sea-born Demeter in the Museum. This over-life-size, fifth-century bronze bust, broken from its body, had recently been found in a drag-net by sponge fishers from Bodrum. Her compassionate face, with its faintly Semitic features, had none of the superhuman detachment of classical sculpture.[1] Cleaned of concretions, the metal was left without patina. It might have come from the workshops after the sculptor chased it and incised outlines round the lips. The eye-sockets were

[1] Edward Bacon, *Digging for History*, p. 150, Adam and Charles Black, 1960.

empty, though they must once have contained eyeballs of polished semi-precious stones. Such realism was difficult to visualize in a head whose brooding expression depended on these cavities. Slightly inclined, the turn of the neck hinted at a movement which was emphasized by the pleated frill of a garment, half hidden beneath the veil she wore around her and covering her head; torn by the sea, it now fluttered freely over one shoulder. Describing the unusual character of this bust, writers have been forced to use the terms Renaissance and Baroque; 'all the thoughts and experience of the world' had been 'etched and moulded there'. No words can describe her better than Pater's (though he was writing of the Mona Lisa, not, of course, of this Demeter):

> She has been dead many times, and learned the secrets of the grave; and has been a diver in deep seas, and keeps their fallen day about her; and trafficked for strange webs with Eastern merchants: and as Leda was the mother of Helen of Troy, and, as St. Anne, the Mother of Mary; and all this has been to her but as the sound of lyres and flutes and lives only in the delicacy with which it has moulded the changing lineaments.[1]

The story of Demeter's discovery belongs to Bodrum and the old sponge diver who a week or so later was to lead us to a Byzantine wreck.

In Izmir the torrid heat sapped my energy and forced me to concentrate on essentials. One of my introductions was to Hakki Beck Bey of the Turyağ factory, who was chairman of the *Kurbağa Kulübü*. When I phoned he was out of town, but on hearing the nature of my enquiry I was advised to come over immediately; the entire factory appeared to be staffed by divers. The next year, when I met its English engineer, Mr Connell, he wryly admitted that there was no restraining their spare-time enthusiasm. They not only took advantage of days when the factory compressors were switched over to air to fill their bottles but also there was hardly a corner of laboratory or workshop which had not been used to make their equipment. The more I learned of the factory itself, the more impressed I became. There was not a question or a test which its chemists, geologists and mechanics could not tackle. The name *Turyağ* appears on the shelves of every village shop in Turkey. It produces oil, margarine, cooking fat, soaps, cattle cake and probably a host of other things which are beyond my understanding.

The gentleman who acted on behalf of Hakki Beck Bey introduced us to a young engineer-diver. Yes, he said, Bodrum was the place. The Club's best divers: Rasim Divanli and Mustafa Kapkin (who was a photographer and,

[1] Walter Pater, *The Renaissance: Leonardo da Vinci*, Macmillan, 1907, p. 125.

exceptionally, did not belong to the factory) had just gone there and were with their friend Capt. Kemal Aras, who had a sponge boat. He added that there were one or two good wrecks near Izmir, but that they could not be reached without a car and boat.

'Have they got their *narghilé* with them at Bodrum?' I asked nervously. He looked rather vague.

I need not worry, he said, they had instead an American photographer-journalist who bristled with the necessary equipment, including a compressor. '*Il en est armé jusqu'aux dents!*'

Furnished with new introductions to Capt. Kemal and Mustafa Bey, we thanked our hosts and went to find out about buses. The first left at seven-forty-five on the following morning, stopped the night at Milas, and arrived at Bodrum in the next evening. There is no limit to the amount of luggage which country buses will accept and carry on their roofs, but I did not trust their straps to hold my bottle. Even if these suspicions were unjustified, it would inevitably be thrown from roof to ground with the other luggage, and this would either damage the tap or cause the whole thing to explode. Moreover, two days' exposure to the broiling sun were hardly to be recommended for a tank filled with 150 atmospheres of compressed air. The cramped seats became so unbearable by the end of the day that the added discomfort of nursing a good-sized steel cylinder was hardly noticeable. On the other hand, the Cyprus situation caused anti-British feeling, and the average peasant, like the *Gümrük*, might imagine that my bottle was a bomb. So, with John's consent, I wrapped it in towels and then in a *kuffeah*, an Arabic head-dress bought in Jordan, and cradled it in my arms. Whether our fellow travellers really thought the bundle was a baby, live or dead, was immaterial. The important thing was that my solicitude for it was evident during the two days that I carried it or passed it to John. On a human level, they could see that I was attached to the thing; even an enthusiastic saboteur could not sustain that attitude to a bomb.

Anyone who thinks rough travel is 'jolly good fun' must be either very young or completely inhuman. It is hell, but sometimes inevitable. All the same, there are compensations. One would not go out of one's way to catch an infectious disease or experience war, but when such things occur they are often mitigated by incidents so touching as to reconcile one with humanity at large. Turkish peasants, among their many qualities, have a physical sensitivity and deep courtesy that overwhelm the traveller. On such journeys my neighbours always shifted their position if they noticed, or even anticipated, that I was cramped. Fruit and drink are circulated both inside the transport and at the many wayside halts, for in Turkey travel becomes one long picnic. Children are beautifully brought up; their screams being stilled and curiosity skilfully restrained. They are urged to share sweets with their neighbours. Courtesies are even more pronounced when a woman travels alone; families immediately take her under their protection and see her baggage is looked after, sometimes carrying it themselves. They haggle with local *hammals*, or porters, so that she shall not pay a *kuruş* too much and bludgeon hotel-keepers into providing a suitable bed. This treatment does, of course, depend on the traveller's respecting local customs; brash behaviour or clothing that is considered unsuitable will lead to trouble. Lastly, their generosity is unbounded: I never managed to pay for a plate of food on these journeys. The honesty shown over John's case at Ankara was not exceptional. People have run after me with cashmere sweaters and harpoon guns that I dropped: items which in a country where no consumer goods are imported represented a small fortune.

Cynics say that stoicism in face of discomfort results from insensitivity, but experience shows this is seldom the case. After days of heat, jolting, dust and cramp, I am convinced that my fellow-travellers all felt like death. They controlled their emotions; what would have been the use of hysterics? with the best will in the world, the country could not afford to switch over to luxury travel. Only once did I see a passenger break down. She was an elderly lady, travelling with her son to Bodrum. The bus had been late and we missed our connection. On the second day, after a nine-hour wait on hard café chairs and much bargaining on the part of the menfolk, we piled, eight of us, into an open jeep with luggage and livestock on our laps and tied on to the boot. After an hour on unmade, dusty mountain roads she started to whimper. I would not have minded joining her. As it was, I passed the ritual bottle of eau-de-Cologne. We sprinkled it on to the palms of our hands and rubbed the dust and sweat into our burning faces. Her show of emotion was exceptional.

Looking back on it now, I can see that the first journey with John was relatively comfortable and uneventful. We passed Ephesus, climbed over some mountains, then down into the Menderes, or Meander, valley with its groves of fig trees. Liquorice also grows there, and most of this trade is still in the hands of a Scottish family. The country is typical of Turkey, with its farmsteads crowned by stork's nests and surrounded by clumps of poplars. Roads are good; bands of gipsies camp beside them, or wander along the nearby tracks, their chains of camels tied together and led by a man on a donkey. In the countryside motors still excite suicidal tendencies in children and dogs. The latter, usually large shaggy Anatolian sheepdogs with their ears cut off so that wolves can't get a hold on them, hurl themselves snarling at the wheels. Children tended to throw themselves in front until there was a national campaign about it in the schools. They were persuaded that the correct behaviour was to jump aside, stand rigidly to attention and give travellers a military salute. It caught on: each bus-load of peasants is saluted as though they were hurtling into battle in desperate defence of their country.

The first night was spent in the communal dormitory of the Milas *Café Oteli*. Most of our fellow passengers had brought '*paplamas*', a kind of kapok quilt. We were put into an alcove with iron bedsteads and clean sheets. Next day the roads got worse; now a new one which is both shorter and surfaced must be finished. The road I travelled for three years was unspeakable, consisting of ill-conceived hairpin bends over range upon range of mountains. After Milas the scenery was in complete contrast with the farmlands of the Meander valley, where stone-built houses looked almost European; now they gave place to more or less elaborate wooden huts, and some of the mountain people had Mongolian features. One range of mountains always struck me as a Stone Age man's paradise. Everywhere there were gigantic rounded or pancake pebbles, often balanced on top of each other like dolmens and moving slightly in the wind. Here scrub was sparse and the ground shone with splinters of mica. The road, I am sorry to say, shone with marble chippings which were not local. Classical towns that line the route from Izmir to Bodrum serve as quarries, and statues and inscriptions are also converted into lime to whitewash the houses. The Government does what it can to prevent this, but in a country so vast, yet so crowded with ancient ruins, it would take an army of educators, police and administrators to eradicate this traditional destruction.

The last stop on the second day was dramatic. To begin with, near the top of each range we invented arguments to substantiate our hopes that it would afford the first view of the Aegean. By evening, when we drew up at a new type of way-side café, our hopes had given place to despair. The white, flat-roofed box of a building had a terrace fronted by six inelegant columns, made out of mud or cement. Timbers ran between them and from each column to the roof of the house. This trellis supported fronds of fading oleander which shaded the café chairs; marble altars with bull's skulls and garlands in relief served as tables. The architecture was tantalizingly familiar. 'My God!' said John. 'It's Minoan!' Houses excavated in Crete had been built on this plan and the relation of columns to foundations had always been controversial. Here was the explanation and here a sign of Mediterranean influence (Plate XI).

While '*çai*' (tea) was brewing we wandered into a field where marbles stuck through the crops, and from there saw Bodrum, or perhaps I should say Halicarnassos, as distance emphasized the classical elements. Hills ran down steeply to double bays, separated by a peninsula crowned with fortifications. On one of those hills below us, Mausolus' widow had erected his memorial, so that it could be seen by sailors far out at sea, with a splendour that made it the seventh wonder of the world and the prototype of all elaborate tombs. Beyond, rising out of the hot blue of the Aegean, was the mountainous mass of Kara Ada, a 'black island' if ever there was one, and, on the horizon, Cos (Plate VII). Reality measured up to expectation.

An hour or so later the bus stopped in front of two *otelis* in the small, white square. There was not much choice of accommodation; in any case, we were past caring, but the bedroom windows did look on to a *Hamam*. Without unpacking, John rushed down and came back with the news that, though it was the men's bathing hour, the place was empty. This is another Turkish compensation for rough travel. Every village has its bath; so do the towns, but there they may be far from the hotel, or the traveller arrive at a time when they are open to the opposite sex. I came to regard the Bodrum *Hamam* as my own bathroom. It was kept by a charming couple with a family which increased at each annual visit. The husband had fought in the Korean War. He had not picked up a second language; one of his elderly relatives, however, spoke Italian, which facilitated the making of appointments and discussions about when one had to have a dress back, for they also took in laundry. Sometimes, when I was working, the family would enquire why I had not had a bath. 'She is always in the sea,' they would be told. At such times I visited them only when my hair became congealed with salt.

Next day, after presenting credentials at the Sponge Co-operative and learning that the Izmir divers and Capt. Kemal were at sea, but expected back soon, we went to visit the castle. It is the heart of Bodrum, whose very stones are an amalgam of history. Until recent times it was an island between the two bays. I have seen photographs of the fort at the end of the nineteenth century, before the causeway linking it to the village was built. Quays, a beautiful mosque and many little houses now cover this ground; their appearance is so ageless that without irrefutable evidence it would be difficult to guess that they were modern. The market-place, hotels, port and fishermen's quarters spread from the castle round the west of the bay. A more bourgeois community lives in well-kept villas to the east; this was a world so remote from my own interests that I never got to know it.

The earliest settlement and first citadel had been on the impregnable island. Later, a town spread to the west and was surrounded by a wall which ended in another fortification on the cape, opposite the island. Beyond this headland and city wall is a third and smaller bay; to this day sponge boats anchor there when the men make flying visits to their homes and wish to avoid the formalities of showing papers and entering the port. Here the fountain of Salmacis, known in antiquity, still supplies the town with all its drinking-water. From the map one would suppose that the largest, eastern bay had been the 'open' harbour in ancient times, but in fact it is too exposed. Vitruvius, speaking of visiting traders, says: 'they left their ships unattended on the beach and went within the city walls'; probably by the fountain of Salmacis, as the sponge boats do today. I find it difficult to interpret such statements literally; leaving boats 'on' the beach may be a figure of speech, for in sheltered, tideless Mediterranean coves it is difficult to imagine a justification for dragging ships out of the water on to the shore.

The city walls enclosed five hillocks, that is to say a very much larger area than the present village. Foundations of temples and, of course, the Mausoleum, rock-cut tombs and a theatre cover slopes now used for rough grazing. Lower down, unpaved alleys separating the whitewashed, neo-Minoan houses have been worn to a level where mosaic floors and courses of classical masonry show through the dust. Sometimes the boundaries of modern houses correspond with their ancient predecessors, and there the sunken streets are 'original'. As at Pompeii, pavements are high and narrow, while the bedrock is worn to a curved gulley by 3,000 years of use. Every house incorporates some relic of the past: altars, marble columns or oblong dressed stones. Dorian settlers, Carian Dynasts and Rhodian imperialists all left their mark. Mausolus moved his capital from Milas to Halicarnassos: after that the architect Satyrus and the sculptors Bryaxes, Timotheus, Pytheus and Leochares must have climbed these streets to supervise work on his tomb; Herodotus was also one of its citizens. Artemisia, sister and widow of Mausolus, continued his administration and policies. Alexander the Great was allied with her daughter-in-law Ada; then for a brief period the town was ruled by the Seleucids, before the Romans took it over and administered it from Rhodes.

In the eleventh century it came under Byzantines, then Seljuk Turks, until 1300, when the Ottomans moved in. After Bayaset I was defeated at the Battle of Ankara, it passed to the Crusaders and was renamed Mesy. These changes can all be traced in the castle. Courses of masonry in the defence walls date back to the early citadels, in other parts there are Byzantine mosaics. Marble from Halicarnassos was re-used: an Italian shield is carved on the top of an Ionic capital so that the volutes flank it at either side (Plate IX). Other shields have been carved on the back portions of a frieze, perhaps from the Mausoleum, and one has part of a warrior on the reverse. Elsewhere a sultan's signature or *tura* is superimposed on a cardinal's escutcheon, itself carved on classical marble. Corner stones and even marble steps bear Greek inscriptions. As in most Crusader architecture, column drums are laid horizontally strengthen the walls.

The general plan of the castle, with its towers and double fortifications, is the work of a German, Henry Schlegelholt, who was commissioned by the Knights of Jerusalem in the fourteenth century. With a zeal characteristic of Crusader architects, he tore down classical buildings, re-using the stone. Halicarnassos was so large that despite his thoroughness he could not destroy it. In 1472 the Italian navigator Cepio reported that part of the Mausoleum was still standing. In 1522, just before the siege of Rhodes by Sulyman the Magnificent, Philippe Villiers de l'Isle Adam, Grand Master of the Knights of Jerusalem, sent a Lyonnais called Tourette to put the fortifications in order. This must have accounted for many of the remaining marbles. The castle fell to the Turks before his work was finished. Ottomans added barracks and baths, but these were on a modest scale, and their materials relatively flimsy.

After that Bodrum sank into oblivion, from which it emerged briefly when Lord Stratford excavated in 1846 and Newton in 1856–58, salvaging the statues, which are now in the British Museum. But for them, Mausolus and Artemisia might have lost their heads to a pious iconoclast, or been reduced to a coat of whitewash on a fisherman's house. The extent and complexity of the remaining ruins in Halicarnassos and the surrounding Carian towns are baffling. There is no neatly excavated area from which a tourist can form an impression of the whole. Yet the classical scholars of the nineteenth century are not without successors. Messrs Cook and Bean seem to have made thorough surveys of a vast area of the southern Turkish coast. I say 'seem', because I could not pretend to evaluate their work. All I can say is that when chance has landed me in the remotest farmsteads of Caria and Lycia, where there were no roads, I have noted inscriptions and ruins, only to find that without exception they were already fully recorded and explained by Cook and Bean.

To get into the castle, we had to call the *Bekci* with the keys. All official monuments in Turkey have their St Peter, though few possess the gentle charm of *Bekci* Amed. In all countries the genus is irritating. Perhaps the best that can happen to a tourist is that he should be assessed as financially unrewarding. In that case, after a cursory viewing, he is left with his book to puzzle out the structure alone. The alternative is an aggressive flow of misinformation salted with all too personal questions, reminiscences about distinguished predecessors, who frequently include Sir Winston Churchill. Usually the traveller finds that he is giving a lesson in common English usage. Amed's technique was unique: he did not attempt conversation. Always considerate of our pace and degree of interest, he led us through the outer fortifications, indicating their extent by an eloquent wave of his hand, slackening his pace and pointing out any item he thought we might miss. He unlocked the second door, to the inner castle, excusing himself while he untethered a sheep.

Now there were four of us. The sheep took the lead; it too knew every stone, but was more egocentric than its master. We pelted along until it paused with insistent bleats. Apologetically, the old man disappeared into a guard room and returned with a leaky battered bucket which he lowered into a hole. It was at the highest point of the rocky island and the water, probably rain, must have come from a cistern; in any case, when later I myself was thirsty, I found it stale. Sated, the animal calmed down and we continued our inspection of the walls. Each tower bore the shield of French, English, Italian, Spanish or German Knights.

The English tower, with the arms of Edward IV, overlooked the sea. Its door was surmounted by an archaic lion, taken from Halicarnassos. Unfortunately the structure was badly damaged by cannon fire and the floors had collapsed. Amed *Amca* steered us to a vantage point from which we could see across to a first-floor window, whereon soldiers from Canterbury had inscribed their names during what must have been the great age of graffiti; the Gothic letters were carefully carved, unlike our contemporary scratchings. At this time I little supposed the castle would become my residence. When I started drawing, the Knight's refectory being the only room with a key, I was installed there with a table, two chairs, lent by the school and, of course, the antiquities. Had it not been for the brackish water, I would have slept there. As it was, I left the intolerably hot, none too clean cubicle in the *Oteli*, and every morning met Amed at the port, where we sometimes had tea. Then we proceeded to the office and he settled on the second chair. To begin with, I resented being watched at work, but very soon came to appreciate his presence. Tactfully, he diverted the curious, whether peasants, local idlers or tourists. The latter turned up in surprising numbers. Several times a week parties appeared from France, Germany or Holland. I would never have believed that so many people were willing to hazard their private cars across such rough country, or put up with the impossible *Otelis* and Khans. Once, returning from the sea, I found a note on my desk left by a friend from London who passing on an Hellenic Cruise had been surprised to recognize some of my possessions in the castle. If I worked late, Amed handed over the keys and I locked the castle when I left.

The refectory was the best drawing office I ever had. After several hours of close work I could go and swim. There was a hole on the ramparts leading to a partly collapsed gallery in the walls, which in turn, through another hole, gave on to the seaward rocks. I shared the knowledge of this passage, which I used twice daily, with one or two local boys. Amed stood guard outside the refectory while I changed, then carried my gun and flippers, which he handed down as I disappeared into the hole. Sometimes he watched, and so, indeed, did the rest of the village. The ramparts rose sheer for 50 metres, and the water below was so clear that they could follow my every movement, even on the bottom. On market days, when the peasants came to town, the audience reached embarrassing proportions. I would look up and see rows of heads lining the battlements, probably taking bets whether I would catch a fish or not. At such times it became a moral duty not to disappoint them.

I had every opportunity to get to know the castle, but the more I explored its cisterns, galleries and tunnels, the more baffling it became. In the third year someone suggested I should scribble down a plan. It was then I realized how little I knew it; even a rough sketch was beyond my capacity. However, the relation of the site to the fifth-century port did fascinate me, and the indications were sufficiently clear to be worth recording (see Fig. 25). Lehmann-Hartleben compares the harbour of Halicarnassos to Syracuse.[1] Vitruvius describes

[1] Karl Lehmann-Hartleben, '*Die Antiken Hafenanlangen des Mittelmeers*', Klio, Vol. XIV, Leipzig, 1923.

Halicarnassos as having the spring of Salmacis to the right and the secret port at the farther side of the town on the left. An embankment had hidden this secret military dock from all but Mausolus himself, whose palace overlooked it; Vitruvius goes on, after this sketchy, topographical description, to tell of an ambush. After the King's death the Rhodians attempted to take advantage of his widow. Artemisia got wind of the plot, and when their fleet attacked the town she allowed it to enter the main port. She then rowed her war galleys, which had been hidden, out of an eastern mouth of the secret harbour, round the island and into the main harbour. By this time the Rhodians, thinking themselves unopposed, had disembarked. She towed their abandoned fleet out to sea, leaving the crews to the mercy of her army. Later she surprised the Rhodians by attacking them with their own fleet and, after killing their rulers, erected a bronze trophy portrait of herself in their citadel.[1]

Now as Lehmann-Hartleben had not been to Bodrum, he assumes from this description that, as only the eastern mouth of the secret harbour was mentioned, there was no western communication with the main, closed harbour. Secondly, he quotes the geographer Scylax as saying that there were two harbours within the fortifications, one being 'between the island and the river'. At this point, since Hartleben was working from documents, his description becomes confused. Seeing no river on the surveys, he assumes Scylax meant the spring of Salmacis at the other side of the bay. He also assumes that the royal or naval docks could not be within the main port enclosed by the city walls. In fact, there is a dried-up river bed in Bodrum, beside the market-place, behind and slightly to the west of the present castle and one-time citadel. Two lines of classical masonry do run out underwater, from this point, towards the island, turning westwards at their extremity, but stopping short of the shore. This fits Scylax' description. These underwater walls can be seen very clearly from the Italian tower of the castle (Plate VIII). They are about 1 metre below the water, and within them are silted shallows, doubtless due to the building of the modern causeway, which, having stopped a through current, allowed matter to accumulate. I cannot see any reason to doubt that these walls enclosed the 'secret port' or that this dock should have been inside the main, closed harbour. Poidebard suggests that at both Tyre and Sidon the secret ports were where one would expect: well within the city's fortifications.

As to Artemisia's having to sail round the island from the naval docks to the

[1] Vitruvius, *de Architectura*, II, ch. viii.

enclosed harbour, she had good reason for taking that route. Now the causeway has been built there is no apparent connection between these docks and the enclosed harbour, and it is impossible to say for certain whether there was or was not an opening on the eastern side. I did, however, find rubble-fill, underwater, along the eastern length of the castle rock, which suggested landing quays. One would have expected quays to be faced with masonry, but there was no trace of the usual, oblong blocks. On the other hand, many Rhodian amphora handles

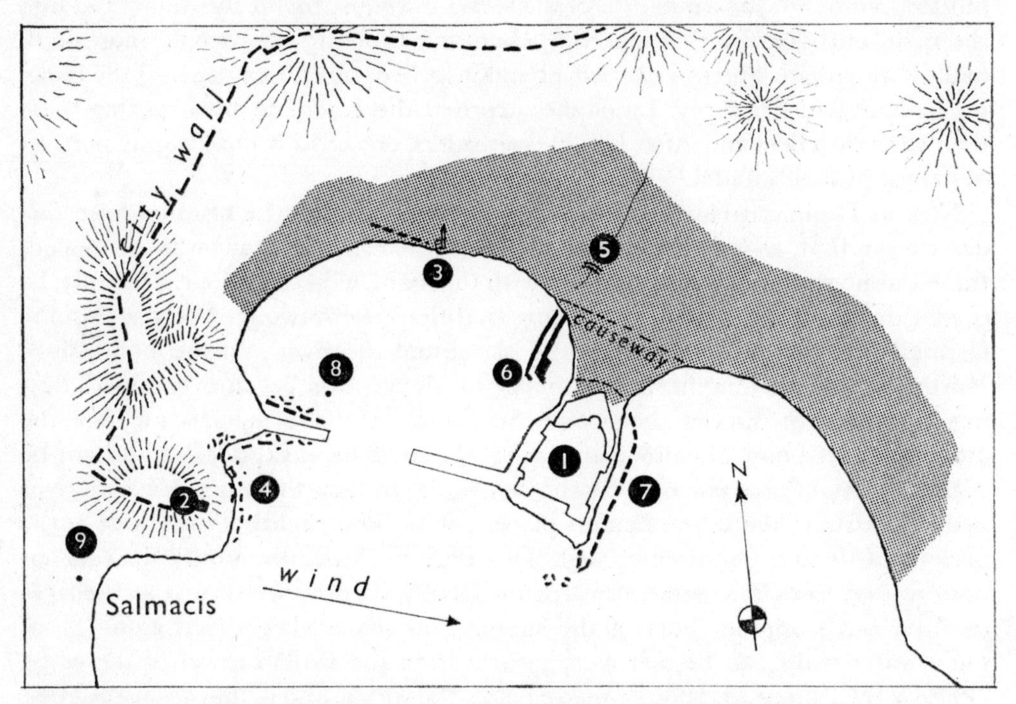

25. Halicarnassos (Bodrum) harbour; area covered by the modern village shown in tone.

Key: (*1*) *Crusader castle; built on the island site of the earliest citadel.* (*2*) *The corresponding strong-point that guarded the harbour mouth (on one end of the fifth-century town-wall)* (*3*) *Now on land, this line of masonry near the Mosque (Plate VI) was part of the fifth-century waterfront at the probable level of the Agora.* (*4*) *Remains of classical buildings, now awash.* (*5*) *Modern bridge over a dry torrent bed; this may have been the stream described by the Geographer Scylax.* (*6*) *Submerged harbour-works which may have enclosed the naval docks or 'secret port' (see also Plate VIII).* (*7*) *Submerged rubble-fill ending in unidentified masonry to the south; possibly the landing quay of the early citadel.* (*8*) *A spring of sweet water rising under the sea; note the ancient masonry (shown in black) at either side of the nearby western mole.* (*9*) *The spring of Salmacis.*

and early sherds were mixed with the fill. There is also a detached and inexplicable mass of rubble off the south-eastern extremity of the island (Fig. 25). If the fill does mean that there were quays it makes it all the more likely that there was an entrance to the secret docks from this side, and it would have been this entrance, or rather exit, that Artemisia used. Being protected from the prevailing wind, the eastern side of the island is the obvious place for the earliest anchorage, before the fifth-century harbour was constructed.

The modern jetties of the main harbour were rebuilt the year before I came to Bodrum. They run from the citadel and from the fortifications on the cape opposite; their position is said to correspond with the jetties of the fifth-century closed port. There is no trace of ancient masonry round the base of the island mole, which is not surprising, as the solid, new building is very large. There are, however, classical blocks strewn on the bottom to either side of the opposite jetty. The narrow harbour entrance between these two jetties is well protected from current; indeed, they are built in the line of the prevailing wind. There is very little current within the naturally sheltered bays this side of Kara Ada; however, the behaviour of silt is so unaccountable that it is not without significance that there is a submarine, freshwater spring just within the western mole [Fig. 25 (8)]. The strength of its flow might divert any small amount of silt that tried to find its way round the harbour mouth. The presence of this spring certainly guarantees a constant depth at that place, which is on the side of the commercial quarters of the ancient town. According to Hartleben, the quays which served the agora were 1,500 metres long; their line can still be traced on the shore under the new promenade [Fig. 25 (3)]. The fact that the agora was to the west again implies that the eastern side of the town by the citadel was reserved for naval use. Here as elsewhere confusion has arisen out of the interpretation of documents. The exact whereabouts of the harbour installations could now be settled by archaeological survey and a few soundings on land and underwater. The problems at Halicarnassos are relatively simple, but like all harbour research, the tests are beyond the capacity of a single individual.

One evening shortly after seeing the castle John and I went to the waterside café, where *meses* and *arak* were served under the tamarisks. A young man with a flashing smile, a striped tee-shirt and a European knitted, sailor's cap with a pom-pom came towards us and said, 'I am Mustafa.' Between the two Captains, two Mustafas and two Arases, I had got my introductions thoroughly muddled and given the lot to the Sponge Co-operative: Bodrum being a small place, they

TURKISH SPONGE DIVERS

XII (opposite). *The flag being hoisted on Capt. Kemal's sponge* caïque, *the* Mandalinci.

XIII (centre, verso). *Ceremonial dressing of a sponge diver. Kasim, wearing his warmest woollies, pulls on his suit while his young dresser waits to help him with his helmet, leads and lead shoes.*

XIV (recto, top). *While a diver is on the bottom, the life-line attendant sits concentrating on every tremor of the rope in his hands.*

XV (centre). *His charge reaches some brilliant sponge-growths on the bottom (these varieties are of no commercial value).*

XVI (bottom). *As the diver surfaces helping hands are ready to draw him in and to relieve him of his bag full of sponges.*

XVII (verso). *Bodrum is nicknamed the 'Wooden Village' because of the numbers of provisional, wooden memorials hastily erected for divers in its cemetery. In this photograph, however, only permanent headstones show under the westernmost fortification of Bodrum Bay.*

XII. M. Kapkin

XIII. M. Kapk

XIV. M. Kapkin

XV. M. Kapkin

XVI. M. Kapkin

XVII. M. Kapkin

managed to sort them out. This was Mustafa Kapkin of Izmir. We joined his table and were introduced to Rasim Divanli of the Turyağ Fabrik, other divers who were returning to Izmir on the 4 a.m. bus, Capt. Kemal, his Mate Kasim and Peter Throckmorton. On hearing we were both draughtsmen and that I had a bottle and was interested in wrecks, we were invited to join their party. John moved into their communal dormitory, and we were shown the pottery they had already found. The Izmir divers had not got their *narghilé*, and were filling bottles from Peter's small compressor; he generously offered to allow me to do the same.

Throckmorton had done salvage diving in the Pacific, but gave it up in favour of taking war photos in Korea and subsequently big game subjects in India. He arrived in Turkey by jeep, via Afghanistan. Geographically and metaphorically, we reached the same point from different directions. He came from the New World and discovered the Turkish wrecks by accident. Being the first ancient wrecks he had seen, they came as a revelation, and Peter was not one to dismiss revelations. Furthermore, he fell seriously in love with Mediterranean civilization, discovering in it some of his own roots. Being of British stock, he found his family shield in the Crusader Castle at Rhodes. His approach to archaeology also differed from ours. Middle Eastern excavation, started by the French and the British over a hundred years ago, is firmly established. New methods have been developed, but always within a tradition; moreover, religious and philosophical thought and the bases of our European civilization come from the Levant. In America, for obvious reasons, archaeology is connected in the schools with anthropology, and among his many activities Peter had once read anthropology. This approach to the subject, though novel to us, may well be salutary. In matters of theory, our views were bound to differ, but in practice we all worked together happily. The conflict between journalism and archaeology, or rather, the balance which has to be struck, is something which I think Throckmorton achieved, but that is his own story. The upshot of our meeting was that we left together, as Capt. Kemal's guests on the *Mandalinci*, to look at some wrecks off the Karabağla group of islands.

Had it not been for the Izmir contingent, our visits to the wrecks would have resulted in no more than photographs and a few drawings. One of the aims of the *Kurbağa Kulübü* was archaeological research; its members had aroused the interest of Bey Hakki Gultekin, Director of the Izmir Museum. He also administered the archaeology in the surrounding district, including Bodrum, where he joined the

Izmir divers and, realizing the importance of their finds, eventually arranged that these should be kept under lock and key in the fortress. In the second year he managed to get government support for the idea that the castle should be turned into a museum of antiquities coming from the sea. The buildings were superb and such a collection appropriate to a village of sponge divers. Peter, too, dreamed of this museum, suggesting that the Izmir Demeter should be returned and placed in the impressive setting of the disused Crusader chapel. Of course, founding a museum involves work and the appointment of a full-time curator to preserve, arrange, classify and catalogue the exhibits. It is to be hoped that this will come to pass. The first tangible result of government support was a small grant for structural repairs. It materialized in the second year, when, with the exception of John Carswell, we all met again at Bodrum.

On this second occasion I came as before, from Lebanon via Izmir, but through northern Syria and South-Eastern Turkey, travelling in buses and *dolmuş* taxis. During these weeks I had no postal address, or any notion of who I would find at Bodrum when I arrived. My object that second year was to go back and draw one of the wrecks I had already seen but had not had sufficient time to study. I was prepared to wait in Bodrum until the Izmir or sponge divers turned up. Rasim Divanli was also interested in this project; he was not an enthusiastic amateur archaeologist, but being an inventor, welcomed any specific question; he regarded the development of instruments for underwater survey as a personal challenge. He and I met in Izmir, but that year a new baby confined him and his family to the comforts of their own house. Peter, Mustafa and Hakki Bey were, so Rasim told me, on an American yacht somewhere in the Aegean. Nevertheless, I resisted the temptation to dally at Izmir and continued towards Bodrum.

The evening of my arrival I again went to the sponge divers' café. To our mutual surprise, the others were already there, having disembarked that morning with samples of a Bronze Age cargo, which Hakki Bey put in the castle. The year before Kemal let drop, in the course of conversation, that there were copper ingots off a cape marked on the charts as Gelidonou Burnu, which is probably a corruption of the Greek, meaning 'the cape the swallows fly over on migration'; the sponge divers call it Anadolou Burnu or the 'Nose of Anatolia'. Both names convey the importance of its position as the southernmost tip of Anatolia and explain the route this ship laden with bronze and copper took from Cyprus to one of the settlements, perhaps on Rhodes, or even Troy, Mycenae or Crete. One or two copper ingots had in the past been sold by sponge divers as scrap, but the metal was too corroded to fetch a good price. Peter, who was listening to Kemal's story of this sale, suddenly realized the implications: copper does not corrode quickly, and would be saleable after a few hundred years. This cargo must therefore be very old. He could not rest until he had seen it. When he did, he found his intuition justified, the ingots were of that ox-hide shape shown in Egyptian tomb paintings. He found the spot, not without difficulty, and raised representative samples, both metal and ceramic. Mustafa, whose underwater sketches were nothing short of brilliant, had been able in two dives to make notes of the site. They concluded this story in the café by saying that I must

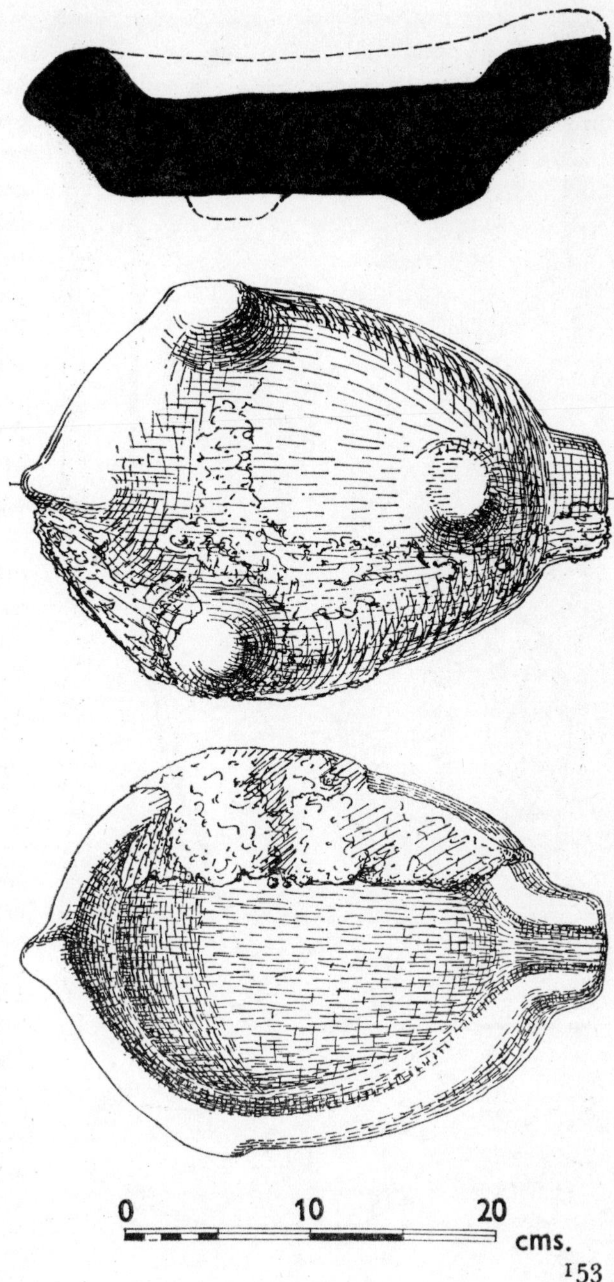

26. Receptacle with spout, vestigial duck-tail handle and three legs, made out of a hard grey stone, from the Bronze Age cargo at Gelidonou Burnu. It is now in the castle at Bodrum with the other objects found in 1959 (Figs. 27 and 28). Both in use and provenance, this receptacle is somewhat of a puzzle; no exact counterpart has been found on any Cretan, Phoenician or Minoan site of that date.

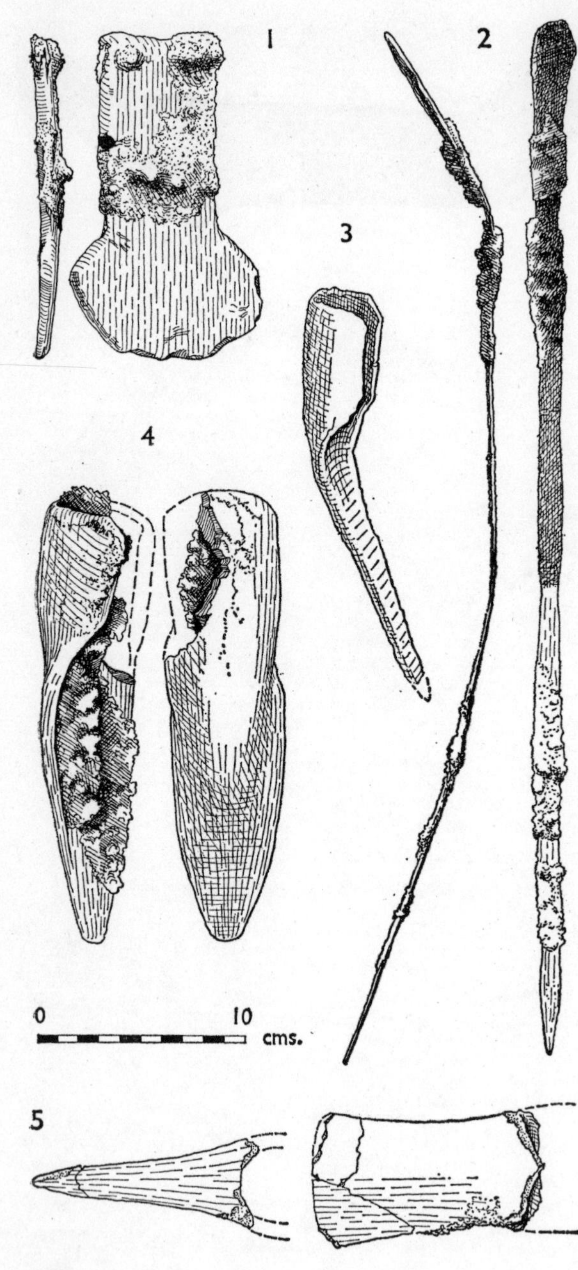

start to record their finds next morning. Exhausted by the journey, my enthusiasm was not great. I pointed out that I had come to draw a Byzantine wreck; moreover, from what Mustafa said of the rocky place where these bronzes lay, precious little would remain of the 'oldest ship in the world'. I preferred to reserve my energies for the other, where the structure could still be found. Byzantine ships were, after all, as much a mystery as any earlier wreck.

Next day, when I saw the ingots, tools, stone bowl and pottery in the castle, there was no denying the importance of this Bronze

27. Bronze implements from Gelidonou Burnu, drawn as they were found in 1959, before the concretions had been removed.

Key: (*1*) *Many of the implements had been broken in antiquity; this unidentified object may have been shipped as scrap metal.* (*2*) *A spatulate implement with traces of chasing; it looks like the tool still used in Turkey for turning meat on a charcoal grill.* (*3*) *and* (*4*) *Agricultural implements resembling those found in Cyprus in the 'Engomi hoard'.* (*5*) *Half a double-headed axe; unlike the rest of the bronze, this metal was light in colour and friable, looking like steatite, a condition which suggests a pronounced admixture of tin in the alloy.*

Age hoard. Even the concretions covering the objects were interesting. The crystals formed by electrolysis from the metal in certain lumps were quite large. Some rope was found under the ingots; its preservation might be due to lack of oxygen or to the copper in the metals which would, on dissolution, have permeated the material, preserving it in much the same way as green copper compounds do the canvas of tents. It was apparent that the cargo contained a variety of alloys which had reacted with each other, producing some odd effects.

The condition of various metal objects was surprising; concreted bronze implements that had been lying on the surface of the sand were in a good state, while

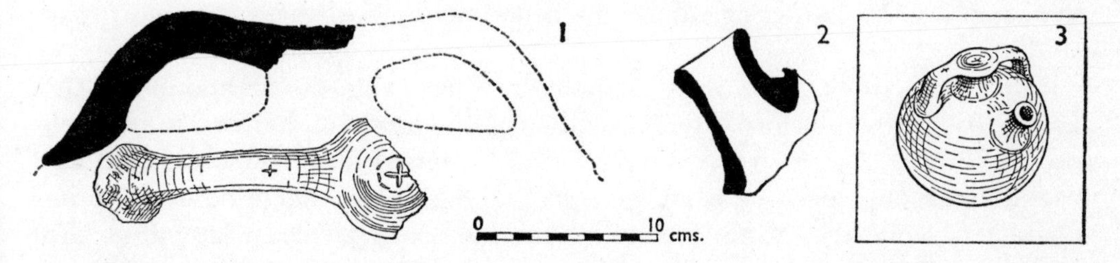

28. Cargoes of stirrup jars come as a welcome change for the diver accustomed to amphorae. Parts of two of these jars, so characteristic of Minoan and Mycenaean civilizations, were found in the cargo at Gelidonou Burnu in 1959.

Key: (*1*) *This handle had attached to it 1½ yards of rope made out of some fibre like papyrus; both handle and rope were preserved in the shallow sand underneath an ox-hide ingot. The crosses incised on the handle could be characters from a Cypro-Minoan script, though with a sign so common it is impossible to be certain.* (*2*) *The side spout of another jar made of coarse yellow paste, quite different from the pinkish ware of the handle.* (*3*) *Reconstruction of a stirrup-jar.*

others that had been buried were no more than shells containing a crumbly black substance. The phenomena, in my experience peculiar to this wreck, are explained by differential aeration. Except for the surface layer, every part of the pile of metal cargo which had fallen on rock had at some period been half-buried by the ever-mounting sand, which had, originally, gathered as a result of the wreck itself. At some point therefore each piece of metal was receiving less oxygen in the part below the sand than in the part that was surrounded by water; it was the action set up by this difference of environment that might have caused the form of decay we found.[1] Here was another indication that the technical aspects of underwater excavation, until they became better understood, required the attention of a great many different kinds of experts.

No one had yet grappled with the preservation of antiquities from the sea. The problem had to be put to specialists, and the sooner the better; meanwhile amateur experiment should be avoided. We left the finds in their uncleaned state so that the questions they set could be analysed in the best laboratories before any further excavation took place.

When the objects were drawn the concretions were a nuisance, but I did not regret their partially camouflaged state, as I am convinced that all underwater finds should be photographed and drawn both before and after cleaning. Unknown and widely differing submarine concretions are in themselves worthy of study.

Little did I think, when making these drawings (Figs. 26, 27 and 28) in the castle, that I would be forced to devote the winter months of that year to research on this Bronze Age hoard. Before we could arouse official interest in an excavation we had to know what we were 'selling'.[2] The ingots bore a Cypriot character, while the crosses incised on the handle of a stirrup jar might also be from a Cypro-Minoan script. Stirrup jars in themselves are characteristic of these same civilizations. The ingots were not all 'ox-hide'; we had a heavily concreted copper disk reminiscent of the 'bun' ingots found at Hagia Triada in Crete. I was delighted to find that this disk also corresponded with a stone mould discovered by Dr Dikaios at Engomi in Cyprus, which dated from the thirteenth century B.C., or late Cypriot II B; it might indeed have been made in this very mould! The list grew. They had raised thirty bits of pottery and fifteen other finds, which included ploughshares and half a double-headed axe.

The following summer, when the University of Pennsylvania excavated the Bronze Age wreck, the entire cargo that we raised justified Peter's dreams. As a closed group it will continue to stimulate research and doubtless give rise to one

[1] Ulic R. Evans, *The Corrosion and Oxidation of Metals*, Arnold, 1960, pp. 172–3.

[2] Peter Throckmorton, 'Thirty-three Centuries Under the Sea', *National Geographic Magazine*, Vol. 117, No. 5, May 1960; Honor Frost, 'Two Carian Wrecks', *Antiquity*, Vol. XXXIV, No. 135, September 1960, p. 216; Honor Frost, *Discovery*, May 1960, p. 194; Stanton A. Waterman, 'Three Thousand Years Under the Sea', *Explorers' Journal*, New York, Vol. 38, 1960, no. 3, p. 28.

or two revolutionary conclusions about Bronze Age economics.[1] Nothing comparable had been found since the Huelva Hoard, another Bronze Age cargo, had been dredged out of the Guadalquivir in Spain.[2]

[1] Reports written after the excavation by the University of Pennsylvania of this Bronze Age wreck in the summer of 1960: George F. Bass, 'The Cape Gelidonia Wreck; Preliminary Report', *American Journal of Archaeology*, Vol. 65, No. 3, July 1961; George F. Bass, 'Excavating a Bronze Age Shipwreck', *Archaeology* (*U.S.*), Vol. 14, No. 2, Summer, 1961; Peter Throckmorton, 'Oldest Known Shipwreck Yields Bronze Age Cargo', *National Geographic Magazine*, Vol. 121, No. 5, 1962.

[2] Henkin, 'The Huelva Hoard,' *Zephyrus*, Vol. VII, 1956.

CHAPTER 10

Karabağla Log – The Sites – A Geological Time Scale – Land Records – Deep-water Recording; its Limitations and Function

A SINGLE cruise, made on Capt. Kemal's sponge *caïque*, in the first year, was sufficient to convince me of the quality and importance of the Carian wrecks; above all, they were drawable. Extracts from my log book of that date give a first impression of sites whose interrelationship and individual content raise almost inexhaustible questions:

Friday, July 11, 1958

"Roused with a cup of tea at 3 a.m.; I packed by torch light and so forgot my gun. We boarded the *Mandalinci*, Kemal's boat, at 4 a.m. Forked lightning played over Cos in a leaden sky, Kara Ada lighthouse winked and the castle was only a dark mass as we chugged out of port. Across the bar, three dolphins joined us, leading the boat to sea. The men leaned over, thumping the prow with the flat of their hands. This is supposed to please dolphins. Greeks say they harbour the souls of drowned sailors; perhaps ours were Byzantines showing us the way to their wreck.

At first light we stopped at a small bay to pick up Şeytan, so called because he was the oldest diver (fifty odd), and only a devil could have escaped so many dangers; he it was that found the Izmir Demeter. He knows every wreck and is going to pin-point those off Yassi Ada for us. The *Mandalinci*'s crew consists of two senior divers: Kasim, who is Kemal's mate (he holds the captain's papers, though the ship belongs to Kemal), and old Memet. There are also some younger divers, one is called Red Devil. I try to make up sleep under a Balmain coat on a pile of sails in the prow. At breakfast-time we put into a second bay to show our papers and buy vegetables, which are cheaper here than in Bodrum. Elegant stone houses with balconies line the sandy shore, but they are all uninhabited, windowless and in disrepair. The only sign of life was in a hut where about a dozen men were drinking tea. I asked them the name of the village: they shrugged and said 'it is the place where there had been Greeks'.

At sea again. Cos harbour comes into sight, we round a promontory and see *Paşa Rock* . . . evil looking and almost submerged, with a cormorant perched on top of it. Back in Bodrum, the divers had collected a mosque lamp, a clay drum(?) and amphorae of various periods which they had found on the sides of this rock; the depth at its base is over 40 metres. Kemal confirms that, as we suspected, there are wrecks on the surrounding sand. The place is so exposed that at most times of the year it would only be possible to dive there at dawn when there is no wind. It reminds me of la Chrétienne, which must have looked much the same before the safety beacon was built. We can now see the Karabağla group of six small islands. Tonight we will sleep on the largest, Karabağla itself, because Kemal says his *caïque* is too big to lie off Yassi Ada ('Flat Island'), where we are going to dive. In reality, I do not think he likes the place, as the man who taught him diving was killed on one of the wrecks we are going to see and, for some reason, they buried him on Yassi Ada.

At 10 a.m. we stop off Yassi Ada, which, as its name implies, is flat rock with very shallow soil growing a modicum of scrub. It is too deep to anchor, so the engine is kept running. The crew dive one after another in turn in the communal suit, Şeytan is last. He comes up after forty-five minutes with a globular amphora that looks Byzantine; the depth was around 40 metres and he has buoyed two wrecks. When the helmet is unscrewed he complains of pains at the base of the spine and in one knee. Kemal puts him back into the water to decompress. A spinal bend is very serious, it could mean paralysis, and there is no hope of treatment in Turkey. Their method of decompression is five minutes per *kulaç* (5 feet), which is, of course, nonsense by modern diving tables. They say the system originated 'many years ago when a captain had a young son who dived'. The boy surfaced with a bad bend and they knew he would die. Wishing to spare his father, and perhaps realizing the anaesthetic properties of deep water, he asked to be put down again to the same depth. This was done, but his father, in an agony of indecision and anxiety, pulled him up a *kulaç*, every five minutes. When the boy eventually reached the surface he was cured. The story is probably Greek in origin. Before the troubles, the mainland Turks worked with the sponge fleet from the islands opposite.

When Şeytan came up he was not cured. We put him back, and this time

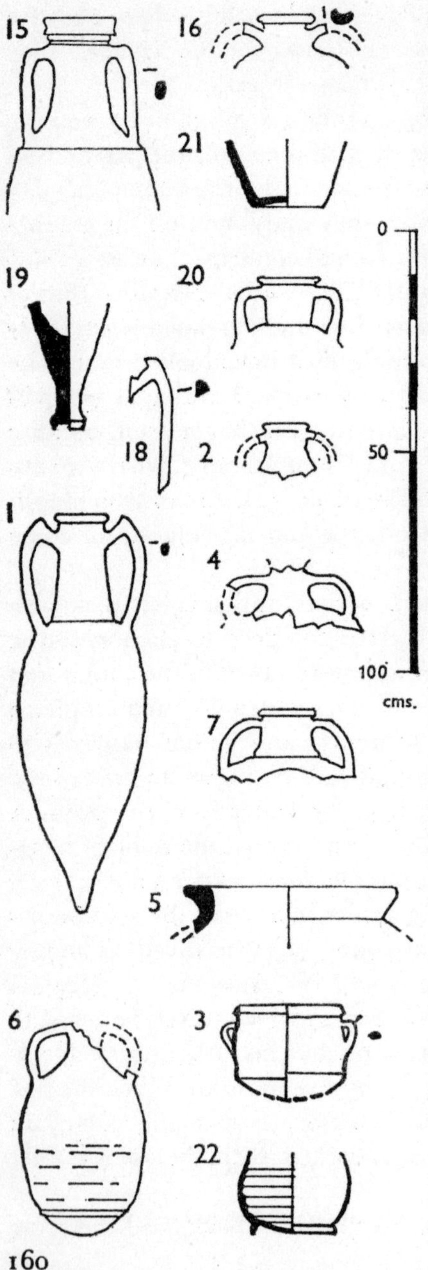

suggested that he be decompressed according to the tables printed on Peter's diving watch. Mustafa and I went down to amuse him by circling the pathetic figure as he hung in the blue. His eyes followed us through one window of his helmet after another. Was he to come up? he asked us. 'No,' we gestured back, 'stay there until Kemal pulls the rope.' The whole business lasted four hours. When he surfaced he said the knee was better. He still had a pain in his back, but this might be rheumatism.

We were free to dive. There was no wind, so we took advantage of the calm by going to the most exposed place. This was a reef 1 metre below the surface, off the seaward tip of Yassi Ada (Fig. 29). The island is itself an extension of Karabağla (from which it is

29. Plan and section of the eastern slope of the submerged reef that extended seawards from the Karabağla islands. It must have been responsible for the numerous wrecks in that area including the Byzantine ships (see Figs. 31 and 33). Ships that sank immediately, on top of the reef itself, were broken up and their cargoes dispersed over the shallow rocky slopes. Numbers alongside individual objects correspond to those on the plan and indicate where the things were found.

Certain groupings are still discernible within the mingled cargoes: stacked plates, pots, jars and roof tiles of the same period denote a galley (Nos. 9–12, 3, 14, 30 and 31). Two groups of Rhodian amphorae are still piled three deep in stacks (Nos. 1 and 18); from between their necks I drew out the undamaged lamp (Fig. 30). Loose amphorae of differing date were scattered over the whole area, while on the crest of the reef stone and metal cannon balls (No. 33 is metal) hinted at wrecks of warships as yet undiscovered.

Drawings made by John Carswell in 1958.

separated by a deep channel). All three formations run out at right angles from the coast. The prevailing wind comes from the west.

Peter, who had been to the reef before, showed John its shallow eastern slopes. John, wearing a mask, sounded, measured and drew from the surface. Mustafa took the west and Rasim the south or seaward slopes. I reserved my energies for exploration in depth with a bottle. On my sheltered, eastern side the bottom fell at an angle of about 20° down to a depth of 60 metres. I did not go deeper than 25 metres. The area was large and my bottle small, so air had to be husbanded. The rocks were encrusted with amphorae and sherds. Innumerable cargoes had intermingled; the ships they came from are long since broken and dispersed.

At 8 metres there were two piles of stacked amphorae. What could have kept them in

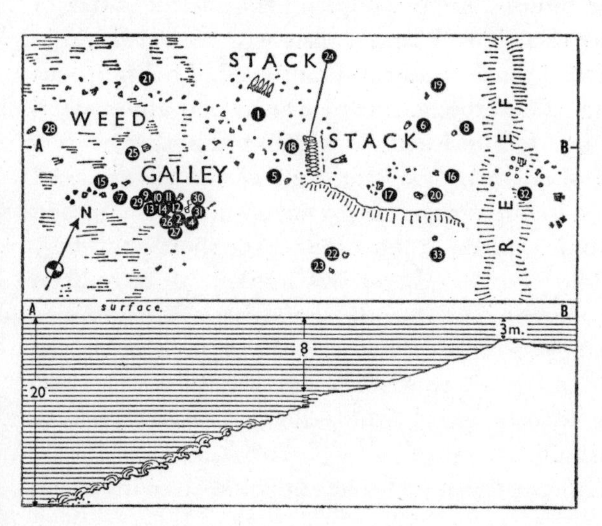

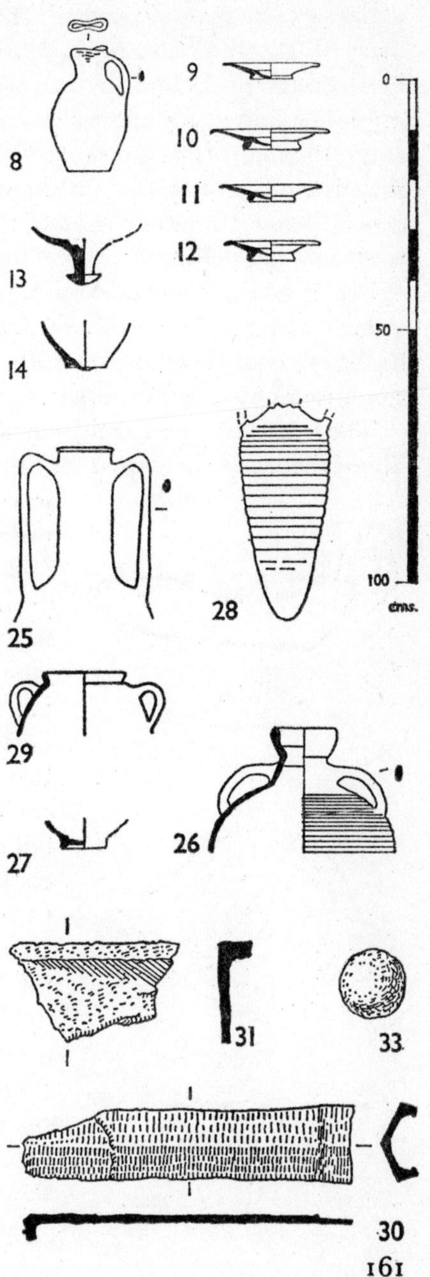

place in such shallow water? Had they been roped and had concretions taken over by the time the rope decayed? I put my hand into one of these stacks, between the necks and the handles, and drew out a lamp (Fig. 30). It was loose, unbroken and had a trident stamped on the base . . . perhaps it dropped into the cargo the night the ship sank. Near by there was another significant grouping of pantiles, plates and kitchen utensils, probably from the galley of a ship. Lower down, below the movement of the swell, it became much more difficult to see what was happening because slimy weed blanketed the rocks like greenish snow. When it was pushed aside more amphorae were revealed in rock crevices. Beyond 25 metres the visibility was better. Sherds continued down the slopes as far as the eye could see; about another 25 metres, for the water was clear. There were quantities of fearless groupers.

The wind had risen and John was already in the boat when I surfaced. Excited about the lamp, I shouted for him. Kasim, taking my equipment, made negative warning gestures. When I got into the boat John was prostrate and vomiting. He and Rasim are both bad sailors, though it is harder for the latter, who is devoted to the sea. Mustafa had found cannon balls, both stone and metal. Rasim reported even greater quantities of amphorae, of another kind, on the seaward slopes of the reef.

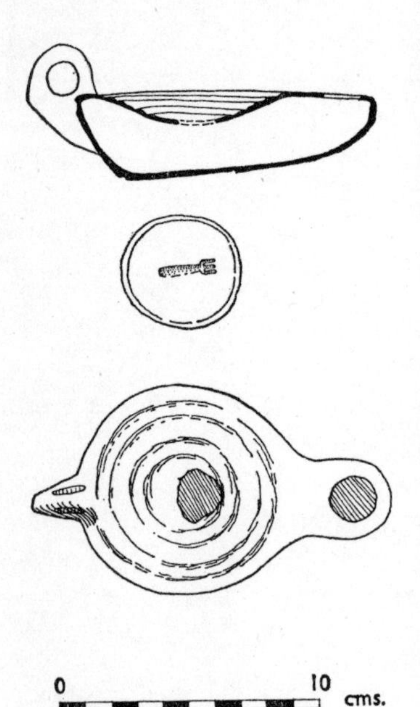

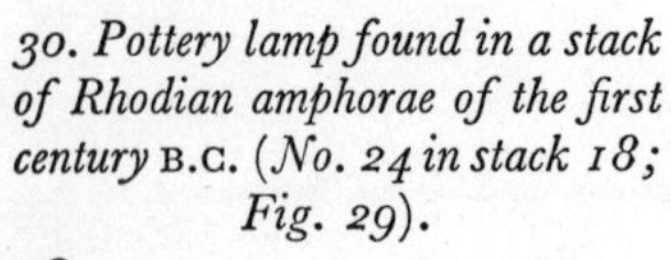

30. Pottery lamp found in a stack of Rhodian amphorae of the first century B.C. (*No. 24 in stack 18; Fig. 29*).

We moored for the night in the sheltered bay of Karabağla. The island consists of two peaks, one conical, joined by a saddle of land. The light was failing. The crew gathered brushwood and started cooking. I found a rock which I mistakenly took to be sheltered, near the crest of the saddle, and started to unpack and do my face. John, who climbed the conical peak, found Bronze Age sherds half-way up. The waterless island was unlikely to have been a settlement, but it could have been a necropolis (depending on the existence of a settlement on the mainland); alternatively, the sherds could have come from a wreck, the sailors having escaped to the island.

Suddenly shouting broke out below; looking down

at the bay, we saw the men gesticulating. Mustafa and Rasim had gone in to fish for supper; a 3-metre shark had chased them back into the bay, right up to the shore. The crew said it was early in the season; sharks normally pass this way in September. Peter thinks we are in ideal shark water, as the bottom slopes steeply to depth; he once studied their behaviour with some American research team.

In consequence, there was no fish for supper, our first and only meal. Kasim, a resourceful cook, cut a species of sponge from the pottery we raised. Sliced and fried with garlic, it tasted like mushroom, though its consistency was crisper. This he supplemented by the contents of Pina shells that grew on the sand in shallow water. There was also pilaf, beans, salad, melon and *arak* which we had brought with us. Şeytan had a private supply of white cheese powder which he kept in a handkerchief. We talked, until the fire went out, of Roman boats, drawing what little we knew of them on our flippers for Kemal, who was interested.

July 12

The ground was hard, the wind cold and I had only one thin blanket and my coat, so got no sleep. Breakfasted on eggs, tomatoes, *halva* and tea. The ship's bread is rock hard and has to be softened in water. The sponge men do not eat. John said he preferred to remain on the island drawing yesterday's pots rather than risk another day of sea-sickness. As there was no shade, he made an awning with blankets fixed to rocks and prepared to enjoy the desert island by sunbathing naked. He was, however, surprised by a bunch of xenophobic fishermen from the mainland. It all passed off peacefully; he managed to get dressed in time, and make them some tea.

At sea we indulged in the usual interminable arguments over the buoyed wrecks. Diving connotes delay. Rasim was sick. Mustafa had ear-ache, and his home-made valve and bottle were not good enough for the depths we were diving (between 35 and 45 metres). Peter had double tanks. My single bottle being too small, I was to follow him down after he had run half his time. In this way he would have been able to show me what he had found, so that I would not waste precious time on the bottom searching in the wrong places. He was also to take overall measurements of the site. I, in return, was to take him down his camera (this because the case we were using was also home-made and could not be subjected to pressure for long periods). Our signals went wrong: I met Peter on the buoy-line as he was coming up. This meant more work for me; I decided to take a risk with my ears and not waste time waiting for them to equalize. The

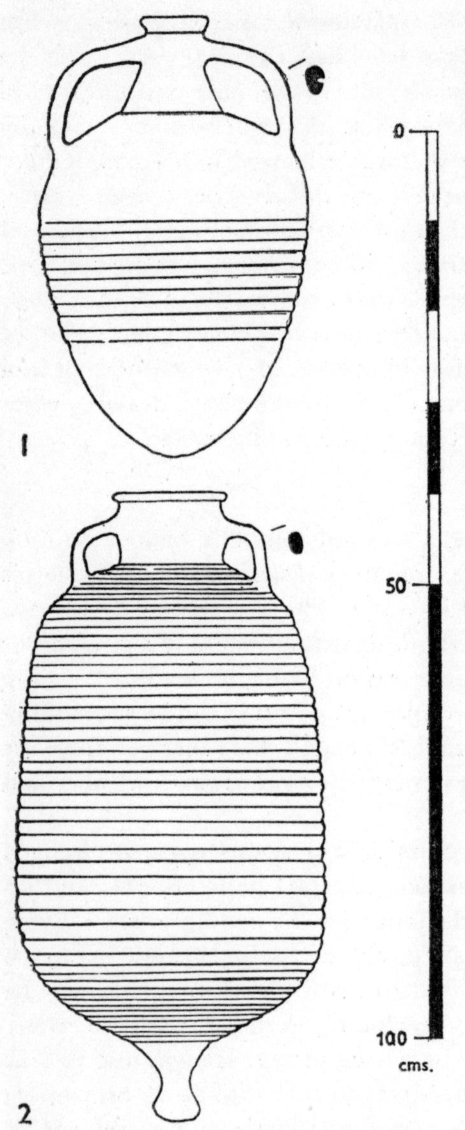

31. Amphorae from the cargo of the sixth-century Byzantine wreck (drawing Plate 24) which lay alongside the seventh-century wreck (Fig. 34).

result was a violent nose-bleed. Thoughtlessly I emptied my mask, remembering later that it was the best way to attract our familiar shark. If he did come back, I did not see him, as I was too busy making notes. By bad luck, the water was cloudy.

The wreck consisted of an oval pile of amphorae, loose on the surface of the sand, which slopes up towards the base of the island (Fig. 34). *El Hamdul'illah!* it is perfect for drawing. The amphorae, like the one brought up by Şeytan, were globular with an incised decoration. There were also some smaller ones: long, with a faintly defined waist. I came across a group of flat roof- and floor-tiles which must denote the galley. My small bottle started to run out after ten minutes. I managed to take some measurements and note the disposition of certain details before surfacing. Peter said there was a pile of concreted metal 'like anchors' at the top end of the wreck, but I missed it. I had no compass.

The bottles were refilled by afternoon. We dived on a second wreck, 30 metres from the first and slightly deeper. Could it be the same ship? The amphorae were different: pear shaped and with a bobble at the base (Fig. 31). Most of their necks point in the same direction: up the slope. This time Peter and I were together for about five minutes. He took photos. A tame, fat silver fish came and allowed itself to be stroked; I hope he got a picture.

Towards evening Mustafa dived again

on the shallow, reef-complex, taking measurements which they had not had time to get yesterday. Peter complained of an itching, or mild form of bend. That is the worst of having to work against the clock. The two deep wrecks were sheltered, in the lee of the island, the anchors and wood of the ships must be *in situ*; they could be excavated.

Kemal had given us a lot of his time: he was keen to get back to Bodrum and his own work. We picked up John and made the return journey in record time, about four hours, with a following wind. Dropped Şeytan at his village. He hobbled up the hill, but I think his walk was the result of multifarious past bends; he seemed none the worse for yesterday's experience. It was dusk when we arrived in Bodrum, but there was just time for a hot bath at the Hamam."

These entries made in my log book during the first visit need to be examined in the light of experience. There were three kinds of site at Karabağla.

The first (Fig. 32) was *Paşa Rock*, where, unfortunately, we did not dive, but from its appearance, the objects found on its slopes and Kemal's reports, it is probably one of those provisional offshore anchorages used by ships that could not sail against the wind. There are also wrecks on the sand around its base.

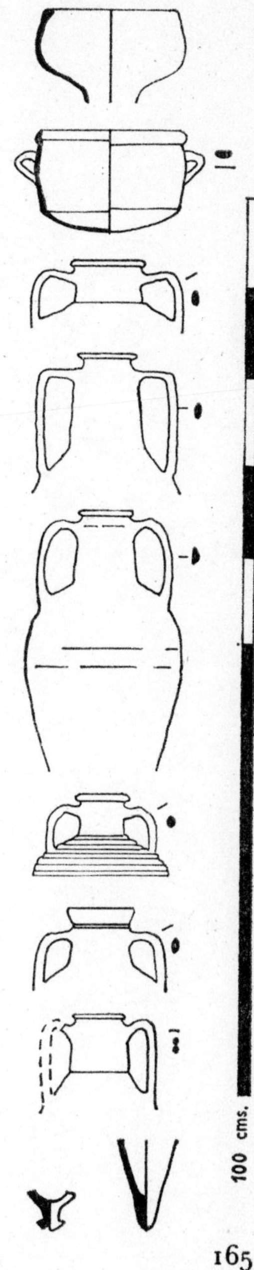

32. Pottery of differing date from the underwater slopes of the offshore and almost submerged Paşa Rock. Rising 40 metres from the surrounding sandy bottom, this rock must have served as an emergency anchorage in the centuries before ships could sail against the wind. These jars represent a span of 800 years of this period. When visibility was bad the rock would also have been a hazard to shipping; the surrounding sea-bed is probably strewn with wrecks. The goblet-shaped object at the top is reminiscent of a clay hand-drum; these were used on ships to beat time for oarsmen. The rest of the pottery ranges from the third century B.C. *to Byzantine times.*
Drawings made by John Carswell in 1958.

Fig. 33

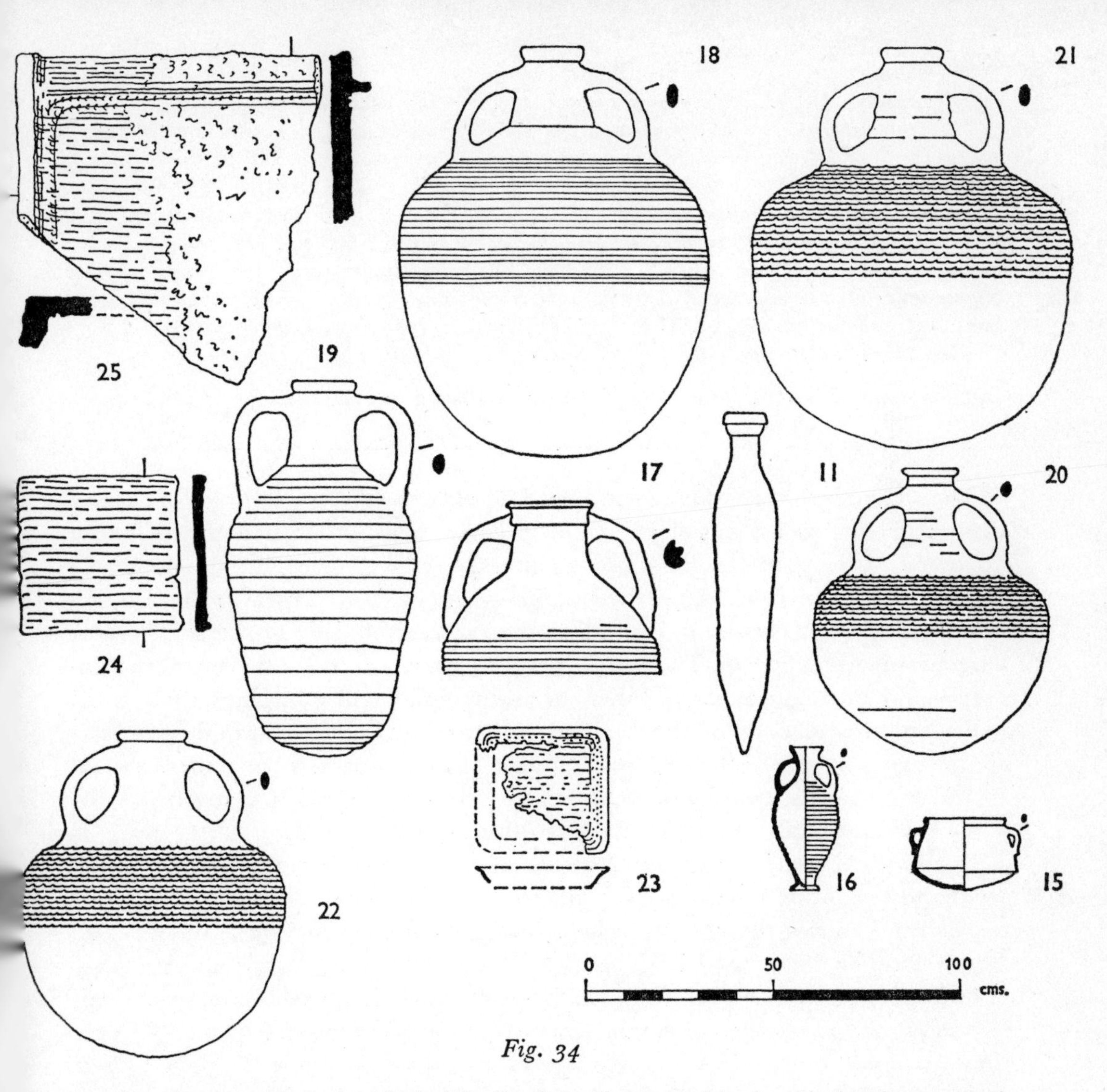

Fig. 34

33. *Seventh-century Byzantine 'Globe Wreck' off the Karabağla islands; this drawing was made during my second visit; the site remained undisturbed except for samples of cargo (shown above) which were lifted for dating.*

Key to plan (opposite): (*1*) *A pile of concreted iron; possibly anchors with movable flukes.* (*2*) *and* (*3*) *'Steps' of concreted metal in the sand.* (*4*) *A line of probes made in the sand with a metal rod between points 3 and 4. The rod struck pottery then* (*at the crosses*), *a substance of the consistency of waterlogged wood.* (*5*) *Small iron anchor; the kedge?* (*6*) *Tapered bronze pipe loose on the sand. Merchant ships of the period being armed, it was suggested that this pipe may have been*

[*Continued overleaf*

connected with Greek fire. (7) Iron bar 1 metre long emerging from the sand at an angle of 45°. (8) Galley area containing kitchen utensils, roof and floor tiles. (9) Timber located by probes; a sample length of 40 centimetres (section 20 centimetres square) was raised, it contained remains of iron nails, and one facet bore traces of a protective covering like paint. (10) Roof-tile and sherds. (11) One of the elongated amphorae. (12) and (13) Small pieces of concreted metal emerging from the sand. (14) One of the sponge divers said he had taken two small lead bars from this area; possibly connected with the wreck. (15) Cooking-pot. (16) Pottery vase. (17)–(22) Amphorae representative of the main cargo (dated by similar specimens from a land excavation at Chios). (23) Copper baking tin. (24) and (25) Roof and floor tiles. (26) Probe striking wood at X.

These numbers also refer to the detailed drawings of objects lifted, Fig. 34.

34. Representative samples of the cargo of this seventh-century Byzantine wreck.

The second is the reef (Fig. 29), which I would describe as a complex of cargoes dispersed over rocks that slope in an easterly direction to a depth of about 30 metres. After 30 metres the rocks are interspersed with sand, but the slope continues until 60 metres, where the bottom becomes level. Towards and on this bottom there is a possibility of finding the remains of some of the ships whose cargoes spilled higher up. The rocks near the surface deserve a survey, as various cargoes are distinguishable and there are some significant groupings, such as the galley and the stacks of amphorae. The contents of at least two amphora-carriers spilled over one side of the reef and, judging from the cannon balls, there should be traces of warships on the other slope. The crest of this reef, 1 metre below the surface, was responsible for the wrecks to the lee of the island.

In this third area, sheltered by the island, the bottom is sandy and deep. Beyond the Byzantine wrecks I have already mentioned are older, and therefore more deeply buried, amphora-carriers. All these ships crashed on to the reef and were then blown into the lee of the island by the prevailing wind; alternatively, once they were disabled, they may deliberately have sought shelter in an attempt to anchor or to save the crew. The base of the island being unexpectedly steep, they sank without anchoring, planing to the bottom and settling with their cargoes hardly deranged. There was one odd wreck near the channel separating the islands, where a sponge diver found a cargo of lilac, green and blackish glass in lumps the size of a man's head. I showed samples to the museum attached to a glass factory in Venice, also to specialists in London. Both agreed they were modern; the former said that glass was exported from Greece in this form in the nineteenth century.

This third area in the lee of Yassi Ada is important for many reasons. To me, of course, the seventh-century Byzantine wreck and its sixth-century neighbour were ideal for drawing; the former, where the galley and anchors still showed, was best. The island being flat and far from land, there was little erosion and none of the calcareous sand and rockfall generated by cliffs. Beneath the sand and cargoes lay ships of unknown structure. There are written accounts of Byzantine warships, but not merchantmen, though the indications are that they resembled Roman 'round' ships; here, the sea holds the answers.

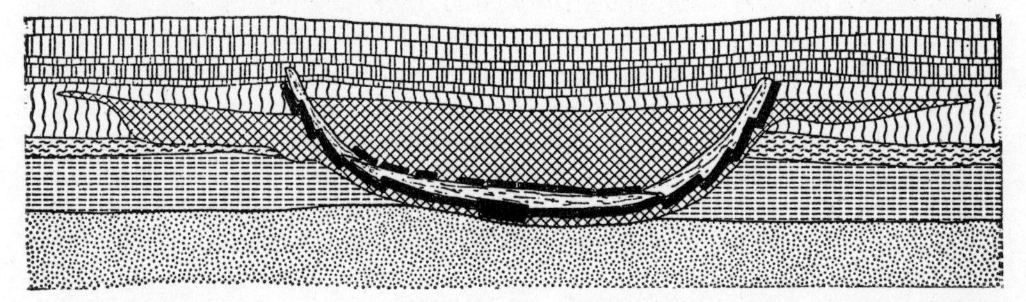

35. A medieval ship excavated in the reclaimed lands of the Zuyder Zee. This section shows the soil disturbances and layers of sedimentation. 200 wrecks were found in the north-west Polder; being of known date, they served as guide fossils in the study of sediments. Note that this hull has kept its shape because it sank into soft mud. The hull might have been better preserved had the water been more than 3 metres deep when it sank. Drawing reproduced by courtesy of G. D. van der Heide.

The area as a whole has less obvious, but equally important significance for marine geologists. Hulls, each buried to a greater or lesser degree on the same type of bottom, are a time-scale for dating sediments. More sand covered the sixth-century ship than the seventh, while so little cargo showed on the older wrecks that they were dismissed as 'uninteresting'.

On land-excavations geological opinion is desirable, in the sea it is essential; each line of research is complementary. This was demonstrated when land was reclaimed from the Zuyder Zee: in one area alone ruins, artifacts and 150 wrecks were revealed after drainage. Geologists used the archaeological evidence to reconstruct natural changes that had occurred in the region. Layers of sedimentation in datable wrecks were of particular interest (Fig. 35).[1] Among geologists and biologists there are many divers accustomed to underwater work and capable of assessing its problems. During a discussion on this subject, Mr Robert Dill of the

[1] G. D. van der Heide, 'Zuyder Zee Archaeology', *Antiquity and Survival*, No. III, 1955.

Scripps Institute of Oceanography, La Jolla, California, himself a diver, remarked that even a flipper disturbing sand over a wreck would, from his point of view, destroy evidence. Unfortunately wrecks are not reported to biologists. Archaeology, geology and biology are highly specialized professions whose members have a full-time job keeping up with reports on their own subjects. Nevertheless, it is to be hoped that a collaboration will begin before too many wrecks are destroyed; they are not inexhaustible.

At Karabağla there was a wealth of material to be studied, both in the form of artifacts and the sites from which they came. Like monuments on land, all belonged to the Turkish Government. Countries where legislation has been revised in recent times have an advantage over the West. In France, for instance, Colbert's laws still apply to wrecks; regardless of date, they are valued in terms of salvage. These laws are being changed, but the new ones may be based on the present practice of giving the concession to the finder. If a discovery results from deliberate search it would be unfair to debar the finder from the benefit of his work. On the other hand, when profit urges and the law allows a finder to sell antiquities on the commercial market the principle becomes dangerous. In the case of a wreck where duplicates, such as amphorae, are numerous there is no reason why they should not be sold after excavation, providing that a public body controls the transaction and administers the profits. Be this as it may, unlike land sites, no wreck has ever been discovered by an archaeologist; as things are, he comes on to the scene as a more or less welcome guest and sometimes as a cuckoo in the nest.

It devolved on us to record the Karabağla wrecks so that an appropriate body could apply to the Turkish Government for permission to excavate. Peter and I were like Jack Sprat and his wife: I thought it sufficient to catalogue and make technical drawings; Peter took the view that, over and above this, everyone had a right to know about the discoveries, as excavations depend on public funds. He therefore took 'popular' photographs and kept an elaborate written account of events, to the chagrin of Rasim and John. All four men shared the same dormitory, and Peter pounded his typewriter late into the night and again at first light; Mustafa slept through it. On the most important point we were all in wholehearted agreement: we thought it inadmissible to undertake excavation without making provision for recording and preservation, and without having direction from archaeologists who, if non-divers, would follow events from reports, photographs and drawings.

Readers would take it for granted that excavation by sportsmen and fishermen is a contradiction in terms, but in the short history of submarine archaeology it has never been otherwise. Members of innumerable diving clubs consider that if an archaeologist is present at all his place is on the surface and his function merely to date finds which they lay at his feet. 'Doing underwater archaeology in the Med.' is a way of spending the annual holiday. That, to be useful, underwater work requires craftsmanship, or that archaeological technicians need training, are ideas that do not readily occur to enthusiasts. If they did it would be impossible, as yet, to provide this training. A *corps d'élite* of professionals must first formulate the problems and then evolve the answers. In other words, a diver with comparative knowledge of ancient wrecks will have to collaborate with an archaeologist to develop standardized techniques. We realized it was easier to find wrecks than to persuade first-rate professionals to produce rational excavation methods. Universities would have to be approached, the diver we needed must come from the French pioneers, as they alone had seen a sufficient quantity of Mediterranean wrecks to have a standard of judgement. Success depended on our ability to present the evidence and raise interest in the project.

The immediate job of recording fell into two categories: the finds and the sites. The former had to be measured, drawn, described, numbered and catalogued according to provenance. Even before our trip to Karabağla, a pile of finds had collected in our hotel. John settled down to work; I do not think it occurred to him that he was on holiday, or had any choice in the matter. Seven years as a draughtsman produced an automatic reaction to sherds. We had no materials, but within an hour he scrounged a table, chair, compass, ruler, indian ink and typing paper (wrapping paper was the alternative he had to consider). Pots are always drawn same size; had he done so, there would have been another unwieldy bundle for us to carry in aeroplanes. Furthermore, large drawings would waste precious film, for both the Izmir Museum and Peter needed copies. Being an experienced draughtsman, John made a direct reduction, drawing the larger finds 1 : 10 or 1 : 20. He marked the provenance of each object, then typed out descriptions of the ware, its quality, colour and firing. Finally, he organized us as porters and carried the collection to the flat, whitewashed roof of the hotel to be photographed; the objects were arranged in groups, behind a centimetre scale he had made (Plate 26).

The problem of maintaining records after John and I left was solved miraculously. Rasim, being an engineer, was always demonstrating his inventions on paper. Mustafa we knew as a photographer and ex-pilot in the Turkish Air Force, but it transpired that his original interest was in drawing; he had aptitude without training. John was a teacher, and recording is mechanical, depending on the observance of simple, universally accepted conventions. Both men learned quickly and continued the work. John saw their drawings a few months later, when Peter passed through Beirut. He wrote to me enthusiastically; the records were up to professional standard; indeed John said they were better than his own.

On the second year, when there was no one else, I drew the finds, often on the deck of a *caïque*, but at the outset I was glad to be left in peace to think out ways and means of planning the sites themselves. This meant evolving some method of underwater work that would give the same results as a theodolite on land. John had made the surface survey of the reef, for shallow-water recording is much the same as on land.

Curiously enough, I had less difficulty in equipping myself for underwater drawing than John had had on land. Lead pencils work underwater and so do india-rubbers. Any sheet of light-coloured metal, such as aluminium, makes a serviceable tablet. Notes and drawings made in the water are traced on to paper later, so that a tablet can be re-used. When I do not have to improvise, my standard equipment consists of a portable metal drawing-board with a spring clamp down one side, such as architects use in the field. Sheets of plastic 'paper', cut to size, are inserted in the spring to form a block; they can be detached after use. The only modification that had to be made to this portable board was the addition of a second clamp, held by bolts, on the opposite side of the board. Without this, the sheets tended to slip out of the spring when submerged. Plastic or metal rulers are equally serviceable in water, but for longer measurements I find that an arrow from my fish-gun (graduated in units of 10 centimetres in nail varnish) is handier. It is also less likely to be mislaid on a boat, where fish-guns are always carefully stowed.

During my first visit to Karabağla I had only one dive on each Byzantine wreck, so I could do no more than correlate the overall measurements of each cargo with drawings I had made on the bottom. Knowing the exact size of the amphorae (from the samples we raised) and the area they had covered, I could estimate rough plans. I also noted the relationship of certain objects to their surroundings: 'that pot comes from the bottom of the slope; it is 3 metres from a couple of neckless amphorae and two from a large sponge'. From this description

I would be able to find the place again and recheck. I realized it would be necessary to go back the following year.

Without instruments one could not give an accurate compass point or section of the bottom. I attempted to work out bearings from the surface: we argued that if the axis of the wreck tumulus followed the slope of the island, then it must run from east to west, as the island was to the west, but of course this was not good enough. Similarly, we took soundings in order to make a rough section, but the boat was never directly above the points I wanted on the wreck. Despite difficulties, the data were sufficient to give a general impression. My aim that first year was, by making rough measured drawings, to find my way about the wrecks, since this would save me a lot of time when I started work in the following year.

Without records, excavation is wanton destruction. I might not be able to solve the problems of submarine survey, but at least I could find out what they were. The following year I went back and dived twice a day for two weeks at Karabağla. I spent most of the time on the 'Globe Wreck' (when one works on a site it always acquires a pet name).

Again I was without an assistant; even on land, this would make survey almost impossible. Peter was there and did help, but he had his own work, and making plans was not part of his training. Nevertheless, the second plan (Fig. 34) was more informative than the first. I had time to do detailed drawings of significant parts: such as the galley, where roof tiles lay over floor tiles and where a copper tray was found [Fig. 33 (23)]. There was also a small (probably a sheet-) anchor and the curious pile of concreted iron which looked like anchors with movable flukes.[1] There must have been about five of these anchors, but without raising them, cutting the concretions, removing the remains of the iron (probably in a liquid state), then, as with the axe from Anthéor, taking plaster casts from the natural moulds, it was impossible to be certain. My job was to record. However great the temptation, our policy was not to touch or displace. I regretted leaving a slightly tapered copper tube which was loose on the sand [Fig. 34 (6)]; back in London, its description aroused interest, and Byzantinologists suggested it might have been used for Greek fire. In the eighth century, when piracy was rife, merchant ships were armed. Piping is also found on Roman wrecks, but it is made of lead and carried water. We did take samples, such as pottery, for dating and marked their provenance on the sketch plan (Figs. 33 and 34).

[1] A thirteenth-century Arab anchor with movable flukes is illustrated in the Makamen of Hariri MS. in the British Museum.

The areas I drew in detail were related to each other, and the site as a whole, by triangulation (this was not easy without an assistant). The central pile consisted of well over a hundred amphorae; planning each separate jar was out of the question in the time. I had to choose between shading the area and writing a lengthy description in the key, or giving an impression of its appearance. Instead of explaining in a report that there were two layers of two kinds of amphorae, that the globular variety predominated, that a certain percentage were broken and the whole tumbled, I chose the latter course and drew them in free-hand. On land, where others could have visited the place, it would have been unnecessary, but no archaeologist had seen a wreck, so visual statement was more vivid. On this second year I had an underwater compass and depth gauge. The plan was an improvement on its predecessor, but my efforts were no substitute for a properly organized survey. Apart from explaining the site, the main value of my work was again that it taught me the exact limitations inherent in deep-water recording. It became apparent that land techniques were not directly adaptable, just as accepted methods of charting the sea-bed are inapplicable to wrecks, since they answer a different type of question. The limitations of underwater recording are essentially: disorientation due to lack of horizon, distorted vision, and the effect of depth on the mind.[1]

Planning and charting, on land, on the surface of the sea and in shallow water, is based on the existence of a horizon. The first thing a surveyor does is to set up a plane table and see that the top is horizontal. At Jericho, when plotting the fifty-odd tombs under the refugee village, we would set up our table, site, say, the corner of a house and a window and measure the distance between all three. This triangulation was repeated until we had all the information we wanted. We used an alidade and measuring tapes. The theodolite is based on similar principles. Whatever the mechanical equipment, there was a skyline all round us and our feet were firmly on the ground. If the land sloped we knew it and our judgement would correct any possible misreading of an instrument.

Underwater, where there is no horizon, the diver moves three-dimensionally.

[1] The Experimental Diving Unit of the American Navy recently demonstrated that, even at 30 metres, the function of the higher nerve centres starts to decrease. Symptoms intensify with depth: divers act mechanically, by routine, and are incapable of interpreting unforeseen events. They accomplish their set tasks, but are occasionally subject to disconcerting lapses of memory. Only after years of practice can man recover, underwater, some portion of his normal intelligence. Good amateur divers who have become perfectly at ease in the water frequently remain unaware of this physiological limitation.

His disorientation can be such that, in deep water or poor visibility, he may not even know whether he is moving up or down. He is taught in this extremity to stop and watch the bubbles rising from his valve, then follow them to the surface. Lack of horizon removes the very basis of survey techniques. Theoretic solutions spring to mind, but their application differs according to the type of site. Without mechanical aid, the diver is often thrown back on his own judgement, and judgement varies with individual experience and aptitude. The only generalization which I would put forward at this point is that all important underwater measurements must be taken by more than one method: for instance, depth-gauge readings should be checked against soundings.

Distorted vision has already been mentioned, but the effect it has on a draughtsman trying to plot only a few square metres is serious. The mask enlarges by a quarter while at the same time reducing the diver's angle of vision, so that he becomes like a horse wearing blinkers. Furthermore, as there is no cast shadow in depth, relief is almost imperceptible. It is easy to see a rock sticking out of the bottom, but not that the bottom itself is on a slope. For normal purposes the diver learns to compensate, but for the draughtsman some side effects remain.

Let us postulate that a draughtsman has to measure the distance between points 12 metres apart and subsequently make scale drawings of all the objects sticking out of the sand along this line. When he swims between these points he keeps himself a metre or so above, and his body will naturally be parallel with, the bottom. Since he is wearing blinkers, his attention is focused on a narrow strip of ground; he loses that standard of comparison given by normal vision. Moreover, a swimmer's slow pace, coupled with the mask's enlargement, make distances seem enormous. The first observation I made on wearing a mask was: 'The body is somewhere behind; out of sight out of mind . . . no module to measure by . . . fish look one coldly in the eye; are they larger or smaller than oneself?' Experienced divers forget this early experience, but it still affects the draughtsman. Being always parallel with the bottom, he cannot realize its slope. If by some miracle the same area suddenly became dry land, variety of sensory messages from his leg muscles and eyes would tell him whether he was on the flat or not.

Let us return to the little task we have set for a submarine draughtsman: he is to measure and draw a 12-metre line of bottom. First he hammers in rods at either end of the line and verifies the distance between with a surveyor's tape. His next step is to make measured drawings of the objects on the ground. If the ground is uneven there will be a discrepancy between his overall measurement and the sum of the detailed measurements. This discrepancy could be remedied on paper if: (*a*) it were possible to find out the depth of the declivities, and (*b*) it were certain that the measuring tape between the two points had been horizontal.

Lastly, reactions become automatic once depth affects the mind. This is the easiest limitation to overcome. The draughtsman prepares his dive in advance. I write objectives like a shopping list on my tablet or flippers and cross them off as they are accomplished.

CHAPTER 11

Nature of Wreck Formations – Dumas' Excavation Method – Solutions to Recording Problems: the Grid, an Alternative Convention – Photography and Deep Water Recording

LACK of horizon, distorted vision and the dulling of his mind in depth are the first things an underwater draughtsman has to consider, but during an excavation he is only one member of a team. If a buried ship is to be reconstructed he has to produce records of every phase of its excavation, and this he cannot do unless the excavators know their business. The surface is usually the least significant part of a wreck, but below it the draughtsman can draw only what the diggers uncover. We must therefore revert to wreck-formations and see how they should be excavated before we can suggest solutions to the problems of underwater recording.

Within the Mediterranean, wreck-formations are so varied as to make general definition almost impossible; all the same, we will have to assume a 'typical wreck' and postulate its sinking. A ship is in the first place a mobile, self-contained machine; when it strikes a rock the impact will displace some of its parts. After it sinks it will either nose dive or plane towards the bottom. During the journey the laws of submarine gravity will dictate another displacement: heavy objects slip forwards and lighter ones fly upwards or off. Another jolt unsettles the cargo when the ship touches the bottom. When she lists, according to the slope of the sea-bed, the cargo will finally slide to one side. Cargoes have to be firmly stowed and submarine gravity is reduced, but it is still calculable, so that these events do not add up to chaos.

Having swallowed the ship, the sea starts to digest her. If the hull falls on sand it will block the natural movement of erosion products across the bottom so that they will start to pile up. At the same time the delicious organic matter, such as wood, attracts tiny animals in shells, who rush to gorge on the unexpected feast.

Sated, they die, their waste matter and crumbling shells falling into the wreck. Thus, the lower parts of the hull are simultaneously covered by two different kinds of sand: the one attracted from the surroundings and the other caused by broken shells. After certain depths there are layers of sand and water where the oxygen content is reduced.[1] Taken together, these three factors explain the astonishing preservation of wood and other organic matter found in the lower parts of most wrecks.

Next, within a few months of sinking, wood becomes waterlogged and flattens out under the weight of the cargo. The mast falls according to the list of the ship. Degrees of preservation depend on many factors, including the nature of the bottom: deep mud, for instance, would preserve the shape of a hull. Out of the variety of wreck-formations which a draughtsman might have to record, I am taking as 'typical' a ship that has sunk on to a sandy bottom. Even so, the top layer of this kind of formation might incorporate biological concretions. These incrustations start to form as soon as the ship has settled and, after a period of time, the results can be so varied as to defy simple summary. Some concreted artifacts, like the implements which Barnier found at Anthéor, lie loose on the surface. In certain waters the top layer of cargo is joined by a 'pie-crust' of concretion and this will be impossible to plot underwater. If one of these wrecks is going to be excavated, so that it becomes necessary to make an accurate survey of a concreted top layer, the only solution is to hammer in fixed points, break the largest possible lumps of 'pie-crust', number each as it is raised, then put the lot together again on land. The reconstructed mass is drawn, then as each lump of concretion is broken and artifacts are extracted from within it, the separate objects can be marked on to the drawing made on land. The procedure is tiresome; happily it does not apply to every wreck.

Dumas has described wreck-formation in detail and its implications in terms of excavation technique. It is impossible to discuss recording without summarizing his conclusions. Up to now, both professionals and amateurs have extracted cargo from ancient wrecks by digging into the site (Fig. 36). The result is that a diver finds himself at the bottom of a hole, surrounded by delicate organic matter and loose sand, which he blows from one side to the other as he extracts finds. His task is difficult and recording impossible. Dumas' method is first to analyse the

[1] J. Brouardel and J. Vernet, 'Variations en Mer de la Teneur en Oxygène Dissous au Proche Voisinage des Sédiments.' *Bulletin de l'Institut Océanographique de Monaco*, No. III, January 27, 1958.

formation: the axis of the ship, its list and the extent of the buried remains which, on one side, will be the length of the mast (see Fig. 37). After that, the entire significant area is disengaged and raised above the level of its surroundings by means of a peripheral trench. For this purpose, the full power of an airlift can be used with impunity, since it will be digging into virgin sand. Once the wreck is free standing, it is a relatively easy matter to remove and record layer after layer of cargo (Fig. 37).

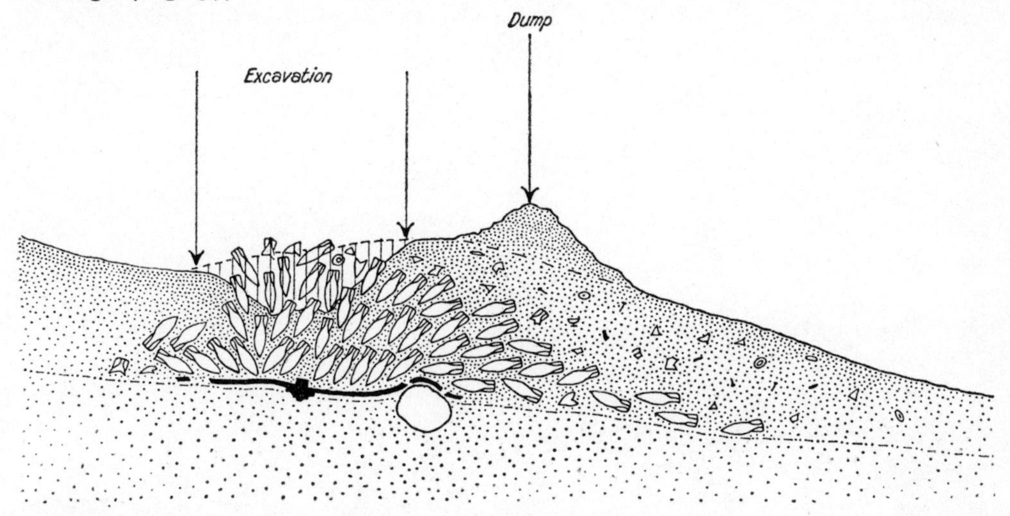

36. Section of an amphora-carrying wreck, showing the wrong method of excavation: a hole has been dug into that part of the tumulus where amphorae necks showed above the surface of the sand, with the result that waste from the hole has been dumped above another part of the cargo. When this is done cargo cannot be removed in consecutive layers, and recording becomes impossible. Diagram from Deep Water Archaeology, *by F. Dumas.*

Analysis of the as yet untrenched site can be made by an expert, whose judgement is checked by coring, a device which has long been used by geologists and oceanographers. The older type of core-sampler is unwieldy, but others are being developed. Given time and money, there is no reason why these well-tried principles should not be adapted to archaeological requirements. A core 2 or 3 metres long by 2 centimetres in diameter would give a section through the cargo, and beyond the limits of the wreck, of course, pure sand. Core samples containing strata of pottery, sand, wood and lead would be drawn on the surface and filed for future reference. Whenever a core was taken on the bottom a metal rod would be inserted in the hole. These rods, running right through the wreck-formation, would be shown on consecutive plans, throughout every stage of the excavation; they could also be used by the draughtsman as fixed points (Fig. 39).

Archaeologists will appreciate that these cores and core-poles are an underwater substitute for baulks (see Fig. 40). When trenches are made on a land site

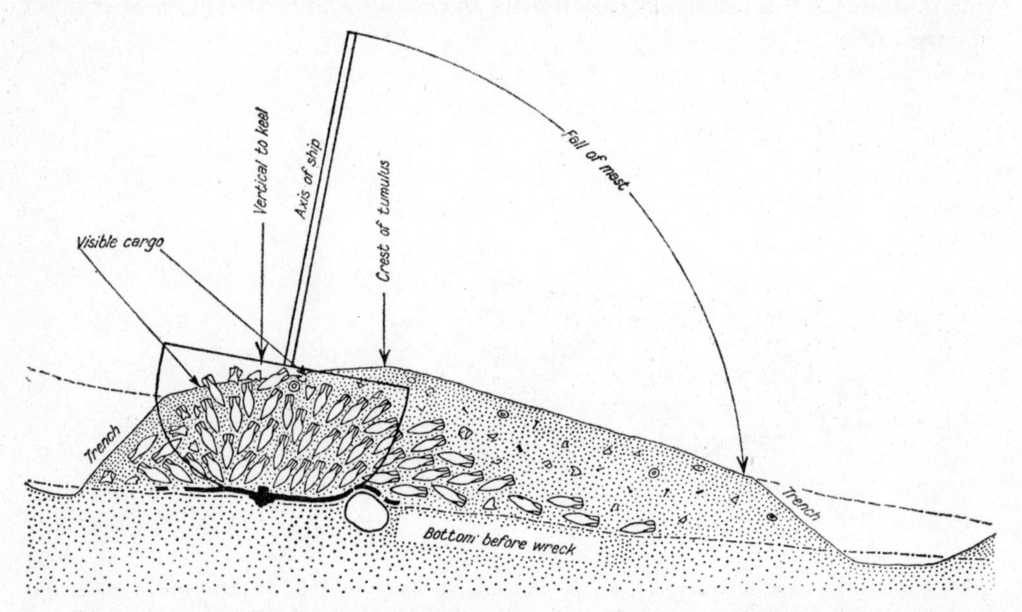

37. Schematic section showing how an amphora-carrying ship, on a sandy bottom, opens when the wood becomes waterlogged. The softened hull (shown in black) takes the shape of the bottom and the amphorae fan out according to the slope; in the course of time sand gathers and a tumulus is formed. Also shown is a peripheral trench dug round this tumulus with an air-lift, in order to isolate the significant area so that excavation can be carried out in a series of well-controlled layers; the sand from each layer is pushed into the trench, which is cleared periodically. Diagram from Deep Water Archaeology, *by F. Dumas.*

baulks are left standing within each excavated section. From these baulks strata can be related at various points on the site. There is no stratification, in this sense, on a wreck, but it is highly useful to know how the buried cargo is disposed: there may be three layers of amphorae in one place and only wood or sherds under the sand in another. Coring and trenching are established forms of underwater work, but their application for archaeological purposes would be impossible in unskilled hands. Once again we are forced to conclude that professional divers are essential on a well-conducted excavation.

What kind of drawing will describe these complicated events for posterity? On land there is a difference of approach between surveying architectural remains and planning the contents of a tomb; the analogy is useful. It is not necessary to draw every stone in the foundations of a Roman villa, but it is essential to get the accurate alignment of the courses. A plan shows the size and type of the original house. Interpretation and reconstruction of the contents of a tomb depend on a different set of data. We are faced by skeletons, each with its weapons and jewellery and surrounded by goods, chattels and funeral meats. All the objects are different in kind, and each is placed there deliberately. In tombs the things themselves and their juxtaposition with one another are relatively more important than their alignment relative to the tomb as a whole; each one has to be drawn in perspective and its relationship to its neighbour clearly recorded. Beads which once encircled a lady's neck are now scattered among vertebrae, but we can see that she had been wearing a necklace. Imperishable parts of rigging, such as the lead rings, will be as beads to vertebrae on the surface cargo of a wreck. In both cases the objects have slipped from their original position. The draughtsman cannot put them back in place, as he might dot in the missing stones in a course of masonry; his task is to describe them clearly and show which was next to which. The law of gravity becomes complex under water, but it is not beyond our comprehension.

It would be easier to reconstruct a tomb from a free-hand drawing of the pots lying on their side than from an accurate, diagrammatic plan where they were all shown upright, as a series of pairs of concentric circles. Varied objects once placed in deliberate or functional relationship are not comparable to architectural remains. I do not imply that a tomb or wreck draughtsman should be casual about measurements, but he must keep in mind a clear idea of his ultimate aim. In a tomb even the draughtsman's time seems unlimited, but it is no use pretending that this will be so on a wreck. His air will run out and there are other crises: recently exposed organic matter can float away between dives, so he may have to choose between making a free-hand drawing or not seeing his subject again. The wreck-draughtsman's job is hard, but not impossible. Half the battle is won if the limitations are analysed; the greatest danger is that they will pass unnoticed.

Even on the surface layer of the 'Globe Wreck' at Karabağla I learned some of the practical difficulties, and first among these are measurements in depth or the

WRECKS

XVIII (opposite). *Capt. Kemal surfacing with a full bag of sponges fastened to his belt. The diver in the distance is, by contrast, truly 'free' and can use this mobility to advantage in prospecting for, or examining, wrecks.*

XIX (centre, verso). *Seen from a cleft of rock on an uninhabited island, two* caïques *are anchored above the wreck of a ship that foundered thirteen centuries before Christ. In the background is the southernmost cape of Turkey, which sponge-men call 'the Nose of Anatolia'.*

XX (recto, top). *Detail of the Roman hull known as the 'Chretienne A'. This picture was taken in 21 metres of water by natural light. Surprisingly, the inner floor-boards have not been moulded over the ribs; these latter are grouped in pairs, which is unusual in wrecks of this date. The yellowish planking of the hull is* in situ *and, to the left, it is possible to see a small cut made through this planking at a mortise join. One twig, in the top left-hand corner, indicates where a large bunch was found; this might have been either a rustic broom or a protective packing of brushwood. Note the oblique cut on the central rib, made to take a wedge-shaped join as on the Nemi ships. (See Appendix.)*

XXI (below). *Modern* caïques *in three stages of construction; wrecks in the making?*

XXII (verso). *Taken without flash at a respectable depth of 43 metres where all is monochrome blue, this picture is unusual for the luminous yellow of the ascidians (which was also apparent to the human eye). Unlike the other wrecks in the vicinity, this 'Chretienne C' is deeply buried in sand; only these few amphorae mark the site.*

XVIII. M. Kapkin

XX. F. Dumas

XXI. F. Dumas

XXII. F. Dumas

making of sections. The tumulus of amphorae only a metre or so high was spread out on an even, sandy slope. In theory, all I had to do to make a section was to take depth readings, from the gauge which I wore like a watch, at various points on a line running across the wreck. Unfortunately, after about 25 metres the best gauges become inaccurate and the margin of error rapidly increases to over a metre. The readings would not be accurate, and it would be impossible to continue this system of measurement in depth, through layer after layer of excavated cargo.

The plan I made of the 'Globe Wreck' was not intended as a substitute for an excavation survey. Even so, the rough form of triangulation which I used to make the surface measurements was only possible because, on that particular site, the bottom was fairly level. I stuck arrows from my gun into the key areas and measured the distance between with a fisherman's line. Checking this triangulation with a compass was more difficult, for the bottles I wore were magnetic. I floated the compass, dissociated myself from it, then swam round to see how much it was affected.

In theory, there is no reason why a theodolite should not be made to work underwater, but submarine visibility and the difficulty of having it on the same fixed point, possibly over a period of years, makes the idea impracticable. Rasim thought up a simple form of alidade for occasional use, but it never materialized; in any case it was not essential on the 'Globe Wreck'. I bitterly regretted it later, when I had to plan a large area of uneven bottom. On that occasion, in order to avoid obstacles on the ground, which was itself both sloping and indented, measuring tapes had to be stretched about 4 metres above ill-defined key points. With an alidade one could at least have sited on buoys. The distances which had to be measured ranged from 6 to 12 metres; there was no way of telling whether the tapes were horizontal, let alone measuring the depths of the declivities in the ground, so there was bound to be a discrepancy between the overall measurements and the sum of the detailed drawings made on the sea-bed.

On all wrecks the main difficulty is this measurement in depth. It becomes more pronounced when layer after layer of cargo is lifted and each has to be related to the last both in plan and section. From a realistic point of view, if one is forced to make plans without adequate assistance and equipment, the only thing to do is to break the area into convenient subdivisions of about 2 metres, regardless of any declivities. This will at least provide a series of individually accurate drawings. The next stage is to fit the mosaic together. If, on the other hand, the draughtsman works backwards from long, overall measurements and attempts to fit details into this suspect scheme, confusion will ensue.

When our joint efforts at Karabağla resulted in a project to excavate the Globe Wreck it devolved on me to show the plan I had made and explain the site to Frédéric Dumas, who had been invited, by the University of Pennsylvania, to join the expedition as head diver. He needed to understand the requirements of the site before writing his report recommending a specific method of excavation and the appropriate machinery. Of course, I stressed my problems as draughtsman, with the result that he sketched out an instrument. This was constructed and, at least in theory, seems fool-proof. We were never able to test it, as the entire season was spent on the Bronze Age cargo. It is characteristic of wreck excavation that the machine could not be used on that other atypical site, which consisted of two heaps of fossilized cargo on an uneven, rocky saddle joining two islands. There was only a centimetre or so of sand, and the place was swept by current.

The 'Globe Wreck' machine was a grid of tubular metal standing on four adjustable legs. The frame was square, each side being 5 metres long and graduated in units of 5 centimetres. Across it ran a movable bar also graduated. A rod with a vertical movement slid along this bar, serving as a plumb-line; it, too, was graduated. The grid was to be positioned over an extremity of the wreck and the square frame set horizontally, by means of a spirit level (Fig. 38). When the tip of the vertical bar was placed above an object three readings would give its exact position in space. When one part of the wreck had been drawn the frame would be swivelled on a single leg over to the adjoining area, leaving three legs standing. One of these would be re-used and two new ones added on the far side. In this way the entire wreck area would be divided into squares; within each square and on any one level, all the measurements would be accurate, both horizontally and in depth.

In order to record successive phases of excavation on a deeply buried wreck, the legs of these grids would, of course, have to be driven right through the cargo and the hull into the original bottom (as it had been before the wreck formed). If this were not done the instrument could not be repositioned with any degree of accuracy during the long months or years of excavation.

We discovered later that year that a similar grid had been used for planning *palafite*, or settlements submerged in lakes, and that the idea had also been reinvented in Italy. Judging from reports, the others were smaller than Dumas' grid; so were the sites. In practice, grids, like airlifts, must be designed for a specific job. Dumas' 5-metre grid could not have been worked by the draughtsman alone, unless he swam from one point to another, adjusting it before returning to his drawing. On the other hand, a smaller grid would not only waste time through frequent resettings but also risk inaccuracies whenever it was moved. Worse still, it would get in the way, pinning the draughtsman or excavators under

38. The measuring machine. From Deep Water Archaeology, *by F. Dumas.*

the sides, or the vertical rod would slip through the diver's breathing tubes. The most logical ideas are often impracticable. When planning small finds held in sand at the bottom of a crevice, I once asked that a levelled rod should be fixed between the rocks above, so that I could take vertical measurements with a plumb-line. The other divers said it would get in their way when they brought down cameras, airlifts and the rest of their paraphernalia.

The grid is a workmanlike instrument for producing sections, and vertically observed plans which are what archaeologists expect. It is adaptable to most, but not all wrecks. My own feelings on the subject of deep-water recording are more radical, and therefore, perhaps, less acceptable. It is axiomatic that no work which can be done on land should be attempted in depth. Moreover, I have a

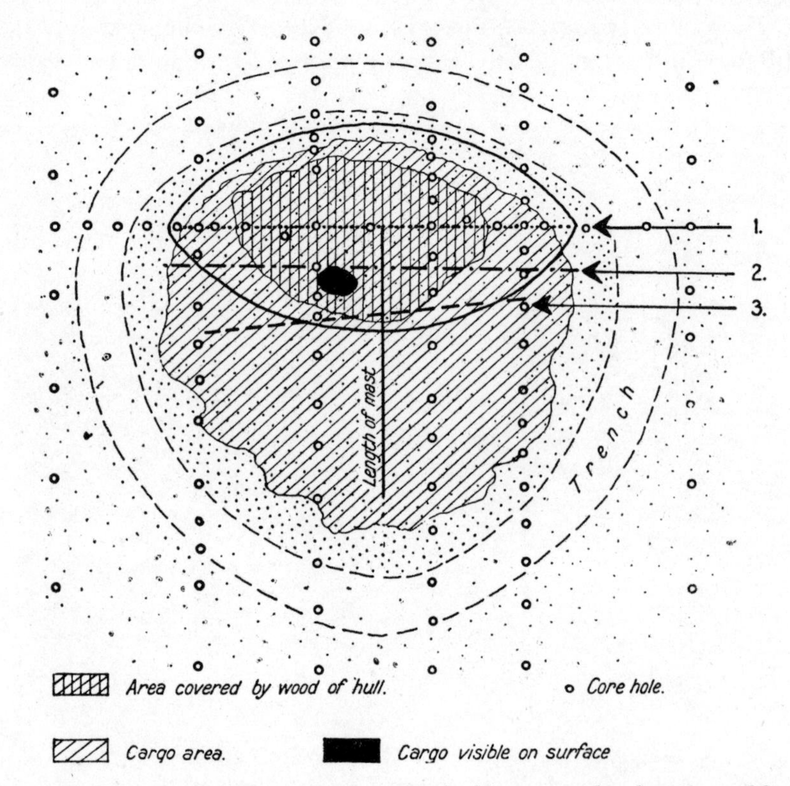

39. *Schematic plan of a buried wreck where the significant area has been located by coring.* Key: (*1*) *Axis of the buried keel.* (*2*) *Surface intersection of the plane mast-to-keel* (*before collapse*), *i.e. the list of the ship when it settled on the bottom.* (*3*) *The axis of the wreck tumulus as visible on the bottom. Diagram from* Deep Water Archaeology, *by F. Dumas.*

distrust of instruments which I cannot control myself and which are designed to reduce, by mechanical means, a certain sequence of operations. To set a large grid on the bottom would be time-consuming, and it would also normally take three people to make it work. Its main purpose is to provide a horizontal level, but the whole contraption might slip in the course of work. Why, one wonders, is it necessary to divide the strange, collapsed machine which is a wreck into squares, and what is sacrosanct about vertically observed plans? They are essential to the understanding of a collapsed building, but are they the only convention that will explain a dislocated pile of machinery? If there is one thing that modern art has taught, it is the multiplicity of visual conventions, each communicating a different type of statement and each depending on the limitations of the medium used. A pencil outline is one way of describing two-dimensional events, shading adds depth. Mathematical perspective is another way of showing

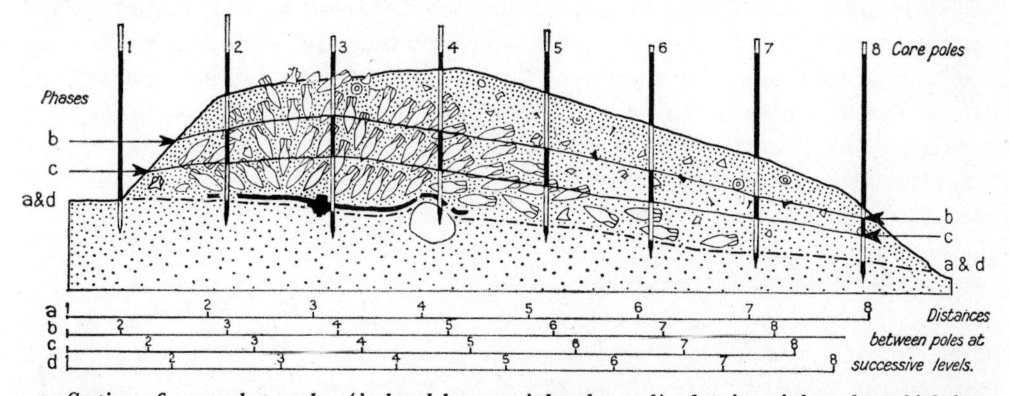

40. Section of a wreck tumulus (isolated by a peripheral trench) showing eight poles which have been stuck into core holes. A given horizontal has been marked on the protruding end of each pole (this level is marked 1–8). The poles are also marked at their intersection with the sand at the surface of the undisturbed tumulus: line a–a. When the first layer of finds has been removed the poles will again be marked at their intersection with the remaining sand: level b–b and so on through c–c and d–d. Measured drawings of the objects will have been made on the actual plane on which they were found. The variations in the size of these drawings (along the lines a, b, c and d) are shown below. Depth measurements having been marked on the poles, the drawings made on varying slopes can be related to each other or projected on a horizontal plane as in Fig. 41.

three-dimensional structures, but architects also use isometric projections. Persian miniaturists put things which are in the background higher up on the paper than things in the foregound. Impressionists describe light and Cézanne indicated recession by his use of colour. Futurists invented conventions to describe movement; the possibilities are inexhaustible.

Conventions are made to fit specific events and are governed only by the limitations of the medium which has to be used and the nature of the subject. In relation to deep-water recording, doubts occurred to me when I had to plot a wedge-shaped mass of packed sand, full of small objects. It looked like a school desk with a top measuring $1\frac{1}{2} \times 1$ metre; the slope was about 20°. I made a base-line by hammering nails into the top extremities of the wedge. By swinging out horizontally from these nails and dropping down to an object with a plumb-line, I projected the sloping plane back on to the horizontal. After the first couple of layers I began to wonder whether this complicated performance, quite alien to underwater conditions and requiring so much calculation, was really going to give archaeologists more information than a drawing of the slope as I saw it in front of me. I could guarantee, with only a fraction of the effort and a minimal margin of error, to draw the finds on the plane on which they lay: to do this, I could not only situate each object in relation to the base-line but also, without the slightest effort, I could measure the distance between one object and the next. A vertically observed plan, made underwater, is contrived and therefore essentially 'spoof'.

When it came to making sections, the only essential depth measurement where this wedge was concerned was the distance from top to bottom, or from the nails to the bedrock once the finds had been removed; in other words, the known vertical, which corresponded to a baulk in land excavation. If I made drawings of what I saw on the slope in front of me, and could find out the corresponding vertical measurements at the back of the wedge, then it would be simple to produce horizontal, that is to say vertically observed, plans later. On land, where my time was not restricted and my mind was clear, I could project a plan from the data I had collected on the bottom (see Fig. 41).

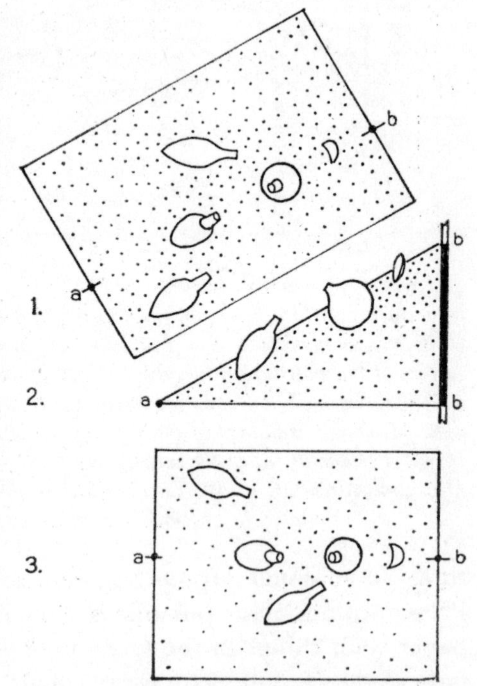

41. (1) Objects drawn underwater on the plane on which they lay; core poles at a and b. (2) Section a–b, with depth measured on core-pole b–b. (3) Projection a–b on to a horizontal plane.

It is, incidentally, easy to draw intricate artifacts and to measure short distances underwater; detailed drawings always impress the layman, though they present no technical difficulty. I have used proportional dividers to make scale drawings of complex structures underwater, and have always found that they compared well with drawings made by a land-draughtsman after the objects had been raised.

Let us see how this system of recording the actual plane (as distinct from attempting a vertically observed plan) could be applied to a wreck tumulus where the cargo consisted mainly of amphorae. If Dumas' method of excavation were used the site would be cored. There would already be some fixed points across the axis of wreck, along the keel and round the periphery (see Fig. 39). These cores might be sufficient for the draughtsman's purposes, but if they were more than 2 metres apart others could be added. Metal poles having been stuck into the core holes, running right through the wreck, the draughtsman's first job would be to take a rod with a spirit level attached to it and mark the top of the poles at a uniform level (Fig. 40, points 1–8). This would be his only concession to the missing horizontal. He would have no further need to rely on a depth gauge or make constant, and possibly inaccurate, underwater calculations.

Next, he would make a measured drawing of cargo within a triangle limited by three of the poles, using a rule, calipers, proportional dividers or any other appropriate and handy instrument. These measurements could be double checked by triangulating from the core-poles. The angle of the slope would be recorded by making a mark on each pole at its intersection with the bottom. If an object protruded to any significant height in the middle of the area this could also be recorded in relation to the poles.

Because the slope of the ground, bounded by the same three poles, would vary every time a layer of finds was raised the drawings made at these successive phases would differ in size if they were superimposed. Since, however, each change of slope would be recorded on the poles that bounded the triangle, the draughtsman would have the information he required to convert his drawings into vertically observed plans. On paper it is a simple matter to project a drawing that was made on to a known slope on to a horizontal plane (Fig. 41). The process may be tedious, but it is feasible on land, whereas underwater attempts both to draw and at the same time to project the drawing on to an imaginary plane are asking for trouble. Needless to say, sections could also be made on land from the same depth measurements that had been marked on the core-poles. We should not forget that records of the original core-samples through cargo and hull would be available as a cross check.

The two most important sections, which together explain the formation of a wreck (and consequently the buried ship) are: the profile of the surface, as it was before excavation, and the profile of the bottom, as it was before the ship sank. Particular care should be taken to double check these sections by soundings, depth-gauge readings and observation, though in themselves these forms of measurement are less accurate than the levels marked on core-poles. If this system were used the draughtsman's work on land might be increased, but at no point would he be expected to do the impossible underwater.

I have put this suggestion bluntly; it might be more persuasive to say that poles should be placed at regular intervals and the area divided into squares, but I think it would be unrealistic, since the original cores were intended to establish the lie of the wreck. Moreover, triangular divisions have certain advantages when it comes to plotting. The draughtsman is not the only diver working on a site; diggers also have their requirements. It may sound shocking to suggest that even small holes 2 centimetres in diameter should be drilled all over a wreck, but in a cargo of 3,000–10,000 amphorae one has to choose between records that will permit of eventual reconstruction and holes in some of the finds. There is no alternative, for even a grid, if it is going to be replaced on the same spots throughout a long excavation, would have to have holes drilled for its legs. No one would core on a treasure ship!

The camera is sometimes suggested as an alternative to an underwater draughtsman. Could this be, the draughtsman would also be without a job on land; camera and draughtsmen fulfil different functions. Photographs of ancient wood, for instance, are never satisfactory; underwater they are utterly meaningless unless accompanied by drawings. Archaeological recording is specialized; both photographs and drawings must describe objects in an accepted way; even expert photographers have to learn these conventions. It would be beyond me to discuss underwater photography in general, but in so far as it affects the draughtsman, certain things need to be clarified. Aerial photography was a revelation to archaeologists; showing as it did buildings below a field of corn, when their remains had been unnoticeable on the ground. Buried foundations could be seen from the air, because crops grow more or less sparsely according to the depth of soil; over masonry the growth is thinner. This, and also subtle relief, can be seen when photographs are taken in a certain light. Neither condition pertains underwater; submarine growths flourish equally on rock or artifact and concretions complete the camouflage. Relief is lost without colour or cast shadow, nor can one material be distinguished from another. Shallow water is a different matter, there aerial photographs are indispensable, as Père Poidebard's work has shown.

The assumption that, because a photographer could hang directly above a wreck, he would get the same results as in the air, was understandable if naïve. The camera cannot take long shots because of the density of water; no entire wreck has ever been photographed, though excellent close-ups abound. When I was trying to explain what the Byzantine wrecks looked like to non-divers I had to draw reconstructions from my plans, as nothing else could give the general impression (see Plate 24). Aware of all this, Dr Roghi, in his most illuminating report of a well-organized excavation which was started (but alas, never completed) on a Roman wreck at Spargi,[1] described the methods he used and the results obtained from a photographic overlay. He divided the surface of the wreck into 2-metre squares by means of stretched tapes, numbering each square on a central plaque. Always at the maximum distance of 3 metres, the photographer centred himself above the plaques by a plumb-line. A draughtsman, working on land, was to make the plan from these photographs. It sounds simple, in theory, but it did not prove satisfactory for many reasons; moreover, it was impossible to continue the process in depth once the top layer of the wreck had been raised, because the overlays would not be made to correspond. Even taking the photographs was difficult, for divers had to contend with current and variable visibility. Apart from fluctuations caused by weather, any work on the bottom raises a cloud of mud. Finally, the overlay was found difficult to interpret by divers and more so by the draughtsman. In a flat photograph a sponge growing on an amphora can look like a hole.

The non-selective lens is less efficient than the human eye; if a draughtsman has doubts he can go up to an object, feel it and scratch its surface. Despite difficulties, it is still easier for a man to measure the distance between things on the bottom than to judge their relationship from a perspective photograph. If a photographic overlay is clear and reliable, that is to say if there is no difference in scale and perspective between one photograph and the next, it is a precious addition to a surface plan, but it is no substitute.

On the positive side, ephemeral, *aide mémoire* photographs, meaningless as permanent records, are most useful to the draughtsman. They have to be taken by him, or at his request, and serve to fill in less-important details which he has not

[1] Gianni Roghi, 'Note Tecniche sul Rilevamento e lo scavo della Nave Romana di Spargi', *Bollettino e Atti*, 1958–59.

got time to draw. His twenty minutes may be spent in drawing, for instance, certain bits of wood on which future reconstruction depends, but near by there are a couple of boulders and a broken amphora. These have to be plotted too, though they are relatively less important, so he quickly measures the distances, has them photographed and enters the details on his plan later, on land. 'Later' means that day, as soon as he gets back to his makeshift table; underwater drawings have to be transferred to paper while the visual memory is fresh. *Aide mémoire* photographs must be printed immediately or not at all. Dumas solved this by putting a polaroid camera into an underwater case.

All records, drawings and photographs should be dated; I would go further and say that the hour they were taken and the subject ought to be entered on the diving log, otherwise confusion ensues later, when they are interpreted and compared. A drawing may show two amphorae near a small stone, while in a photograph taken an hour afterwards they are beside a big rock. Sand is so mobile in water that it can be cleared, or fall back, changing the character of a scene in the twinkling of an eye. Arguments follow: 'Was that amphora P. 245?' 'No, because there was no rock there, it must come from another area . . .' and so on. Small finds are hidden, or float away if a diver swims over them. Even fish upset a place which has been carefully prepared for recording. They rush to the sand like birds to newly turned soil; mullets are unbelievably efficient diggers.

All said and done, no excavation of a ship buried in sand has ever been carried to completion; one can only present a patchwork of present experience. Hundreds of Mediterranean wrecks have had their cargoes removed and the sites utterly destroyed. Loss will be turned to gain if we learn from these mistakes. It is now possible to deduce how systematic excavation should be tackled in given circumstances. Experience also teaches caution, for every wreck is a new problem. When rational methods are evolved the reward will be a knowledge of the ships themselves. Let us have no illusions about its being easy; a wreck carrying 10,000 amphorae covers a huge area, and the hull will be at least 2 metres below the cargo. Hundreds of tons of sand have to be removed underwater. Weather is not always fine and recording takes time; meticulous work may last years. Nor can underwater excavation be seasonal, as on land, where a trench is filled in after three months and then left for an indefinite period. If, however, only two wrecks were excavated in twenty years the contribution to science would be considerable. If the work is not tackled with foreknowledge, then it is best left alone, for, as Dr Nino Lamboglia has remarked, wrecks have been preserved for 2,000 years, and will be perfectly safe for another 2,000 if they are not destroyed by premature and thoughtless digging.

Divers meanwhile are in the position of nineteenth-century travellers, who considered it their pleasure and duty to record what they saw. Looking at early travel books, one is rather discouraged, for the standard of classical education and drawing-room accomplishments were considerable: everyone seemed able to make excellent topographical and architectural drawings. Our forebears and the mysterious compilers of *Baedeker* and the *Blue Guides* have left little to be discovered on land; what does remain is buried, and therefore the prerogative of specialists. The sea-bed remains unknown; there, too, excavation is highly specialized, but visible indications of ancient trade routes are more likely to be discovered by amateurs than by organized expeditions, and it is up to these amateurs to record what they see.

PART V

SPONGE DIVERS AND ANOTHER ANCIENT TRADE

Gilgamesh opened the sluices so that a sweet water current might carry him out to the deepest channel; he tied heavy stones to his feet and they dragged him down to the water bed. There he saw the plant growing: though it pricked him he took it in his hands; then he cut the heavy stones from his feet, and the sea carried him and threw him onto the shore.[1]

[1] *The Epic of Gilgamesh*, N. K. Sandars, Penguin Classics, 1960.

CHAPTER 12

Petra Divers – Wreck Prospection – The Sponge Trade – Fishing with a Sponge Boat

THE obscure Gilgamesh epic contains this vivid description of how the hero became a 'petra diver'.[1] Some allusions are tantalizing: what, for instance, were the sweet-water sluices? one is tempted to recall the harbour-works at Seleucia. Elsewhere there is talk of stones which Gilgamesh destroyed, but which might have helped him to make a journey by boat. Was he, like Heracles, whom he resembles, also associated with symbolic anchors? The tree of life which pricked him when he took it in his hands is easier to interpret. Coral trees, because they are imperishable, always had this meaning: in Roman times they were put in tombs. Black coral, found in the Red Sea, is still considered holy; it grows in deep water, and when the *Calypso* had some on board local Arabs begged permission even to touch it, reverently rubbing it against their foreheads. Both sponges and coral used to be gathered by petra divers. The latter is more difficult to collect, as it grows under rocks; it is occasionally taken in trawls, but this must be a very chancy method of obtaining it.[2]

The petra diver's stone carries him straight to the bottom, thus saving time and breath for work. Quick descent strains the physique, especially in deep water, and these men are reputed to work at 30 metres. I have seen one of their boats off a wild part of the Turkish coast and regret not having dived with them. The opportunity may never recur, as there are few who still use this system. In Crete I got to know a petra diver, but he had already retired as a result of occupational injuries. We used to pick sea-urchins in only 6 metres of water. I

[1] These primitive divers use no form of breathing apparatus; by weighting themselves with a heavy stone they reach the bottom quickly without having to swim, thus saving their energy for work.

[2] E. Marchis, *La Pêche des Algues Marines, des Eponges et des Coraux*, Editions Géographiques Nationale et Coloniales, Paris, 1929.

watched his movements with great interest and, it must be admitted, disappointment. Even allowing for his condition, the performance was surprisingly inexpert; he did not seem to know what he was doing or how to do it quickly. Perhaps he had never been brilliant. So many accounts attest these divers' feats that it would be foolish to doubt them because of one man's technique.

The working life of sponge men is short, while petra divers last only a few years before they break down or are killed. My friend was in his late thirties and came, of course, from Kalymnos. Standard apparatus is used there now, but earlier traditions remain and are passed from father to son; indeed, from mother to daughter, as the girls swim there, which is very unusual in the Mediterranean. When the sponge fleet leaves for its annual trip to North Africa the womenfolk dress in black, knowing that no crew will return complete. Despite this, they love the sea, and my friend was determined that his daughters should swim, unlike their Cretan playmates. In Crete, as in most parts of Greece, the easy familiarity with the sea which existed in ancient times has disappeared. Minoans were not only sailors but they also knew how to dive. Wall paintings at Knossos depict sponges and sea-urchins growing on rocks. Many of the stippled effects in these same decorations were done with paint-filled sponges. The way octopus, fish and dolphins are drawn shows that they had been seen in their natural habitat.

Survivals of ancient skills are as interesting to the archaeologist as to the ethnologist. However, the direct importance of primitive diving communities lies in their knowledge of submarine sites. All divers guard their secrets, but the Greeks are also motivated by a keen sense of their pecuniary value. They know that a bronze is worth money, and they usually know where to sell it. Turks are less familiar with foreign buyers, and graven images are forbidden by religion. If they did see one on the sea-bed they would not deface it as on land, but neither would they raise it. The most obvious way to prospect for ancient wrecks is by questioning sponge divers. Comparison between history book and chart shows that wrecks must exist along the Carian and Lycian coasts, but it is difficult to find them without local help.

From a scientific point of view, the nascent submarine archaeologist will want to know how best he can chart representative wrecks in a given area so as to get a picture of trade routes. This prospection need have nothing to do with excavation: it is an end in itself. On a more popular level people ask what are the chances of finding a particular cargo whose loss has been recorded. At the present stage of technical development vague generalized prospection is unrewarding. Nevertheless, geology of the coast and sea-bed, together with knowledge of ancient ports, sea routes, winds and currents, might, in certain cases, provide one or two useful clues. Even when bearings are known it is difficult to find a wreck in open sea. The wreck of the Izmir Demeter is located within half a square mile, but it might take weeks or years to find it. In any case, were it found, only salvage would be possible, as the depth is considerable.

In so far as methodical prospection is considered at all, it has been assumed that the best way of doing it is to have a ship equipped with asdic or echo sounders, as for oceanographic research. Dumas has pointed out the disadvantage of these methods; only well-defined obstacles are registered by such costly instruments, and that on a narrow strip of sea-bed beneath the ship. If a shallow tumulus did happen to be detected divers would have to investigate. On an irregular bottom, and few parts of the sea-bed are completely flat, every bump would mean an exploratory dive. Furthermore, in order to search a square kilometre of sea-bed, the ship has to be navigated back and forth on parallel courses with superhuman accuracy. Much the same applies to prospection by means of underwater motors: most of them are without navigational instruments, and if they do have them they occupy most of the diver's attention. When an area has got to be searched it is probably best to tow the diver on a weighted rope beneath the boat; he will have nothing to do except to observe. If his eye is trained he can drop a marker buoy on to a likely site. Despite difficulties, there is a need for this type of prospection, but it is confined to those parts of the sea-bed where there is no alternative.

Before Peter and I appeared on the scene, the Izmir divers, who had spent four years with the sponge men of Bodrum, got to know many wrecks, which they charted for the museum. The area they covered stretches from north of Izmir round the western and southern coast of Turkey as far as Antalia, and amounts to the area where Capt. Kemal fished. Peter visited most of these sites, questioned fishermen and divers, and listed over twenty other wrecks. In some cases the sponge men were dubious about these lists; Kemal said: 'I have fished these waters for twenty years, and I would say, that there are only the five ancient wrecks that you know.' In this case, I think he may have been mistaken, for great as was his knowledge of the sea, he had never pondered the mysteries of wreck-formation. Nor had he had occasion to dig below the surface of these tumuli. Like most divers, he judged the site by the visible cargo. The pile of ox-hide ingots which Mustafa drew one season had disappeared with all the surface finds by the following year. The site had been known to sponge divers, who like Şeytan may have got a price even for corroded copper. On the bare expanse marked only by the imprints of the ingots which Mustafa had drawn, only Dumas' trained eyes distinguished what others had missed, namely two fossilized lumps of cargo looking to laymen like natural rock.

The number of known wrecks in Turkey is impressive, and analysis of their contents would start new lines of research. Cargoes of roof-tiles, for instance, first came to my notice in Turkey; later I found they cropped up in Greece and France. Indeed, architectural units, whether marble or ceramic, are fairly common on wrecks. This trade has not received much attention, as I found to my cost when I tried to trace the origin of the tiles through their shape, stamp or factory mark. It is, for instance, known that tiles were manufactured in Corinth, but the range of their distribution has not been questioned. On subjects such as this the task is to correlate information from sea and land.

However, we cannot pretend that the sum of known wrecks along this part of the Turkish coast is representative of all the ships that sank there. Wrecks discovered in France and the West are even more selective: firstly, because interest is concentrated on amphora carriers, and secondly, because they were mostly found by gentlemen-divers who were either exploring or looking for fish in picturesque and rocky parts. The Turkish wrecks were found by men who work on sponge beds and have no reason to waste their time elsewhere. The beds are in specific places which have been known for years. Fishermen are also surprisingly familiar with the bottom, but they, too, know only fertile areas. Judging from their habits, it would seem that the ratio of sea-desert is greater than productive regions. Trawlermen know there is sand in one place, a certain sort of weed in another, and rock somewhere else. Because they work deeper than divers, their scope is greater; however, the things they find are difficult to trace. When an object is drawn up in the net it can only be said to come from a certain line of trawl; the exact point is unknown. This was the case with the Izmir Demeter. Her survival was due to the merest chance. Şeytan was at that time in charge of the *congoa*, having given up diving for less arduous work on this kind of sponge trawl. On his last voyage, before retiring from the sea altogether, they drew up Demeter's heavily concreted head. It had torn the net; enraged by this bit of bad luck, one of the younger men said: 'Come on, let's throw it back, it's only old rubbish.' 'What!' said Şeytan, 'I'm not retired yet. While I'm captain of this boat, I take the decisions. Leave it on deck.'

The hierarchy of captain, mate, head diver, down to cook and dresser is scrupulously observed, and a breach of protocol amounts to mutiny. Demeter stayed on board and was dumped on the quay at Bodrum until she was seen by a passing archaeologist, who notified the Izmir Museum. An ex-*congoa* man once told me that he had found a big clay horse on another part of the coast, but threw it back. This kind of thing will not be repeated at Bodrum, thanks to the Izmir Club, to Hakki Bey, to the divers themselves and most of all to the enthusiasm of Throckmorton, which he communicated to the village elders. Anything from the sea is now brought back in triumph. The Castle Museum and the tourists it will eventually attract have become, in the minds of the villagers, the long-term cure for their moribund economy. They want a museum 'like the one in Rhodes or Cos'.

Synthetic sponges are replacing the real thing. The decline of the industry in Turkey was accentuated by political cleavage between the mainland and the Greek islands. After the revolution the Turks ran a fleet of their own, but they had no efficient sales organization; distribution of sponges throughout the world remains a Greek monopoly. In recent times lack of foreign currency confined Turkish boats to their own waters, and the Cyprus troubles destroyed, at least temporarily, the few remaining links with Greece. The Government founded a Sponge Co-operative, but did not supply buyers and travellers; their commercial attachés were no rivals for the experienced and highly organized Greek merchants. Warehouses at Bodrum were piled high with unsold sponges. The same was true of the other centre, at Marmoris, to the east. This illustrates the tragic rift between mainland and islands, which are by nature interdependent.

The fleet shrank; I could never understand how it kept going at all. Some sponge boats were converted for fishing, and a refrigeration plant was opened at Bodrum. One such conversion from *congoa* to fishing-boat occasioned an astonishing relaunching ceremony: a garlanded bull was slaughtered so that its blood spilled on to the prow. It is said that when Sulyman the Magnificent was preparing his attack on Rhodes his fleet was launched with a slaughter of sheep, representing Christian blood. His admiral, incidentally, came from a village not far from Bodrum. Seeing this ceremony on the site of Halicarnassos where so many marble altars were decorated with garlanded, horned skulls, it was impossible not to associate the sacrifice with much earlier traditions.

Diving is not hereditary in Turkey as it is at Kalymnos. Şeytan's son Mustafa became a diver, but he was an exception. On the third year I questioned two new men on the *Mandalinci*: Young Memet was already a diver, while Ali the ship's boy, was only fourteen. They both said it was a dog's life.

'You know we call Bodrum the *Tata Köyu*'; 'wooden village' is a euphemism for cemetery. Before erecting a turbaned headstone, relations mark the grave with a temporary plank, and many Bodrum graves were new. In twenty years Kemal had seen five hundred deaths, though none on his own boat. Ali said his uncle had died of a bend, and his family did not want him to become a diver. Perhaps they hoped he would be a sailor or join a *congoa* once he had finished his apprenticeship. Watching the way the boy looked at the sea and his admiration for the men he dressed, it seemed improbable.

'I certainly wouldn't let my son dive,' Ali said.

Young Memet remarked that he only dived for money.

'But you could earn as much on a farm or driving a lorry.'

'No,' he mumbled, 'no, it's dirty; I dive because it's clean.'

'Old' Memet, whose own survival was a record, remarked: 'When a man gets a pain in his back it is best to prick him with a needle so that the black blood can come out. After that he must drink a glass of water, then he should not dive again that day, or he will be very ill.'

'But he should be put down again, until he is well.'

Old Memet was too polite to contradict. Even the traditional five minutes per *kulatç* was to him a new-fangled trick.

'We don't have accidents: we look at the book, then we spend half an hour at the bottom here, where it's only 28 metres, and five minutes under the boat to get the bubbles out of our blood.' Luckily we could take a 'holier than thou' attitude, as they had never seen a free-diver have a bend!

'Oh, it's all right for you,' Young Memet replied, and they all nodded. 'You don't have to earn. If we don't pick enough sponges we don't get enough money.'

'And if you do, you die. Is that sensible?' It was pointless to get the last word, but the habit is ingrained.

One year, just before I arrived, Kasim had some sort of accident, probably due to the expansion of air in his guts after too quick an ascent; he was buried in hot sand for thirty-six hours, which cured him. Greeks believe in smoking immediately after a dive. Indirectly, they may be right, if nicotinic acid is a vasodilator; in theory, it might help air bubbles to pass through the veins. I do not know whether there is any medical support for this, but after Şeytan's accident I carried tablets of nicotinic acid. There was no hope of treatment in Greece or

Turkey, and unless help is immediate it is useless. Peter went one better and, after innumerable and complicated machinations, managed to acquire a portable decompression chamber. He calculated without the *gümrük*, who took a particularly firm line and would not allow it to go to the hospital. Tubular and coffin-like, it lay on the quay beside the Customs house in Bodrum, and as far as I know, is still there.

When Mustafa and Peter wanted to film sponge men we joined Kemal on a routine cruise in the Ceramic Gulf. The *Mandalinci* carried its full complement of divers, about twelve in all, so it was decided to take a second boat, which also had the advantage of letting them film the *Mandalinci* from alongside. She was called the *Şimşek* (Lightning), and never could there have been a frailer craft. Her hull was so soft that one could make holes in it by scratching with a fingernail. The rigging was a combination of knotted string and rusty wire. The engine worked fitfully, after it had been started like a Primus stove, with a blow-lamp and much smoke. The national shortage of materials and spare parts causes almost universal mechanical decrepitude. There is a little Turkish song of an engine, which Mustafa had frequent occasion to sing, which goes 'I can't do it Captain, it's too much for me Captain, this is the end Captain . . .' and so on. The *Şimşek* was crewed by a charming, pious, middle-aged captain called Hussein and an elderly, volatile mate, Ibrahim. To begin with, Hussein, who had not been out with us before, found my presence difficult to justify, until Kemal took him aside and explained that I, too, was a *dalgutç* (diver): after that, all went well.

Peter and Mustafa filmed every aspect of the men's life: getting under way, breakfastless and before dawn; divers being dressed, jumping into the water, surfacing; cleaning sponges and finally eating after dusk. The single meal was a precaution against diver's indigestion. The men were allowed drinks of water, and it was left to their discretion if they wanted a snack of bread and olives. Doing two deep dives a day, I got very exhausted without food, but on the whole we kept to their routine. The only time when both Peter and I put our feet down was at breakfast. Without a cup of tea, it was impossible to get going. I jokingly explained to Hussein Amca (*amca* or uncle is a respectful term of endearment) that in England people not only expected breakfast but also a cup of tea in bed beforehand.

'Who makes it? the husband or the wife?'

'It depends. Sometimes marriages come unstuck over it.'

We all laughed, but I was extremely touched next day when a tin mug was thrust over the side of the boat as I lay on what Mustafa called my 'gommi-bed'. Both he and I had rubber mattresses and slept on either side of the hold. The deck was not quite wide enough to take them, but we were haunted by the fear that they might be punctured on rough ground, our repair kits being minimal. The crew slept on land, probably because of me. None of the men from the *Mandalinci* would have done so. They disappeared into the incredibly small cabin, while the Captain, mate and chief diver had the place of honour on its flat roof. These habits are partly explained by the animal instinct which makes people choose dark, enclosed lairs, and partly by the crew's mistrust of the shore.

In ten days we saw two inhabited places. For the rest of the time we put in at springs or wells known only by fishermen. Water supply connotes habitation, so there were usually ruins, ranging from large Rhodian citadels, through Byzantine villages to a single cabin inhabited by bee-keepers or charcoal burners. The Gulf was surrounded by steep, forested hills indented by bays and fiords. One night we watched a forest fire, first a red glow in the sky, then flames leaping over the crest and spreading downwards. With childhood memories of fires in Cyprus, where one had had to sit up half the night to see whether the Army could stop them by trenching or whether the wind would change, it was nice to feel detached. Then one had been worried about getting domestic animals and baggage into the car, now it was merely a spectacle; if things got hot the boat could be moved round the corner.

There must have been wild life in the woods, but we had no opportunity to observe it, as we never anchored during daylight hours. Bears were a subject of conversation, and further explained the men's reluctance to sleep on land. One of the divers, who was no longer with us, had been a practising Moslem. When Friday came he decided to take a bath at a well on the shore of a wooded bay. He lit a fire, boiled water and undressed. While he was thus occupied the others slipped into the woods. When he started his ablutions they lobbed stones at him, first from one spot, then, after an interval, from another, to the accompaniment of growls. Bears, apparently, make a habit of throwing stones. The poor man eventually lost his nerve and rushed naked into the sea, whereupon his mates emerged, roaring with laughter. His plight was poignant, as none of these divers knows how to swim. Hussein, who was a sailor, could manage an infantile breast stroke. Swimming is, after all, a useless accomplishment for a helmet diver; if things go wrong at the bottom it would only add frustration to his final terror.

Practical jokes, superstitions, bends and wrecks were the main topics of conversation in the evening. Those who were good at it used to sing. Sammi, the young dresser, who possessed a good memory and a radio in his home, had the largest repertoire. I had a tiny transistor wireless, but, as usual, batteries were unobtainable and, surrounded as we were by mountains, it was only possible to get a whisper from the American station on Rhodes, whose programmes did not amuse the men. Economics, usually local, were discussed, but not politics. Of the Greeks they said: 'They are amusing; in Rhodes there are many cafés and lights and they sing. But it is very strange that when they talk, it is always about politics.' In a place where there was a timber yard Kemal looked up from his supper on the *Mandalinci* at the prosperous manager's house. 'There is a rich man,' he remarked, 'he has a radio and a jeep; but he is not as happy as we are tonight. We are friends eating together on this boat.'

On such occasions we all transferred to the *Mandalinci* for the meal. They cooked in the stern in a petrol tin half full of sand. While the brushwood flamed they made *pilaf* and *çorba* or fish soup. Afterwards they grilled fish steaks on skewers and threw delicacies such as lobsters and small octopus on to the embers. Senior men and guests sat on the roof of the cabin. The hatch was wiped down and placed in the centre, and on it enamel wash-hand basins containing semi-liquid courses and fruit. We all had wooden spoons, but shared the same tin mug for water and, on feast days, arak. The men ate below us by the fire, either out of the cooking-pot or from what remained in our bowls. Afterwards everything was washed in the sea and scoured with a fibrous variety of sponge whose skin, when fresh, is an excellent detergent. This was the normal routine, but with five visitors conditions were cramped, so when the anchorage was beautiful and uninhabited, as it usually was, Kasim would light a fire on shore and we would settle round it in a circle. Another topic of conversation was water: 'Tomorrow night we will stop at the bay after the Five Islands. There is a lot of honey in the woods, so that the water from the well tastes sweet.' Admittedly, some wells were brackish and very nasty, but I was more interested in the mention of honey than the quality of the water. They said that peasants (if one could be found, which was no easy task) would be delighted to exchange two kilograms of honey for one of fish. As luck would have it, that year some mysterious blight was said to have rendered bees unproductive. Looking at the decaying wooden hives fixed to the trees, it seemed more likely that they had not received sufficient encouragement from the bee-keepers. The fact remained that fish were a luxury, though the water teemed with them.

On this particular trip I was out of work. I was not a cameraman and could not fill my bottle, as Peter's compressor was in a parlous state, so its declining energies had to be reserved for essential tasks, such as noting deep wrecks. In the absence of antiquities the only useful job left to me was shooting fish. We carried rice, beans, vegetables, sugar, tea and rock-like bread, but fish was our source of protein. It would have been hard work feeding seventeen people regularly if Mustafa or Peter had not put in the odd hour with their guns. That it was possible at all showed the place to be a sportsman's paradise. In deep water big fish are unafraid and sit watching, but the men were too busy to catch them. Only Kasim occasionally borrowed a gun; mine was so weak that the arrow could not penetrate the thick skulls of giant groupers, although the blow stunned them. Kasim quickly slipped a string through their gills and tied them up. Small, fast-moving fish in relatively shallow water were more difficult to catch. *Keffal*, or grey mullet, swim near the surface, darting first in one direction then in another when they are chased. They never make for open sea and seldom for deep water, so they can eventually be cornered among rocks. *Mercan*, a kind of sea-bream, congregate in caves; once found, they are shot one after another. I have taken as many as twelve in one hole. Brown and yellow, or grey and brown parrot fish, which the Turks call *Iskariot*, nibble at rocks in groups. They have a leader who takes the decisions, and if he is shot the others panic and do silly things. Gilt-heads make good eating, but in my opinion they are the fastest and most difficult to catch.

Groupers deserve a book to themselves, and do indeed take up the best part of innumerable diving memoirs, for they are the sportsman's favourite target. Not being a sportsman, I neither like killing nor eating them. Their flesh is insipid and lacking in texture. Being deep-water rock fish, they are seldom caught by hook or net, which may account for the price they fetch in some places, including Turkey. Individually and collectively, they have great character. Since shooting is at a range of 2 metres (the length of the nylon on my gun), one is on more intimate terms with the catch than most hunters, and the expressions of these fish when shot are heartrending. If one is not wearing a bottle the chase follows a certain pattern. The grouper sits on the bottom and can sometimes be shot before he moves. If not, he swims off to his hole, changing colour like a chameleon: white on sand, green on weed and brown on rock. Once in his hole, it is foolish to shoot him, since both fish and arrow get stuck in the struggle and cannot be extricated. One has to swim back and watch from above, out of sight.

He will stick his head out to see whether the coast is clear; then he can be shot behind the skull. De Latil and Rivoire[1] have suggested that the grouper, or *orfus* as he is called in Turkish, was the *Anthias sacer*, described by classical authors as the diver's mascot. When he was seen on the bottom, through a *calefat*, divers knew that they were on good, safe ground. Certainly there are always groupers on sponge beds, and as I have said, their behaviour is friendly and fearless in deep waters.

On the Globe Wreck we had a grouper that measured at least 1·30 metres and must have weighed over 40 kilograms. I used to take pieces of bread, or break pina shells for him on my way down. He would swim up and open his mouth. At first it took me aback; I was uncertain whether to proffer the food on the palm of my hand, as to a horse, or stick it down his throat. It transpired that he expected the latter. He would dart off and eat it on the sand near the wreck, never sharing a crumb with his two wives, who kept a respectful distance behind him; Ataturk's matrimonial reforms would seem not to have reached territorial waters. At this time circumstances forced Peter to think of turning an honest penny by photography. He dreamed of the one great photo, the full-colour 'cover shot'. A woman feeding a grouper was apparently corny, having already been taken in an American aquarium. One day as I hovered upright over the wreck, busily drawing amphorae on the aluminium tablet which Rasim had given me, I heard groans and, looking up, was surprised to see Peter tearing his hair. Apparently the grouper had come up behind me, cocked his head over my shoulder and examined the drawing. Peter got us into the view-finder and shot twice. He had colour film in the camera, and on both occasions the flash bulb failed to work. It was too deep for the film to give a satisfactory monochrome. The grouper had been attracted by the shiny metal tablet, but the novelty soon wore off. In vain, day after day, we tried to make him repeat his performance. His tricks, however, were not exhausted: once when I forgot to feed him he sucked and nibbled at my hair, which was standing on end as I hung in my usual position above the wreck. I felt nothing, and it was Peter's howls of rage that drew my attention to what was happening. Again he had shot, and again the flash bulb had failed. He never got a photograph of that grouper. By this time, Kasim had a gun of his own, but we begged him to spare the grouper on the Globe Wreck. His subsequent messages always contained news of its health.

[1] Pierre de Latil and Jean Rivoire, *A la Recherche du Monde Marin*, Plon, 1956, p. 80.

When we were not at sea Peter and I worked in Bodrum respectively writing and drawing. Money was short. We longed for a day at sea, but couldn't afford a boat. Fish being scarce, we struck a bargain with Hussein and Ibrahim, who had touching confidence in our efficiency. They would take us for a jaunt to Kara Ada, in return for the fish we caught, and we would all visit the magic cave. When we reached the island the water was extremely cold. I had to get out once or twice to warm myself in the sun. After three unpleasant hours I caught only a few pounds of fish. My popularity, if not my reputation, was saved by finding two splendid and identical conch shells. Both men brought their twelve-year-old sons, who had been asking for horns for some time. Fishermen signalled to each other like tritons with the shells; every other aspect of their lives reminded one more of Bronze Age than classical times. The boys were delighted, but Peter, who had caught nothing, was in despair. Whereas I shot at anything edible, he was a real hunter when his blood was up, disdaining all but big game. As we were about to give up, he signalled that he had found something, then disappeared in 20 metres of water for well over a minute. He surfaced and submerged again in a flurry. The boys, who could swim, jumped in and the boat went towards him. Together they hauled a 30-kilogram grouper on to the boat. He had stalked it and shot skilfully, according to the submarine equivalent of the Queensberry Rules. The two families had enough to eat for days and honour was saved.

Gay but chilled, we made for the Hermaphrodite's cave. Mustafa, John and I had visited it the year before when hot, salty sulphurous water had issued from a rock tunnel into the sea, over pebbles which it coloured a grassy green. After wallowing in the heat we had maintained a nervous ribaldry on the homeward journey; John had said he had no wish to lose the beard he had taken such trouble to grow. This year, all six of us were filing into the cave in bathing-suits when groans swelled out of its blackest depths. Like an articulate conch, they formed themselves into words, repeating in Turkish and with unnerving emphasis, 'It is not a woman.' Somewhere in the recess, an ancient and naked invalid had been seeking health; his surprise at the intrusion certainly equalled our own. Shaken by his assertion, I flung myself down in 2 feet of water, flattened against the side of the tunnel and riveted a masked stare at the pebbles, while he shot past me, out to his clothes.

Reading Vitruvius, back in London, I found I had confused the two springs. It was the fountain of Salmacis in the bay outside the walls of Halicarnassos which was reputed to change a person's sex and, like many myths, there was a good foundation of fact. Savage men came to the town, drank in Greek civilization with its waters, and returned softened to their mountains. To my great surprise, the water at the Kara Ada spring was not as it had been the year before. For the first time in living memory it was running cold. This was confirmed by Sali, captain of the Cos ferry, who lived on the island; the Istanbul art critic had been mistaken about its being uninhabited. Sali's family occupied a derelict bathing establishment which dated from 'the time when there were Greeks'; cows were kept in the cubicles. It was very beautiful, but life must have been difficult, as there was no fresh water on the island. Like Bodrum itself, all drinking-water had to be rowed across from the Salmacis spring. The passage to Kara Ada was more exposed and took three-quarters of an hour at the best of times; how they managed in winter is a mystery. The seals I had been told about lived on the extreme easterly tip of the island; to my sorrow, I never met them. Bodrum had become for me a place of work, and visiting seals seemed as absurd as bolting one's breakfast in London in order to go and look at the Changing of the Guard.

In contrast with the Lebanese fishermen, no one from Bodrum would have dreamed of killing a seal. Children watching me eat sea-urchins, limpets and winkles would throw up their hands and shout 'Unclean!' Shell-fish never appeared in the village. The sponge men were more broad-minded than the villagers when it came to eating things from the sea, but even they had taboos. Like all Mediterraneans, sponge men would rather have starved than kill a dolphin; they still had the same regard as the ancients for these mammals.

The worst breach of custom I ever witnessed was committed by Dumas when he caught a turtle. By this time we were on the official expedition, which employed two Bodrum boats, including Kemal's. Dumas' motives were a mixture of hunger and bravado, but the men's reactions were unexpected. When he swam the turtle up to the dinghy, where it was laid on its back, they smiled with mirthless politeness, admitting that it must have been very difficult to catch. Back in camp, Dumas took it out of the boat, bored a neat little hole through the back of its shell and tied it up in shallow water with a length of nylon, remarking that it could be cooked once the gristly goat was finished. He was not over-enthusiastic about turtle meat himself, which even the Calypso cook had not been able to disguise during a long period in the Seychelles, when it was their only food. Peter had eaten turtle steaks somewhere in the Pacific and came out with quite a good recipe, while I thought I might be able to make a version of Mr Lusty's soup. The Turkish cook was adamant; he would take no part in the matter. We appealed to Kasim. Any man who could produce a good meal from sponges and pina shells must know what to do with turtles; but he shook his head. Gradually the truth emerged: it was unlucky even to see a turtle, and disastrous to touch or eat one. After a few days I was allowed to cut the nylon, and she swam off, with a little white knot in the shell above her tail.

CHAPTER 13

A Forfeit and Ruins – Consignment for a Byzantine Architect – More Building Materials Lost – Back to the Gallo-Romans

CRUISING in the Ceramic Gulf, life had followed a satisfying, if dull, routine; it became my ambition to try the big diving-suit. Mustafa had been allowed to use it, but I was suspect, the victim of a practical joke. The sponge men were unjustifiably impressed when they first saw us dive: being non-swimmers, they thought it dangerous, while envying our mobility and ability to work in currents which defeated them by pulling on their long hose. The respect was mutual, for they used apparatus that involved such things as 'squeezes', troubles which do not affect free-divers. Furthermore, their disregard for decompression was a constant danger. Despite the weight of helmet, lead boots and slabs of lead hung round the neck, the buoyancy of standard suits is difficult to control. Air has to be released by hitting a valve inside the helmet with one's head, which is why all divers wear little skull caps. In shallow water, where relative variations in pressure are considerable, the suits are hard to control. Mustafa was put down in 6 metres and promptly 'spread-eagled', that is to say the suit became so full of air that the limbs shot out rigid; probably the man on the compressor was purposely giving him too much air for the depth.

When Kemal offered to let me try, I determined to hit the valve continuously, especially as the crew were taking bets on my chances of success: bottles of arak all round if I succeeded, but I paid if I failed. With Peter's and Mustafa's help I got my briefing: I was to jump in, then throw my weight forward and bend, clutching my chest-leads and sponge bag; for one of the difficulties is that if a diver is thrown off balance he cannot right himself. Once I had control of buoyancy and reached the bottom, I was to push myself forwards on tiptoe, with my knees bent, as they did. I, too, dived in 6 metres. My one anxiety was that my arms might be too small for the watertight cuffs of the large suit; Kemal said it would be all right if the sleeves were hitched above the elbow, so they dressed me. I panicked when the helmet was screwed down, as I had forgotten to look for the valve, and being by that time incommunicado, I held firmly to Kemal and shook my head around until I found it. They helped me on to my feet and stood me on the bulwarks. Then I jumped, as I had so often seen them jump. When Dumas witnessed the performance later he winced; it was 'suicide' not to go down the steps, as jumping could dislocate one's neck. In the water I pounded at the valve and all was well, I walked along the bottom collecting things; unfortunately there were no good sponges. Visions of glorious arak and prospects of diving independent of a portable compressor so occupied my mind that I did not notice the costume was filling with water; it meant little, accustomed as I was to wet suits. Suddenly it dawned on me that one could drown inside standard apparatus. By now the water was up to my chest having got in through the cuffs, which were partly over the sleeves of my jersey. The crew would have to get me out at the double, but as they had seen me walking happily, they might not realize my predicament. Only one thing would make them act quickly: to 'spreadeagle', for that can burst the suit, which no sponge man would allow. I took my head off the valve and shot up; filled with air, the suit was uncontrollable, I floated face down in the water-filled helmet. They pulled me up to the boat, but by now I was too heavy either to move or to be lifted. Peter, in the water, tried to place my lead boots on the steps, but the suit being big, my feet had long since left them and were now in the knees. It seemed an age before the helmet was upright and I could breathe again. They were very nice about it, but I had lost face and soaked the inside of the suit, which was to be used at dawn next day.

I did not get a chance to buy arak until we returned to Ören, an inhabited place and the port of Keramos. The village was over a kilometre from the port, up a long, straight road. Kasim and Hussein were going to get bread and cigarettes, so I went with them. Heat blazed down, and none of us liked walking; however, it became apparent that the excursion would be interesting. Cliffs to the right were riddled with rock-cut tombs; the town itself was on high ground and surrounded by walls, some classical and some of earlier, polygonal, masonry. More walls encircled it on the hills behind, where there was also a fortress which looked Armenian or Seljuk and a very large aqueduct. People still lived in the ancient houses, to which they had added an upper storey. It was all quite unexpected; the *müdür*, or head man, joined us for a cup of tea: 'Oh yes,' he said, 'Antony gave this town to Cleopatra.' Seeing my interest, a villager volunteered to show us the 'old stones' and led off through bush and briar. Kasim and Hussein, though the walk could not have been to their taste, determined we should miss nothing; the remains were very extensive. We saw a cemetery of partly buried stone sarcophagi, a midden with exquisite but defaced Byzantine paintings, a church large enough to have been a cathedral, which had later been turned into baths. Were there 'drawings or letters', I asked (sculpture is loosely termed 'drawing'); our guide pointed to an inscription ANTO̲NEIN ΣΕΒΑΣΤO̲ΕΥΣ, then to others which were too long to remember, and I had no paper except the cover of a book. On the outskirts of the town he beckoned us to help him turn a large marble slab lying among building stones. On the back were symbols in bas-relief in perfect preservation: the head and shoulders of a humped bull, regardant, with a sun disk between its horns, a vase, a libation cup, a banner and fascis. We let it down again to await the attentions of a stonemason and set off at a jog trot, stopping now and then at altars carved with bulls' heads and garlands, female figures offering sacrifice and decorative libation cups. It became oppressive, there was nothing one could do except hope that archaeologists would see the stuff before it was too late. With relief we collected our bread and bottles and started the downhill trudge, stopping now and then for a glass of water or a handful of figs at hospitable gardens on the way. When I told Peter he snatched his camera and set off, but the sun was sinking and we were leaving at dawn.

The uninhabited, southern side of the Gulf also had ruins. Byzantine fortifications covered the Five Islands, and slightly to the west was a natural, enclosed harbour with classical landing quays and walls of polygonal stones round one of the precipitous headlands. In the middle of the citadel thus enclosed stood a gateway with a curved, monolithic lintel which looked like ninth-century B.C. Rhodian work. In the sea, below walls and cliff, lay hundreds of early amphorae; whether they had fallen as a result of earthquake, been deliberately thrown away, or cast as offerings from boats entering the harbour, is a mystery. Off the extremity of this point a *dolium* 1 metre in diameter lay half-buried on the sandy bottom. These huge round Ali-Baba jars are sometimes found on wrecks, but as yet their presence is unexplained and they have not been subject to the same serious study as amphorae.

In France I saw a wreck which, because badly preserved in shallow water, was of no interest to divers. It did, however, contain two *dolia* strengthened with lead armatures and stamped with the mark CERIDO, a name associated with an

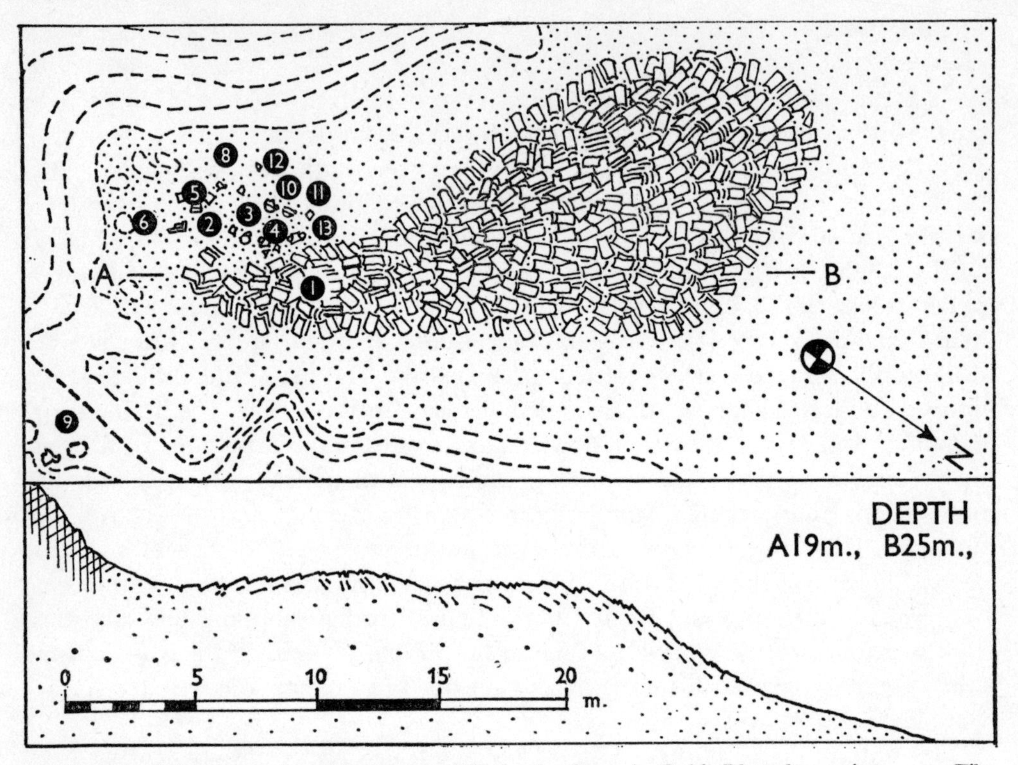

42. Wreck of the Byzantine tile-carrying ship in the Ceramic Gulf. Plan drawn in 1959. The numbers also refer to objects illustrated; with three exceptions: (2) *A shapeless lump of concretion*

Italian potter. Both jars had pottery lids. The diameter of the larger was 2·50 metres, and it must have weighed over a ton. Judging from the enormous sherds strewn about the bottom, there may have been further jars on board. On land they were used for making wine, but, being too large to move when full, is it unlikely that they were shipped as containers either supplementary or alternative to amphorae. As they were difficult to make and fire, they may have been exported to places where viticulture was being introduced but where the inhabitants did not yet know how to make the jars. A later wreck found in the River Hérault contained both amphorae and *dolia;* two of the latter can now be seen in the Museum at Agde. Of local manufacture, it is suggested that in that region they were used for storing grain and other foodstuffs. In themselves these suppositions point to another profitable line of marine research. Were all wreck

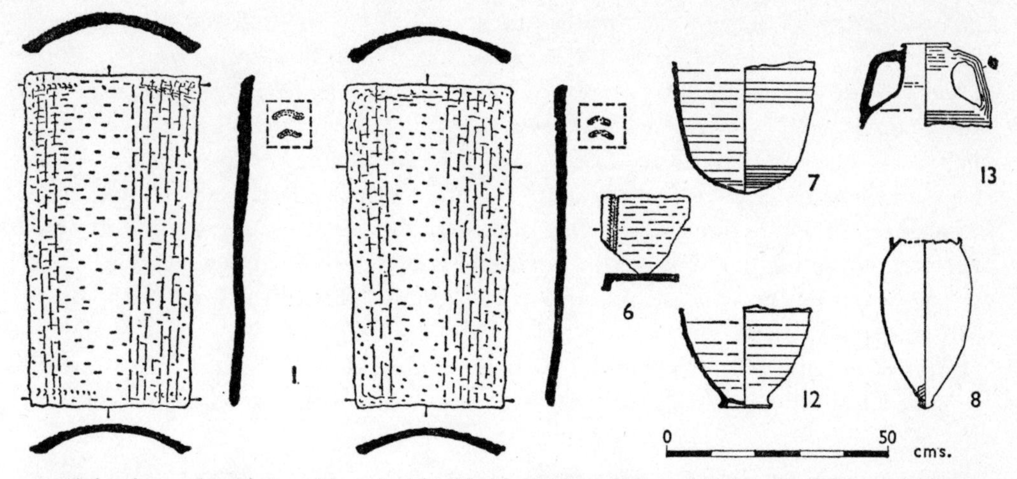

containing iron: the object could not be identified in field conditions. (4) Sherds of flat roof tiles and a casserole. (9) The base of an earlier, Cnidian amphora lodged in the nearby rocks; it probably came from another ship.

Above: *(1) Curved, Laconian tiles representative of the cargo. Indented chevron markings on inner surface. Coarse well-fired pinkish ware with some black and white grits. (6) Sherd of a flat roof tile from the galley; compare with those found on the Globe wreck (Figs. 33 and 34). (7), (8), (12) and (13) Amphorae from the galley. It has been suggested that No. 7 is sixth century, and No. 5 is fourth century.* *See also Fig. 43.*

cargoes to be catalogued on discovery, their analysis would add a great deal to our knowledge of trade in classical times.

To revert to our cruise in the Ceramic Gulf: its object was to make films, but Peter was the last man to insist on this point if it meant missing a wreck. An ox-hide ingot had once been found in the Gulf, but it was hopeless to start searching for another Bronze Age wreck without more exact information. Kemal said he knew of two sites: the first had amphorae and lay off one of the Five Islands. This was vague; we could only afford to spend a few hours in the area and that without bottles. Mustafa went off with the *Mandalinci*, while Peter and I searched. According to the sponge men, the Gulf was full of shark. Peter and Mustafa longed to film sharks with the sponge divers, whom apparently they had never been known to attack. Free-divers also had a sporting chance where sharks were concerned. The presence of these fish was, however, another matter during surface prospection, when we were not wearing bottles. Peter and I agreed to keep in sight of each other, but after half an hour, when no shark appeared, gave it up. There were broken amphorae, both Byzantine and Rhodian, at the base of the island, to corroborate Kemal's information. We strained our eyes at dark patches of Poseidon grass 30 metres below, and when they seemed likely to contain things dived 10–15 metres to have a closer look, but in vain. If we had had the time to search methodically, wearing bottles, we might have found the wreck. Without absolutely precise sitings, chances are small and prospection may be further delayed by weather. Kemal's daily choice of sponge bed was governed by the wind, which drove us from one side of the Gulf to the other with its every change.

Soon after this fruitless search, Kemal reminded us we were near one of Şeytan's sites. His directions were always accurate: we were to come out of such

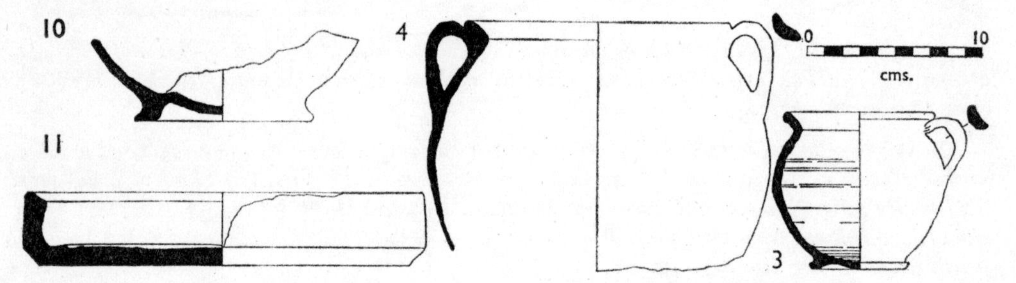

43. Cooking-pots from the galley of the tile-carrying wreck.

and such a bay, round a point, and before we got to a well in another bay there would be a rock 10 metres or so from a cliff. Between these points was a wreck in less than 20 metres of water. We found it on the first dive. A cargo of tiles, whatever their period, may sound dull, but in the context of trade and land sites it can be fascinating. This wreck was directly opposite and only an hour's sail from the large Byzantine church I had seen at Keramos[1]; where had its architect got his materials? Had the order of our visits been reversed, I might have compared these marked tiles with the sherds inside the roofless church. Search on land might also have produced their factory and clay pit. This cargo indicated a considerable output of tiles, and together with similar wrecks in the vicinity opened a new field of research.

[1] I am indebted to Mr R. W. Hutchinson for pointing out that Κεραμειδια is a colloquial name for tiles.

Quâ wreck, our tile carrier was a fine specimen. The ship had sunk into a cleft of rock which echoed the shape of the hull and, despite shallow water, sheltered it from wind and current. Surrounded as it was by rocks and covered by the sand they generated, its contents would be well preserved. The deep, curved bottom meant there would be more of the hull than on a flat site. The ground sloped steeply, making excavation easy: waste could be disposed of downhill, obviating the necessity of a peripheral trench. The load was not deranged in sinking: tiles had been stacked upright round the sides of the ship and lengthwise within it, nesting inside each other, convex side uppermost. The fact that the pile was indented to one side at the top of the slope was explained by flat roof tiles and utensils, denoting a galley (Fig. 41). Wrecks and contemporary representations of Roman and Byzantine ships both indicate that deck-houses were built aft and to port. The flat roof tiles were like those on the galley of the Globe Wreck and quite different from the main cargo. Piled to a height of over 2 metres, the visible load covered an area of 25 × 10 metres and must have contained roughly 5,000 tiles.

Of well-fired, pink paste containing large white grits, each tile was 75 centimetres long and marked on the inside with a double circumflex made by a workman's finger. Their shape, known as Laconian, means little, for similar tiles are used to this day, though I have never noticed them in that part of Turkey. A marble matrix, showing the regulation size for various shapes of tile, stands in the middle of the Agora at Athens as testimony to the importance given to this commodity. However, our ship was proved Byzantine by the pottery found in the galley. Miss Grace, of the American School of Archaeology in Athens, thought the amphora with ribbed handles [Fig. 42 (13)] could be of the fourth century, while the base (Fig. 42 (7)] might be sixth. The cup, cooking-pot, pan and bowl (Fig. 43) look very like twelfth-century crockery found in the Great Palace of Constantinople;[1] rough pottery does not change very much, but further research and certainly excavation would date this wreck precisely; suffice it to say here that it was Byzantine.

More to the point, is that the Izmir divers charted further tile wrecks, four of them round the corner, on the south side of the peninsula bounding the Ceramic Gulf. They found another near Chios; while in Greek waters off that same island, the British School of Athens' Underwater Expedition in 1954 reported a 'pile of

[1] David Talbot Rice, *The Great Palace of the Byzantine Emperors*, Second Report (Walker Trust), 1959, University of St Andrews.

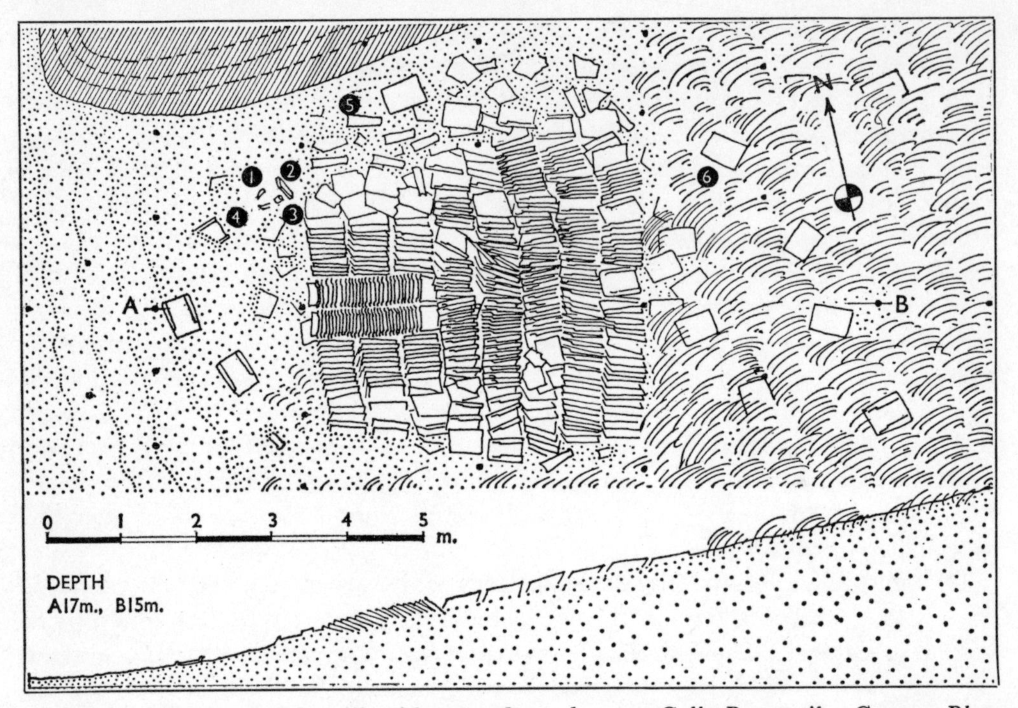

44. Wreck at Frioul near Marseille with cargo of second-century Gallo-Roman tiles. Compare Plate 28, which was taken from the west, looking along the central rows of upright tiles. The black dots on this plan indicate points where core-samples should be taken as a preliminary to accurate survey and excavation.

Key: (*1*) *Curved pinewood plank (see opposite).* (*2*) *Oblong black stone, about 40 centimetres.* (*3*) *Part of a timber 10 centimetres square in section; one end broken, the other cut.* (*4*) *Two small planks.* (*5*) *and* (*6*) *Flat and curved tiles representative of the cargo.*

tiles'. I had never come across tile-carrying ships in the west, but had not long to wait: when after my return to France I mentioned the Turkish cargoes to a Marseille diver he immediately told me of three wrecks. Two were off an island called Frioul, outside the port, and the third, farther up the coast. There are probably more, but local divers being interested in amphorae other cargoes get neglected.

The Frioul wrecks had been a couple of hundred metres apart; one disappeared when it was found that the tiles were serviceable. A concession to excavate the second, which was virgin, was given to the finders, two young business men who kindly allowed me to look at it. The ship had been small, or so it appeared from the visible remains, and this was borne out from reports of its neighbour, whose cargo was already removed. In only 18 metres of water its lie resembled the Byzantine ship; it, too, was on sloping sand, in a shallower basin of rock. Most of the tiles were flat, and dated by Monsieur Jean Chauffin, from a section of their rim, as being of a Gallo-Roman shape of the second century. One of the tiles from the sister ship turned up in Marseille, and I was able to compare the specimens, which were identical in paste, markings and size. Why had these two ships of similar cargo sunk within such a short distance of each other? I suppose one will never know whether they were tied together, but it should be possible, on land, to trace the tile factory and the distribution of its products.

As on the Byzantine ship, the cargo had been carefully stowed and was hardly deranged in sinking. Two upright rows were backed by five rows on their sides and flanked by three others (Fig. 44 and Plate 28). A relatively small quantity of pantiles were scattered around the edges of the main pile; they may have lined the sides of the ship, as on the Turkish wreck. I had only one dive on the site, but the pattern was so clearly defined that, once the size of sample tiles was checked against the number of rows and the overall measurements, it was not difficult to reconstruct the pile. I would stress again that these hasty sketch plans are not put forward as substitutes for proper surveys, which would have to be produced before serious, organized excavation. However, as no such

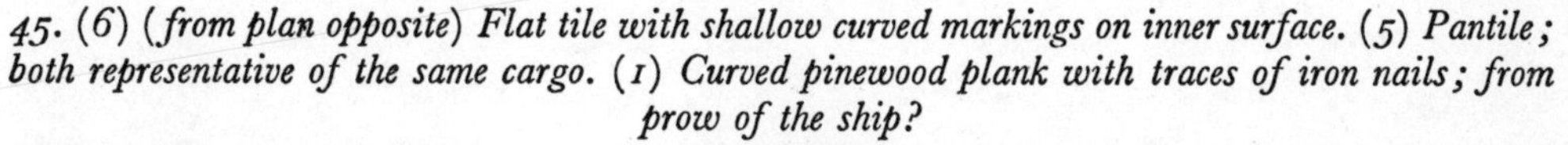

45. (6) (from plan opposite) Flat tile with shallow curved markings on inner surface. (5) Pantile; both representative of the same cargo. (1) Curved pinewood plank with traces of iron nails; from prow of the ship?

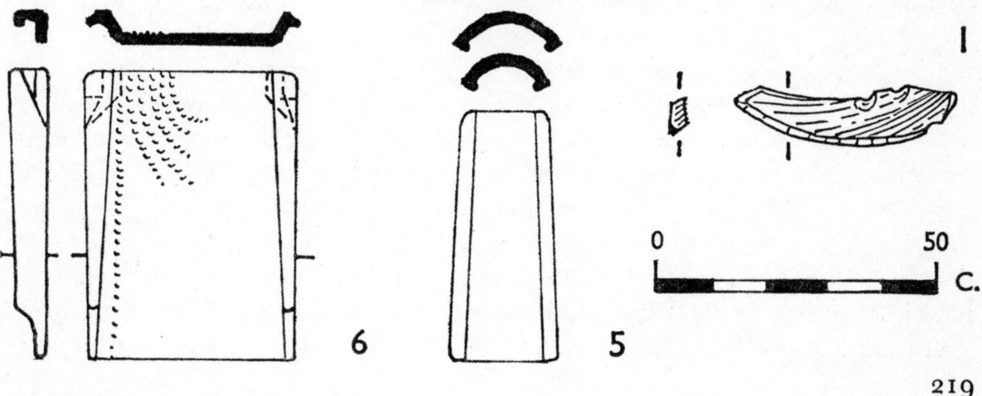

surveys exist as yet, even the notes made by a traveller give some standard of comparison.

Various suggestions have been made as to how flat tiles were placed on roofs. Their notched ends and slightly tapering shape allow them to fit into each other lengthwise. I have also noticed that they fit very well when placed in parallel rows: one row with the edges facing upwards and the next row upside down and overlapping. If such a system were used it would explain the small percentage of pantiles to flat tiles on this particular cargo; the former being required only to cover the crest of the roof. Soon after drawing the Marseille tiles, I saw identical specimens lining Roman water cisterns on the site of the Temple of Poseidon at Isthmia, near Corinth; even the curved markings were the same. They are, of course, a common shape, but the water cisterns proved that their use in building was not confined to roofs.

The axis of this Frioul cargo was very apparent; so I moved sand at the part which I supposed to be the bows. Sure enough there was a curved piece of planking, such as one might expect to find at the prow. There was also an oblong, black stone which was not local. As far as I could ascertain, no pottery had been found on this or its sister ship. A cup or a water-jar, for instance, would be easier to date than the tiles themselves. Sherds or coins may yet emerge in the course of excavation. Regarding sherds, it is worth mentioning another peculiarity of wreck excavation which land archaeologists find difficult to grasp, because it results from submarine gravitation, as distinct from the laws they know. If a sherd is found underwater a competent diver should be able to collect others so that the pot can be reconstructed. On land, unless there are clear indications that a pot broke after structural collapse, the chances are that the fragments have been thrown away and dispersed. Underwater, breakages are caused by the way the ship has sunk; if the genesis of the wreck-formation is understood and also the local water movements, a good diver will know where to look for the remains of an object. I have heard Dumas ask land technicians if they have all the sherds from a certain underwater pot; if they said 'no' he would go and get the remainder. On the other hand, I have never heard anyone ask him to do this, because the implications of his question were not appreciated.

Where the tiles themselves are concerned, there is no question of looking for sherds, because they are usually unbroken. As a diver, one reads with some surprise in Monsieur Jean Chauffin's classification of Gallo-Roman tiles[1] that he had

[1] Jean Chauffin, 'Tuiles Gallo-Romaines du Bas Dauphiné', *Gallia*, Vol. XIV, 1956, pp. 80–8.

to collect two thousand sherds in order to reconstruct one tile; while in the sea, not so far away, there were at least three ship-loads of unbroken specimens, probably 1,500 in the Frioul cargo alone. Moreover, tiles may be difficult to date on land, but if excavated by professionals every ship should produce enough evidence to date its cargo to within a year or so. In one dive on this as yet untouched Frioul tile carrier no datable object was found, but this is exceptional. Even a cursory survey of tile carriers would produce, at the present moment, as much evidence about the building trade in ancient times as years of work on land.

This is an ecological problem; to divers the essence of marine archaeology remains: the ships themselves and all that pertains to their build and methods of navigation. Evidence of ships' structure is buried beneath a colossal pile of cargo, sand and concretions which takes years to excavate. From experience we know that this evidence exists, but to extract it there must be a revolution in the way we dig. This kind of revolution has already taken place on land, but submarine excavation is still in an experimental stage. The potential information contained in a wreck-formation can, in practice, be assessed only by examining sites where the surface cargo has already been salvaged and where, in consequence, at least some of the wooden parts of the structure have become easy of access. Needless to say, on sites where the surface layers have been removed, all clues as to the rigging, not to mention the superstructure of the ship, will have been destroyed. All the same, these remains convince us that the problem is one of method: the evidence was there.

PART VI

ROMAN WOOD UNDER THE SEA-BED

I conceived a passion for business. I will not keep you a moment—I built five ships, got a cargo of wine—which was worth its weight in gold at the time—and sent them to Rome. You may think it was a put up job: every one was wrecked, truth and no fairy tales. Neptune gulped down thirty million in one day. Do you think I lost heart? Lord, no, I no more tasted my loss than if nothing had happened. I built some more, bigger, better and more expensive, so that no one could say I was not a brave man. You know, a huge ship has a certain security about her. I got another cargo of wine, bacon, beans, perfumes and slaves. Fortunata did a noble thing at that time; she sold all her jewellery and all her clothes, and put a hundred gold pieces into my hand. They were the leaven of my fortune. What God wishes soon happens. I made a clear ten million on the voyage. I at once bought up all the estates which had belonged to my patron. I built a house, and bought slaves and cattle: whatever I touched grew like a honey-comb. When I came to have more than the whole revenues of my own country, I threw up the game: I retired from active work and began to finance freed men.[1]

[1] Petronius, *Satyricon*, Heseltine, Loeb ed., p. 151.

CHAPTER 14

'Round' Ships – Their Joinery – Roman Hulls Found on Land – Pioneer Work at the Congloué

TRIMALCHIO, in either feasting or financial speculation, is larger than life; I would like to imagine I had visited his lost ships. With amphora-carrying wrecks there is always a possibility of finding the owner. This was the case at both Anthéor and the Grand Congloué, where the merchants were traced through stamps on the jars. However, whether our interest is aroused more by history or by excavation technique, there comes a point when the character of the ships themselves has to be defined and how they differ from the ships we know. At the present stage definition is dangerous, but it is a risk which must be taken.

From an academic point of view, it is true to say that we have no knowledge of pre-Renaissance ships. Wrecks have not yet provided much exact evidence about structure; nor will they until there is a revolution in excavation method. Some wooden elements, however, have been salvaged. Admittedly they are out of context, but they can be compared with each other and with parts of ships that have been found on land. Lastly, there is the experience of Mediterranean divers, who have, over the past twenty years, salvaged many classical cargoes; the views they have formed have never been published. A rough assessment of the general character of ancient ships, based on the latter, most recent, sources of information is therefore a calculated risk.

Primitive boats, such as coracles, are made by stretching skins over light framework while others are hollowed out of tree-trunks. Modern ships are essentially skeletons, with planks or metal nailed over them. Amphora-carriers were conceived on totally different principles: they were shells. Inside a walnut are divisions weaker than the shell itself, and so, by analogy, is the framework within this type of ship. The frailest ribs and flimsiest keel add rigidity, in length and breadth, to a unit made out of heavy planks 'welded' edge to edge. There was

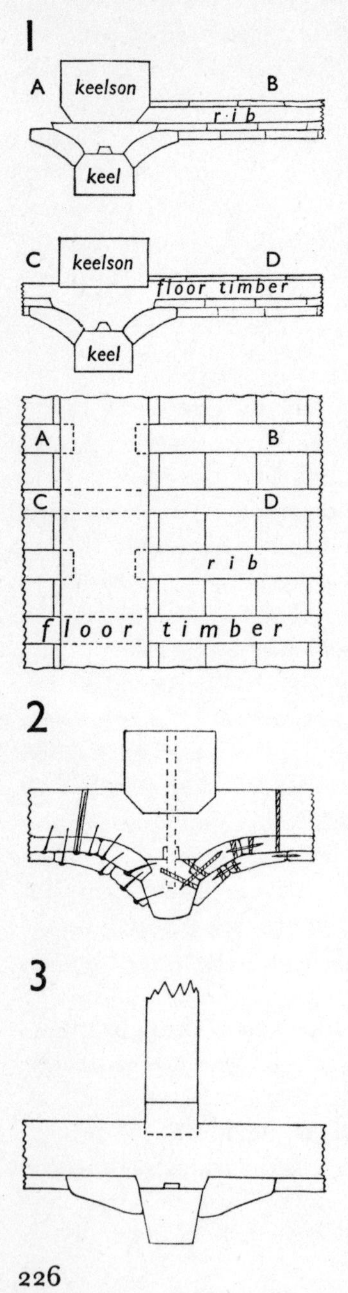

no question of constructing a skeleton of keel and ribs, such as can be seen in any little shipyard today. Indeed, the keel proper, and sometimes the outer, parallel keels (which protected the bilge or bottom of these ships when stranded), were jointed on to the planks themselves. In other words, they were not keel-built. Keel and planks are one unit, the ribs are laid within it and the junction of the keel with the ribs is sometimes covered with a floor timber (Fig. 46). It is difficult to visualize this process of construction and even harder to understand how these hulls could have been repaired. If part of the 'skin' of a keel-built ship is damaged the plank or metal sheet is removed and another nailed on to the skeleton in its place. If, on the other hand, a plank that is joined to its neighbours by tongues of wood [secured through the planks at either side by treenails, see Fig. 46 (2)] is damaged, how can it be replaced? This is one of the mysteries of classical construction which will be solved when we find a repaired hull.

In a Roman ship of 70 × 20 metres (the Dome of St Paul's is 112 metres from the ground and the

46. Three Roman keels: (1) Cap Drammont wreck. Section a–b taken through a rib and c–d through a floor timber, as shown on plan. (2) 'Titan' *or Ile du Levant wreck. Section through keel, keelson and floor timber. Copper nails joining the garboard filling pieces and planks to keel and floor timber are shown in black on the left. The edge-to-edge joinery by means of wooden tenons and treenails is shown (shaded) to the right. (3) Second Nemi ship: section through keel, floor timber and a relatively small keelson bearing an upright post. Of these three wrecks, only the Nemi hull was lead plated. Compare Congloué keel Fig. 48 (4) and Plate 25.*

Drawings based on material published respectively by: P. Tailliez, Office Français des Recherches Scientifiques, and Guido Ucelli, op. cit.

Panthéon in Paris 80 metres) the ribs and keel are, respectively, only about 16 and 20 centimetres wide. This is judging from the Nemi ships (Fig. 47). From its enormous cargo, the ship wrecked at the Grand Congloué must also have been about 60 metres long, but its ribs and keel were even smaller than at Nemi, measuring only 8 and 16 centimetres (Fig. 49). The ships wrecked at Drammont and Anthéor (Appendix) carried smaller cargoes, though there is no great variation in the size of their wooden parts. Unfortunately the exact length of these wrecks was never established, and the point along the length of the keel from

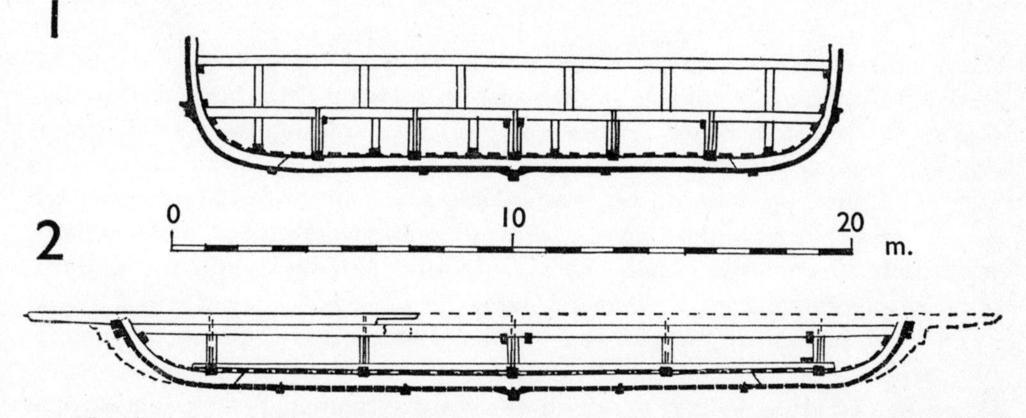

47. The Nemi ships. Neither of these transverse sections is absolutely medial; the maximum width of the second ship is shown by a broken line. Wood cut across the grain shown in solid black.
Key: (*1*) *A partial reconstruction; only the lower parts were* in situ. (*2*) *Note the timber which projected above the water-line. These timbers carried a passage-way round the ship and aft, platforms for the steering-oars* (*as on the bas-relief of a warship at Lyndos in Rhodes*).

which samples of wood were raised is not on record. These shell-like Roman merchantmen were known as 'round' ships, as distinct from long, fast warships propelled by oars. No warship has been found as yet, for reasons already stated, so we do not know whether the details of their joinery differed from 'round' ships.

The rare divers who have dug on hulls (for the majority see only the amphorae on top) have a clear, if inarticulate, idea of the size of these ships. From documentary evidence the most persuasive estimate has been made by Lionel Casson:[1] his text comes from Lucian's *Navigium*, wherein the *Isis*, a Roman grain-carrying

[1] Lionel Casson, 'The Isis and her Voyage', *American Philological Association; Transactions and Proceedings*, Vol. 81, No. I, p. 43, 1950; Lucian, *Navigium* V.

ship, is described. Lucian's figures are in cubits, which can be translated roughly as: length 60 metres, beam 15 metres, deck to keel 14 metres. However, the capacity of a ship depends on her build and length of keel. Casson judges that, from Roman pictures of ships, their proportions were almost the same as a Venetian man-of-war of the sixteenth century. He therefore bases the length of keel on this known type of vessel and applies the measurements to the formula which gives the unladen tonnage of a sailing ship:

$$\frac{\text{Length of keel} \times \text{Beam} \times 1/2 \text{ beam}}{94}$$

which makes the *Isis* 1,228 tons. He points out that this tonnage was not exceeded until the great clippers of the nineteenth century. Earlier naval archaeologists, be it noted, made calculations from the same figures and arrived at tonnages varying between 250 and 3,500. The point at issue is: can we settle this type of question by underwater investigation of ancient hulls? My own view is that it could be done in the long run, if investigations were carried out by experts, as on land. A conclusive answer is as yet impossible; all one can do is to set down personal experience and let the reader judge for himself.

The way planks are seamed in these shell-like hulls is a miracle of joinery, comparable with the best furniture craftsmanship of the eighteenth century. It is even misleading to have to refer to the wood as 'planking', a word associated with rough carpentry or clinker-building, where planks are nailed. In Greek and Roman ships tenons, or tongues of wood, sticking half into one plank and half into the next, each kept in place by a wooden dowel running through joint and plank, are arranged in asymmetric groups of twos and threes. Seen from the side, the mortise slots are alternately high and low along the edge of a plank [Fig. 48 (3)]. The intervals of joinery being irregular, each has to be measured separately, and it is a hard job to analyse and draw even two such planks, and to continue this across a section of hull would be a stern intellectual exercise. The ship is curved, and the curve changes from one portion to another, so the joinery has to vary accordingly. I have never been called upon to draw a large section of hull, but I have seen planks and joints from the same part of a single ship where each component had a subtle but significant difference in size.

Divers who have practical experience of digging deeply into ancient wrecks know all this. A man who has seen three layers of amphorae above timbers, as in M. Girault's excellent photograph of the trench cut, on Dumas' suggestion, through the hull of the Drammont wreck, will have a clear impression of the section of a ship thus loaded (Plate 22). Most divers do not realize the importance of their own experience: they tend to regard archaeologists as omniscient and never commit their own observations to paper. Luckily, seamed construction is also known from land remains: two portions of hulls have been found, one in London when the foundations were being dug for County Hall[1] and the other, 'Caesar's Galley' in Marseille, in the mud of the Lacydon, or ancient harbour.[2] The third and most important source of information is the Nemi Ships.[3]

Under Mussolini's Government the level of Lake Nemi was lowered so that two large ships could be recovered (Fig. 47). They were almost perfectly preserved in fresh-water mud, and eventually housed in a museum built on the shores of the lake. It is one of my sorrows that I never saw these hulls and the elaborate fittings from their superstructure before they were wantonly destroyed at the order of a German officer during the last war. I comfort myself that they would not have meant so much to me at that time. As documents, they are immortalized in Ucelli's book. I bought a copy at Nemi, in the empty museum that still contains a few interesting relics and the metal frames which once held the ships.[4] The guardian described the book as a '*capo lavoro*'. He was right, for every nail and structural component has been analysed and recorded and the work is invaluable for comparative study.

It used to be thought that the Nemi 'barges' were atypical, but underwater excavation shows their construction to be similar to merchantmen of the same period. Caligula may have ordered these as pleasure barges, but he did so in an age when individual craftsmanship and skills were handed down from father to son and a conscious conception of 'functionalism' was unknown. A ship was a ship, and there was only one way of building it. It is possible that the shell-type of construction derived from Egypt; certainly it was practised in Greece and, it has been suggested, passed thence to Rome. The Aphrodito Papyri[5] prove that the

[1] *London in Roman Times*, London Museum, Cat. No. 3.

[2] *Gallia*, Vol. XVI, 1958, Fascicule 1, p. 11 and Fig. 9.

[3] Guido Ucelli, *Le Navi di Nemi*, Libreria dello Stato, Rome, 1950.

[4] The Nemi Museum has been restored and now contains large-scale models of the ships; when I was there, there were only the iron frames that had supported the burnt originals.

[5] The study of papyri in the late ninteenth century threw light on Graeco–Roman Egypt and the hereditary system whereby a son succeeded to the public office held by his father. This system became, if anything, stricter under the Byzantines and was continued by the Arabs. The 'Aphrodito Papyri' were found in 1901 at a village in upper Egypt called Aphrodito in ancient

Byzantine–Greek shipwrights of Alexandria were a hereditary guild which continued to practise traditional skills under their Arab masters after the seventh century.

That the Nemi ships were constructed like seagoing merchantmen is indicated by their leading. The wood of many seagoing ships in the Mediterranean was protected from the burrowing of xylophagous worms, or teredos, by lead sheeting below the water-line. No such animals exist in sweet water, but these lake ships are still lead plated. It did not occur to the workmen to do otherwise. The structural components of the Nemi ships, whether wood, nails or other metal parts, are repeated on amphorae-carrying wrecks with only the tiniest variations, and their anchors are also the same. Elaborate, decorative features in the superstructure of the Nemi 'barges' differ, probably, only in degree from big passenger-carrying ships of the time. Roof and floor tiles, like those used on land, are found on all large Mediterranean wrecks, also quantities of lead piping for either pumps or plumbing. A pretty little mosaic in a portable frame recently found by Barnier in the sea near Cannes may come from a wreck. Why not? If the living-quarters in such workaday ships were tiled, surely it is reasonable to assume that luxury liners of the period could have mosaics? Within the Roman Empire the ruling class was peripatetic.

The sources already mentioned and the evidence of wrecks both suggest that 'round', shell ships persisted at least from Greek to Byzantine times, and that the Arabs adopted Byzantine construction for their Mediterranean fleet (as they continued to use the hereditary guilds of shipbuilders). From Julius Caesar's comments on the Veneti ships, quoted in the chapter on anchors, one can also hazard a guess that the deeper ships, clinker-built on a skeletal frame, were gradually introduced into the Mediterranean from the north.

It would be presumptuous to pass straight from these generalizations to a discussion of details of the hull which lies under the Grand Congloué. There the excavation itself is important. It is difficult to convey quite how much my arrival at the site mattered to me. I spent years trying to get there, and only reached the best-known wreck in the world in 1960 on my way back from Turkey. It was through Cousteau's dog that I got my first invitation. In 1955, when I was diving in Crete, the *Calypso* touched in at Heraclion. The big three, Cousteau,

---

times. These papyri, in both Arabic and Greek, are mostly in the British Museum and the rest in Heidelberg, Strasbourg and Russia. They consist of letters and accounts which give important details concerning the organization of the Navy under the early Caliphate.

Dumas and Tailliez, were not on board, but the crew did the honours, and after a few glasses of Samian wine we were shown radar equipment, the observation chamber under the bows, the precision crane that can flick ash from a cigarette, and most complicated cameras. Not having much grasp of mechanics, I returned to deck, where I soon discerned a figure in the darkness. It was Falco, one of the chief divers, crouched over a prostrate, black dog.

'He won't last till we get to the vet in Athens.'

'What's the matter and what sort of dog is it?'

'Something to do with his head and stomach. He's a Portuguese diving dog. The fishermen use them. . . .' (After dynamiting one supposes.)

'If only Madame Cousteau were here she would do something.'

We took the dog to the light: there was no need to be a vet to diagnose canker and worms.

First aid was simple, but the dazzling array of drugs in the ship's medicine chest did not include a mild antiseptic. Next morning I returned with a bottle of T.C.P. The dog, a model patient, not only survived until he reached professional hands in Athens but still enjoys a tax-free life in Monaco. During these visits to the ship, the crew told me they would be in the Vieux Port at Marseille when I passed through on the way home and could arrange for me to be taken to the Congloué, which was then in the last stages of Cousteau's excavation, before Monsieur Yves Girault took over. They were as good as their word, but the Mistral blew when I reached Marseille and I had a streaming cold. The next time I tried there was not only a mistral but also snow, and so it went on. In 1960 Monsieur Girault, who then held the concession, was, in Sir Mortimer Wheeler's phrase, 'still digging'.

Nearly every author writing about diving in the Mediterranean gives an account of his personal experience as a visitor at the Grand Congloué. In the *Journal de Bord de Marcus Sestius*, Ferdinand Lallemand, who worked there as a diver and field archaeologist, freely reconstructs, from the data found on the wreck, the history of the ship and the log of its last journey. As I write, the long-awaited, authoritative report on this dig (or should one say 'suck'?) by the archaeologist in charge is in the course of publication.[1] But it was the initial publicity which the work received, through Cousteau, that made the excavation a test case in the history of submarine archaeology.

[1] M. Benoît's *L'Epave du Grand Congloué* has been published since the completion of my text; see Bibliography.

The Congloué was the first virgin wreck of any importance to be excavated exclusively by modern methods. The ships at Mahdia and Anticythera were originally tackled by sponge men using standard apparatus. Frédéric Dumas heard of the Congloué from a professional diver called Christiani, who had been brought for treatment to the French Navy's Underwater Research Station (where Dumas worked) suffering from a bad bend. His life was saved, and one day he said, 'You know, Dumas, we divers never tell our secrets, but I won't be able to go down again and I want to tell you mine.' He described, among other things, a colony of lobsters living in 'old jars'. Dumas flared a wreck and later went to dive on the spot with Cousteau. It was Cousteau who actually found the site. As his air supply was running out he saw dishes scattered around and amphorae necks emerging from a tumulus. Before surfacing he only had time to grab three stacked cups (which turned out to be Campanian) and a corroded, bronze hook. In 1952 he organized a team of aqualung divers to excavate the site, with Monsieur F. M. Benoît of the Boreli Museum at Marseille as the archaeologist in charge.

It would be unpardonable to make a detailed criticism of pioneer work; however, in this case circumstances force an assessment. For one thing, the excavation still continues, but, more important, in the early days it received world-wide publicity. This was at a time when it was impossible for the excavators to foresee what they would find or to analyse problems which confronted them for the first time in history. Times have changed, but the record of what can now be regarded as their mistakes has been accepted by a generation of non-diving archaeologists. The mistakes are taken for the inevitable limitations of underwater excavation. It seems obvious, now, that to start digging a hole in the middle of a wreck would be fatal. As we have seen, the deeper it goes into the cargo, the more the sand falls back, is blown from one side to the other, or dumped on another part of the ship; visibility is lost and chaos ensues. Dumas, through his experience at the Congloué and elsewhere, has now evolved a more rational method of excavation. However, the danger of the early misunderstandings being perpetuated remains, for the Congloué hoard is so important that scholars will visit Marseille, read all the relevant documents and continue to study that part of the cargo associated with their own speciality. Questions will arise which could have been answered if excavation had been systematic, and negative results will reflect on underwater archaeology in general.

Before describing the things I saw in 1960, the existing reports have to be examined. These can be reduced to two accounts: the first by Cousteau himself,[1] and the second, 'Premiers Résultats des Recherches Sous-Marines',[2] the most recent conclusions by the archaeologist in charge. Respectively, they summarize the equipment and technique that was used, and the type of information which, in the opinion of a non-diving archaeologist, could be culled from a wreck.

Let us first examine Cousteau's article: reading it again, after many years, one is astounded by his foresight and resourcefulness in matters pertaining to underwater machinery. In practice, little has been added to the equipment he devised for that first experiment; he also made the equipment work. The air-lift is still a dangerous instrument for archaeological purposes even in expert hands, but when he wrote, it was being used for the first time on this type of work:

> Without going into the long struggle Dumas and I had with the theory and performance of undersea suction pumps, debating whether they would simply flatten their nozzles, or gallop away with their operator like a Loch Ness monster, I shall simply record that this pump worked.

The terrifying force had to be tamed, the loss of small finds avoided by adding a strainer or directing the discharge on to the deck of the ship. Suitable baskets and balloons for lifting heavy objects all had to be developed. The limit of a diver's time at the bottom was marked by an alarm clock, with a gun which he could hear substituted for a bell. On the island rock face, above the wreck, a base for shelter, equipment, generators and compressors was built with the help of the Army. A television camera, complete with telephone and floodlights, was used for the first time, and distinguished visitors viewed the work from the surface. As they crowded round the screen while a diver took the camera down, an engineer snatched the hand-mike and shouted:

> 'Delmas! Delmas, what are you doing? Correct your focus.' 30 metres down, Delmas heard this as the voice of Poseidon, for there was a loud speaker in the camera case. The watchers on the surface saw the images grow sharper.

Television was found to work better than a camera in the reduced submarine light. Lamps were only used to cast shadows, in order to make the otherwise clear picture less flat. Cousteau writes:

> For the archaeologists, the new window on the sea was a revelation. Staid specialists, they could sit in warmth and dry comfort and watch an underwater workshop.

[1] J.-Y. Cousteau, *National Geographic Magazine*, January 1954.
[2] M. F. Benoît, *Premiers Résultats des Fouilles Sous-Marines*, Imprimerie Nationale, Paris, 1960.

Their minds were clear, they could consult each other and direct the work by telephone.

In addition to these inventions, Cousteau used the resources of the Services, various scientific institutions and laboratories, and such ancillary scientists as geologists and biologists.

Much has been written since then by good amateur divers after more or less respectable excavations, but none of their accounts describe such ingenious and elaborate equipment as Cousteau produced for this initial experiment. Reading later reports, one is tempted to conclude that their common merit consists in the invention of a new literary form: a Lament prefacing a brief Epic. Mechanical difficulties are set forth at length and with deep feeling, before the description of a gallant little band extracting amphorae and the occasional scrap of information from a wreck. Often, attracted by a title such as 'The Frogman Club of San Blank Wrests Secrets of World's Oldest Wine Merchant from 50 metre Argosy', I have ploughed through these dispiriting accounts with the help of a dictionary. One extreme case began and ended with a heart-rending lament on the non-performance of the air-lift; the machine had belched, vomited, refused to suck, lashed out furiously at its masters, and finally conked. These antics covered several pages and ended abruptly without mention of the cargo.

Cousteau is a many-sided genius, to whom, as divers, we owe a great deal. This said, it would be preferable to pass over his remarks on archaeology, printed in 1954. Unfortunately, until M. Benoît's full report is published, they remain the only available statement on the Grand Congloué, and are found in most archaeological libraries, where they almost convince readers that submarine excavation is impractical. In the absence of any other account, these statements stuck in my own mind up to the time I dived on the site myself.

The first mystery in Cousteau's account concerns lead sheeting. For reasons impossible to fathom, Cousteau repeatedly asserts that the ship, including the decks, was covered with lead:

> After a year's work we estimate that there were twenty tons of lead on the Delian Argosy. *The entire hull and decks were covered with lead plating* [the italics are mine].

Byzantine records[1] specifically mention the use of lead plating below the water-line, where it was needed to protect the wood from burrowing molluscs. Con-

[1] Ali Mohamed Fahmy, *Muslim Sea Power in the Eastern Mediterranean from the 7th to the 12th Centuries*, Alexandria, 1950, p. 85.

stantine Porphyrogenitus says that: One hundred and ten lead sheets were required to plate twenty ships. This reference is worth quoting, as there is every reason to suppose that the Byzantines inherited, unchanged, the techniques of Greek shipyards. The Nemi ships were also lead-plated below the water-line, but not the decks. To cover decks with lead would not only be useless and clumsy, but in hot sun also very uncomfortable for the feet. That Cousteau's statement is wrong is quite unimportant, but his reasons for making it raise doubts. What kind of archaeological records were being kept? How did they know that the leaded planks they had seen were from the deck and not the hull? Years have passed and no plans, measured drawings or any other kind of underwater record have been forthcoming. According to those who have worked on the site from the beginning, no underwater draughtsman has ever been present.

In another controversial passage he says:

> In the same ship were found two types of amphorae which they (archaeologists) had previously attributed to different ages.

Archaeologists were far from agreeing with this assumption that the jars were henceforth proved to be contemporary. At an early date drawings of the various types of amphorae were sent for classification to the accepted authority, Miss Virginia Grace, of the American School of Archaeology in Athens. She never wavered in her diagnosis. In 1958, knowing that I had dived on French wrecks, she asked me whether I had ever actually seen the Congloué site (at that time I had not):

'I can't believe that both types of amphorae were carried on the same boat. Where exactly were the older ones found in relation to the others and to the Campanian pottery? Were they above or below the rest of the cargo? Or were they alongside? There must have been two wrecks.'

Again, where were the records that would have settled this question? Had no diver, on finding jars of a new shape, noted that they were at the bottom of a certain hole from which such-and-such objects had already been extracted?

Even among divers who have known the site for years, the lie of the ship is still in dispute. Before excavating any wreck, it is now realized that the first step should be to assess the axis of the ship below the sand and surface cargo. This is not easy, but it can be done by a diver who has experience of ancient wrecks, or even by mechanical means. If no attempt is made to establish the axis the excavation grinds on blindly. In theory, if absolutely accurate records were kept, the surface finds, rigging and so on could be related to the hull of the ship after the excavation was over. In practice, this is asking too much of any plans and, furthermore, it would eliminate the possibility of cross-checking. Even on land, an archaeologist will examine a *tell* before he puts down a trench, assessing the site from the point of view of defence and water supply, and try to estimate, for instance, the position of the main gates. He will certainly not start digging into it in a haphazard way.

Cousteau's article is illustrated by reconstructions drawn later, presumably from verbal descriptions, showing the ship pointing upwards towards the cliff face. In France I have seen a coloured, almost playful version, in which the wreck practically climbs the cliff. In 1954 there was no doubt in Cousteau's mind on this point:

> Marcus Sestius' freighter sank upright, landing keel down on a sloping shelf of rock, the pedestal of the Grand Congloué. Her stern, counter and captain's house probably crumpled away on the way to the bottom.

How does he know? Did they find tiles?

> She rested with her bow pointing back towards the sacred Isle of Apollo and her stern framed in a wide recess almost designed to fill her lines. The depth at her stern was 37 metres and the ship fell away at a 20° angle towards a depth of 47 metres at the bow.

Unfortunately he does not say how he arrived at this conclusion. If he was right, then there may well have been two ships, one in the position he describes and one where the planking lies today. At this stage, who can tell? Lastly there is mention of the keel:

> On the 15th of May 1953 we reached the keel of the Argosy. It is a complicated structure of oak 50 centimetres wide by 75 centimetres high, indicating a ship larger than we had previously dreamed.

Imagination boggles, for this huge lump of wood does not correspond to the size of any of the ancient keels we know, nor to Monsieur Benoît's later description of the Congloué keel itself,[1] or indeed to another portion of the same keel which I found there [Plate 25 and Fig. 48 (4)]. The piece of wood Cousteau mentions must have been raised. Perhaps the mystery will be resolved when Monsieur Benoît's complete report on the Congloué appears and we can see his interpretation together with the drawing.

[1] Ferdinand Benoît, 'Une Nouvelle Etape de l'Archéologie: Les Recherches Sous-Marines', *L'Erma di Bretscheider*, Vol. I, 1961.

One could go on questioning Cousteau's statements (but the above suffices to show the kind of problem they raise) before passing on to Monsieur Benoît's views, as stated in *Premiers Résultats des Recherches Sous-Marins*. He has published many articles on specific underwater finds in *Gallia*, *Etudes Ligures* and elsewhere and is recognized as a leading authority on submarine archaeology. As director of the Boreli Museum at Marseille and the surrounding circumscription, his task has been onerous. From the early days of free-diving, more antiquities have been found in these coastal waters than in any other part of the Mediterranean.

Marseille is a centre for underwater activities. There are probably more professional and semi-professional divers living in and around the town than anywhere else in the world. The French Federation of Divers and the World Confederation of Underwater Activities were born there. These professionals, excluding standard-apparatus divers, either work at the Centre for Underwater Research (known as the O.F.R.S., where the saucer-bathyscaphe was built) or manufacture or distribute diving equipment. There are also specialist schools of diving which train men for work connected with the Fire Service, Port Authorities, or firms which contract to do certain types of salvage. Other schools produce *Moniteurs*, who teach diving as a sport. Non-specialist diving schools and clubs along the coast do a brisk trade during the season, and one of their main attractions is taking tourist-pupils on conducted tours of Roman ships. Out of season, the *Moniteurs* from these clubs prospect for new and more attractive wrecks for the following year. Nor can the souvenir trade in amphorae be overlooked.

One way and another, all these people are interested in wrecks, so that Monsieur Benoît receives a constant flow of anchors, pots and other portable objects from the sea. Surely no museum in the world can rival the Boreli's intake of disparate finds from different sites. For years Monsieur Benoît has wrestled with this situation, but the conditions under which he works would be the despair of a field archaeologist. The finds are nearly always snatched from their context. Some Sunday-afternoon diver will casually pick up a jar, hardly bothering to notice whether it is jetsam or part of a wreck. In consequence, one reads such vague terms as '*cimetière marin*' and '*gisement*' in the annual list of sites published.[1]

What are Monsieur Benoît's views after twenty years of this sort of thing? Where the ships themselves are concerned, and these, after all, are basic to submarine archaeology, he is of the opinion that raising the hulls or large samples of

[1] *Bulletin de la Fédération Française d'Etudes et Sports Sous-Marins*, October 1960, No. 10.

wood is impracticable owing to lack of museum exhibition space, laboratory and preservation facilities and money.

From the wood he has received, he concludes that it can only provide evidence about carpentry, but not about the shape of the boat. He asserts that the hulls of all ancient wrecks are flattened in the course of time and only their middle and lower portions are found *in situ*. From this he concludes that it is impossible to estimate the section of a ship from stem to stern, whether it is symmetrical or not, or the curve of the transverse sections. Judging from what he has seen on land, one can sympathize with his pessimistic conclusion, but it would be premature to accept capitulation before at least trying to apply the recording routine of modern field archaeology. Nor should we accept a non-diver's description of the state of all ancient hulls. Even a professional diver would not know this, unless he had special comparative knowledge of ancient wrecks, and in addition an understanding of the techniques of archaeological reconstruction practised on land. Dumas had classified wrecks according to the type of bottom on which they fell and the manner of their sinking; in certain conditions, and when the ship was buried in mud, it might not lose its shape, nor would the middle portion necessarily be the only part preserved. The *Vasa* is an extreme case, but even Mediterranean conditions vary sufficiently to give different degrees of preservation.

On land, many accepted reconstructions of buildings have been based on scraps of wood, carefully excavated and recorded, but individually in a far worse state of preservation than the hulls of ancient wrecks. These land reconstructions are not, of course, based on a boxful of old wood, but on the interrelations of the pieces as they fell when the structure collapsed and disintegrated. The wood of a ship, when finally reached, is in almost perfect preservation. The parts are neither shrunken nor distorted, the grain is apparent and the wood when cut is not discoloured; last but not least, many of the elements are joined, though they may have to be broken to be raised.

If wreck excavation is systematic and everything recorded *in situ* the relationships of the parts should give an idea of the shape of the ship. To produce the necessary information it is essential to make a preliminary analysis of the lie of the ship and how she listed when she settled on the bottom, because whatever part of the hull is in contact with the bottom will be well preserved, while the remainder will be far less significant. The exposed portions of a hulk that were not preserved in quickly gathering sand may either have been eaten by animalculi or they may have splayed out as they became waterlogged.

Once the wreck is understood it should be possible to assess and cross-check what remains. The transverse section of the ship, and in particular its depth, can be judged from such things as a series of related planks, their shape and the decreasing size of the mortise joints, etc. From even a portion of rib the curve of the whole can be estimated on paper. This, taken together with other factors, such as the relation of a find to the axis of the keel, the timbers which traverse the ship to give her rigidity and the way the cargo was loaded, builds up a picture of one section. Like most archaeological interpretations, this would be worked out after excavation, from records made underwater. Similarly with the longitudinal section, where the curve of either end is in question, the upright timbers from keel or standing keels to deck level would give the depth. Naturally they would be broken or displaced, but it should be possible to work out the size of the whole from the parts. On some wrecks, if careful search were made in the right place, enough useful fragments of stem or stern should be found to show their curve. The evidence might not come from a single wreck, but would be built up on a comparative basis. It is not easy, but the method should be tried; moreover, portable electronic devices are being developed which, if available, would be of great help in the early stages of excavation. Used in addition to coring, they would give the foreknowledge of the buried remains which is so necessary in marine conditions.

CHAPTER 15

The Cargo of Sestius' Ship – First Visit to the Congloué; A Piece of Keel – Two Parallel Groups of Planking – A Third Group with Ribs, Rider and Double Planking – Clues to Lie and Construction – The Need for Expert Evaluation

THE reader who has persevered thus far now knows the kind of background information and questions which the writer had accumulated before diving on the Congloué. More difficult to imagine is the emotional state these produced. All had sunk and settled like mud into the disobedient depths of my mind. I realized the information was there, but when I set out for the Congloué nothing coherent surfaced, only blatant generalizations like: 'I think someone said there must have been two ships.' In any case, there seemed little point in delving for these memories, since, after eight years' energetic digging, the conformation of the bottom and all the clues as to the ship itself must have disappeared. Only an occasional amphora or scattered cup would remain. But a surprise awaited me.

The waterless island of the Grand Congloué is an outcrop extension of that part of the coast where there are rocky fjords or *Callanques*. The place is noted for its beauty, both above and below the surface, and is about an hour's journey from Cassis on a small boat. I determined to take the trip as a tourist, to enjoy myself and be able to say I had 'been there'. The trouble about nagging half-remembered information is that it is apt to rise 'like ghosts to trouble joy'; I had certainly no intention of making the outing a busman's holiday. I do not know what it is that attracts people, after a murder, to visit the scene of the crime and gaze up at a dirty lace curtain behind which some unfortunate has been dismembered. Incidentally, the most exquisite bryozoa, or sea lace, in the Mediterranean grows on the submarine part of the Congloué cliff above the wreck; also scarlet and orange gorgonia, like elongated flattened coral trees, which for me has the same nostalgic association as mimosa with the South of France.

I went to the Congloué as the guest of Monsieur Yves Girault, the well-known diver who took over the unloading of this vast cargo when Cousteau's excavation ended. Of the cargo (which with the exception of some duplicates is mostly in the Boreli Museum) it must be said that three thousand amphorae were raised by 1954, and Cousteau estimated the entire load at ten thousand. An amphora full of wine weighs about 50 kilograms, and was the tonnage measure of Greek ships. Monsieur Benoît says that:

> Vessels carrying ten thousand amphorae (260 tons) mentioned by Strabo, would seem exceptional. By the Law of Thasos 181, the Senators limited the size of merchant ships by restricting the cargo to three thousand amphorae.[1]

Elsewhere it is suggested that a 10,000 amphora ship, or *Myriagogos* would be 700 to 800 tons, but as we have seen, Casson puts it higher. The amphorae on the Congloué were mostly Hellenistic or Italic[2] with the exception of some Cnidian and Rhodian (estimated as second century B.C.), which were about seventy years earlier than the rest of the cargo. Some amphorae bore the stamp SES, followed by either an anchor or a trident; from this, the ownership has been ascribed to a known merchant called Marcus Sestius. The remainder of the cargo consisted of Campanian tableware. These dishes, bowls and wine cups bear no mark of the potter's fingers, but instead small circular indentations caused by wooden forms, which show them to be an early example of mass production. Their glaze is dull and black, the decoration stamped, with an occasional blob of white paint for good measure. They must have been packed in some form of container, for many were found stacked, their double handles at right angles to each other, or nested by an expert hand, the smaller inside the larger. Those found on the surface were naked but for concretions, while others in deep sand and mud were glazed, in mint condition, as they had come from the factory.

Apart from family and visitors, there were about eight divers on Girault's boat that day. Their task was to go down, clear away sand from a certain area and bring up unbroken pots. Years of salvage had made them *blasé* about the sherds so dear to archaeologists. This is perhaps a characteristic of divers: I was with Dumas when he first saw the collection of amphora types in the basement

[1] 'Regulations of the Port of Thasos: *de la Marine Antique à la Marine Moderne*', H. de Saussure, *Revue Archéologique*, 1937, II.

[2] M. F. Benoît, 'Amphores et Céramiques de l'Epave de Marseille', *Gallia*, Vol. XII.

of the Agora in Athens; he was more impressed by their condition than their variety: 'But they're all broken and mended! Why, I could get hundreds of quite new ones from the sea.'

At the Congloué each man on Girault's boat was to dive twice: first for eighteen minutes, with three minutes decompression, then after an interval of three hours, for fifteen minutes with six minutes decompression. The area to be worked was at 43 metres, a respectable depth for strenuous activity, and possibly too deep for lengthy, meticulous excavation. The visitor notices on arrival at the island the memorial plaque on the cliff face to Pierre Servanti, who lost his life there in the early days. He was not the only one. Even during the three days I was there there were two accidents. One wretch had to spend ten hours in a decompression chamber. The other got off more lightly: he surfaced in a state of '*affollement*' due to a mild narcosis and was picked up by swimmers. When he had recovered he was put down again with another bottle to decompress properly. Not much sympathy is wasted on accidents at work, but it is as well to note that they occur, since people are all too ready to take on these jobs lightly. When diving is done regularly, day after day, very strict timing has to be maintained. My own work involves hardly any risk, since it requires no physical exertion. Divers go down two at a time as a safety measure. In theory, they watch each other, and if anything goes wrong with one of them the other stuffs the air pipes back into the victim's mouth and gets him to the surface.

That day, I made the first dive with Monsieur Girault, who was taking down a water jet. This consisted of a fireman's hose powered from a motor on the boat, which blew sand away by the force of water expelled. Air lifts had already done their work and decreased the height of the original tumulus by 3 or 4 metres, so that it was now possible to blow the sand downhill off the last layers of cargo. Abandoned lengths of piping from these machines were strewn about the bottom, together with disused lifting baskets, sheets of corrugated iron and other scrap which later, when I made measured drawings, served as useful key points.

This first dive was far from enjoyable. I had borrowed large bottles of, to me unknown, Spanish manufacture. They were clogged with internal rust (I only discovered this weeks later; at the time I blamed the demand valve); moreover, I thought them buoyant, when in fact they were extremely heavy; and lastly, to add to my discomfort, the type of harness, which I had never seen before, was adjusted upside down. The result was that when I jumped into the water the bottles flew off and had to be held in place with one hand and the mouthpiece kept in position between clenched teeth. I was not getting enough air, and I could not swim. I proceeded to sink like a stone. This terrified me, because of my ears and also because Girault had warned me that when I joined him I must not touch the bottom and kick up mud where he was working. Of course, I could, indeed should, have gone up and changed bottles, but I was reluctant to lose face or to throw out the time schedule on dives for the day, so I struggled over to a disused cable hanging down the cliff and stayed on it at a depth of about 15 metres until the pressure in my ears had equalized.

For my type of work, this ear trouble is a blessing in disguise. From 15 metres I could see the bottom and take stock. On other occasions I spend the time making notes and preparing my dive so as not to waste a second on the bottom. The rock beside me was under-cut and covered with bright fans of gorgonia, whose colours were still visible at that depth. Seven metres below was a narrow ledge, then the ground fell away again at an angle of 75°; the rock on this slope was covered with mud and less spectacular plants. Around 37 metres the direction of the slope changed again to a gradient of 20°, and some way out, on the bottom, I could see Girault in a cloud of mud raised by his water lance [Fig. 49 (6)].

He had warned me that he had no time to take me on a conducted tour, but in the hole where he was working he would show me wood. I let myself sink and bounced down the slope towards him, raising clouds of mud. When I reached the hole I saw three hulking planks joined together (Fig. 49 (3)]. They stretched for a distance of about 2 metres, one end was lost in sand, and at the other they had been moulded over a stone whose shape they had taken as they became waterlogged. Two people can get in each other's way even on the sea-bed. What with my weight and the water jet, the visibility around us soon rivalled a pea-souper. I crawled out of this fog and sat on the sand a few metres to the westwards panting for air. There, no man-made object was visible except a broken, metal lifting basket. I realized that I must start making an effort to regain the surface if I was not to jettison my leads. So I crawled back to the air-hose and climbed up it, hand over hand. At the 3-metre stop Girault joined me for decompression, his work finished. I mention this experience for two reasons: first, as a demonstration of the importance of good equipment. The sensation of diving is pure bliss to those who like it, but bad equipment can turn it into the worst form of torture. Secondly, and of more importance, had I not been forced to do so I would not on

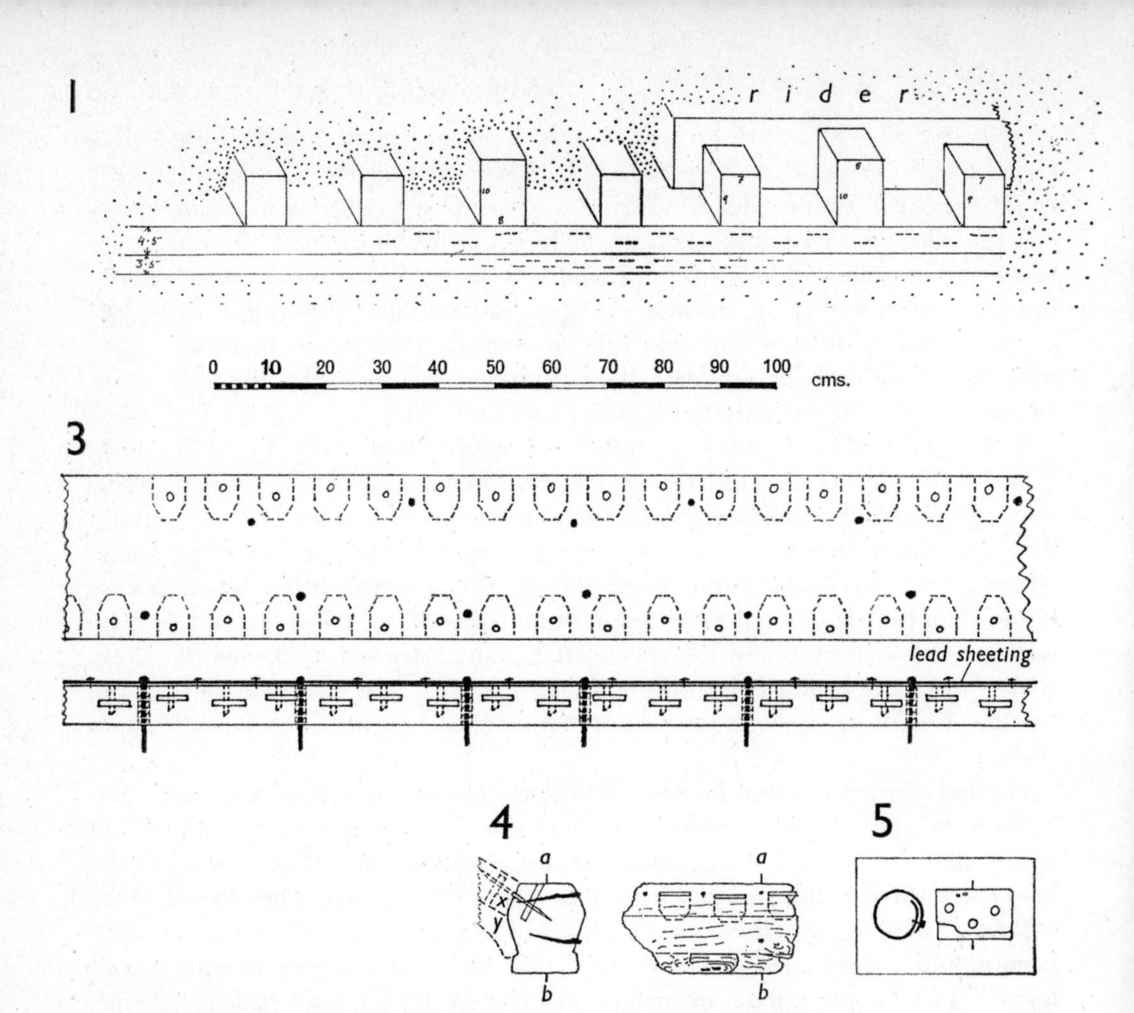

48. Wood of the Congloué wreck, drawn in 1960. The numbering of the details on the above figure corresponds with their position on the plan opposite.

Details from Plan: (1) Ribs, rider and double planking, measured and drawn underwater. Without raising these planks it was impossible to tell whether their underside had been leaded; they had disappeared by 1961. (3) The lowest of the group of three planks shown on plan; it was lifted and drawn on board boat. The section shows the lead covering, which, in the case of this plank, was of paste-like consistency, also the copper tacks that joined the lead sheeting to the wood. There were linen fibres and traces of woven fabric between the lead and the wood. Copper nails shown in solid black; the ribs they had held had disappeared from this part of the hull. (4) Section and elevation of the bit of keel (found loose on the surface at 4, but which must have come from the hole at 6); x is the seam of plank with keel and y, a garboard filling-piece. (5) Object made of lead with traces of wood inside it; possibly a counterweight from a dinghy oar.

49. Plan and Section: (1), (2) and (3) Groups of planks from the hull. (4) A portion of keel. (5) Lead object. (6) The 'hole' or area under excavation when these drawings were made.

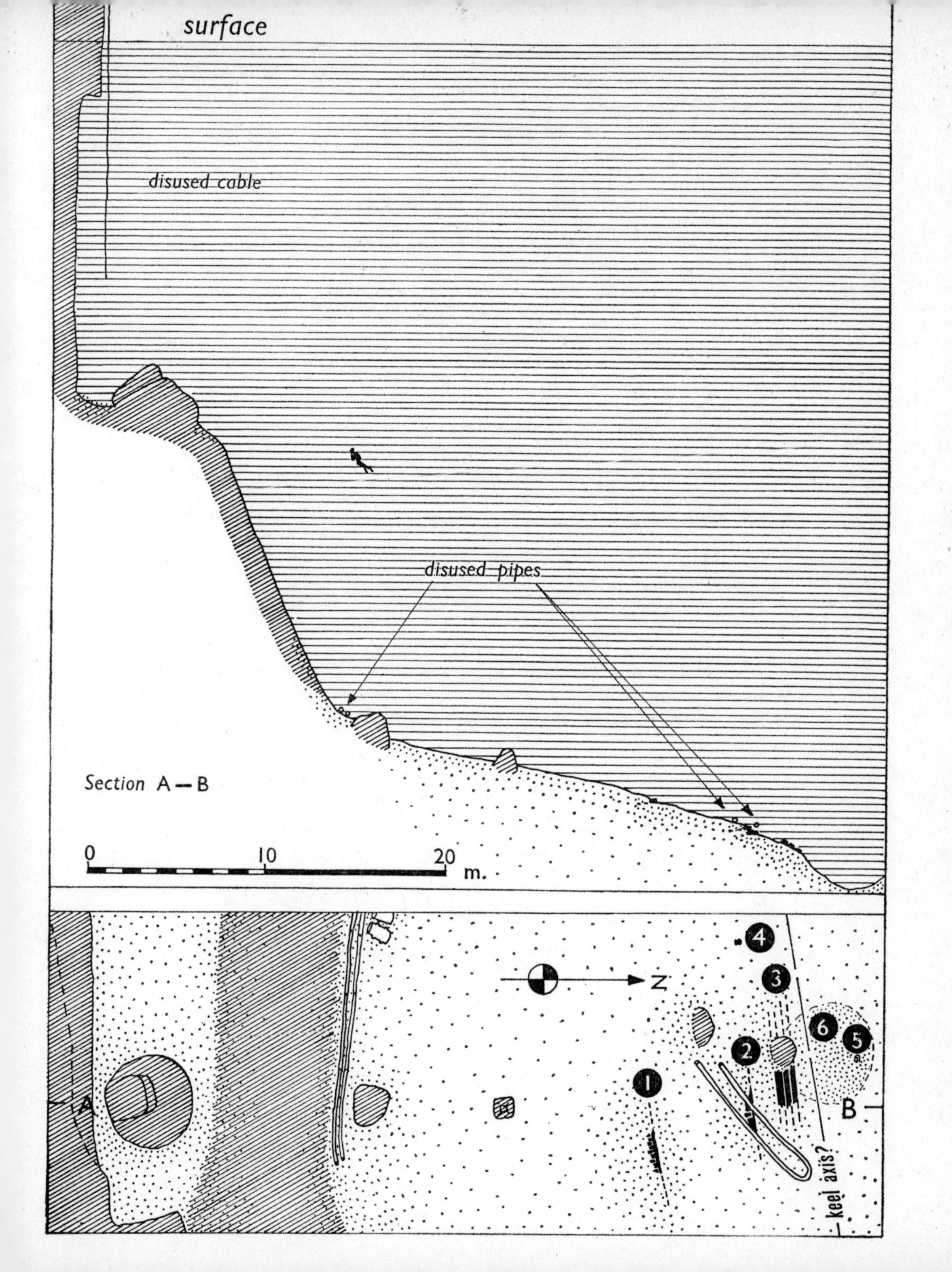

surface
disused cable
disused pipes
Section A — B
0
10
20
m.
N
1
2
3
4
5
6
A
B
keel axis?

ANCIENT WRECKS.

22 (opposite). *A trench taken through the Roman wreck (first or second century) at Cap Drammont. This section through the cargo shows the top layer of amphorae to be soldered to each other by a pie-crust of concretion, while the second and third layers are held together in sand. At the bottom of the trench, in the centre, scraps of inner floor-boards can be distinguished above the ribs of the hull; compare the fragmentary state of these boards with the well-preserved bilge of the Anthéor wreck Plate XX.*

23 (verso, top). *The author triangulating with a surveyor's tape on a sixteenth-century wreck. The weed grew so high at that season that the breech-loaded cannons marking the site had to be indicated by the numbered white plastic buoys. Finds covered an area of about 100 square metres, however, the bottom being horizontal this method of surveying proved accurate.*

24 (below). *Drawing of the sixth-century Byzantine wreck off the Karabağla islands in Turkey (p. 164 and Fig. 31). Whereas a diver actually sees a wreck in its entirety, like this, only close-ups can be photographed under-water.*

25 (recto, top left). *Part of the keel from the wreck at the Grand Congloué (compare Fig. 47 and p. 247). That this ship was large is apparent from its cargo, yet, by modern standards, the keel is surprisingly small.*

26. *John Carswell making the first register of the antiquities that had already been collected before our arrival, and provisionally stored in the Hotel at Bodrum. When later they were moved into the Crusader Castle, they became the nucleus of the Museum collection.*

27 (below). *The hull of the* Titan *after excavation; note the keelson still in position (compare Plates 11 and 13).*

28 (verso). *The tile-carrying ship at Frioul (compare Fig. 44, also see p. 218).*

22. Bulletin F.F.S.M., photo Y. Girault

23. F. Dumas

24.

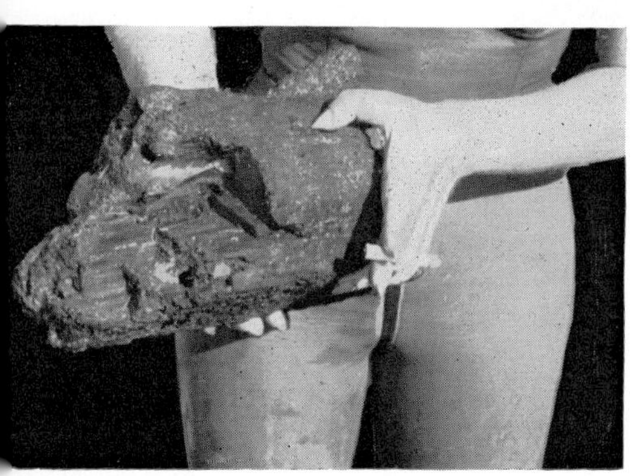

5. F.Clouzot

27. P.Tailliez

26. M.Kapkin

28. *G. Beuchat, photo C. Chiapetti*

that dive have sat still contemplating an arid patch of sand, and had I not done so . . . but the events that followed explain themselves.

In the afternoon I returned, mobility restored by apparatus that worked, to the patch of sand by the basket. I saw something which had not been there in the morning. It was an oddly shaped but symmetrical piece of wood about 30 centimetres long by 16 wide, with nails and tenons sticking out of it [Figs. 48 and 49 (4), Plate 25]. In the interim the divers who had been working in the hole near the planks must have thrown the timber aside, seeing that it was not pottery. When I got it on board, no one seemed to recognize it, but they had been working in poor visibility. I also noticed on that first dive a second area of wood just above the first [Fig. 49 (2)]. It consisted of planks and the remains of a battered rib, almost hidden below disused air-lift pipes. The two lots of planks seemed to be parallcl to each other and to the base of the cliff. When, later, I told Dumas about this wood he decided to dive himself, as he had not visited the Congloué site for several years.

During the following week, I dissected and drew the bit of timber I had raised. It appeared to be part of the keel. If so, it was a very important clue to the lie of the ship, coming as it did from the vicinity of the lowest planks [Fig. 49 (3)], which were still *in situ*. This timber (Plate 25) was shaped to take the garboard filling piece. Garboard filling piece is an unwieldy description which one is forced to use because the nomenclature of structural parts, especially those that have not survived in modern shipbuilding, is not standardized. In shell-like classical ships, where the planks of the hull were seamed by edge-to-edge joinery on to the keel, there was bound to be a weakness at their junction. This weakness in the seaming was reinforced on its underside by pieces of wood that were wedge-shaped in section [see Fig. 46 and Fig. 48 (4)] and which, for want of a better term, must be called garboard filling pieces.

I did not see any of these filling pieces on the Congloué wreck, but in the timber I found there was a long bronze nail which must have held this reinforcement in place. On the bottom of the same timber was a trace of lead. If this wood was indeed part of the keel (and subsequent research proved it to be so), and if it had, as seemed logical, been joined to the lowest plank in Girault's hole, then we had at last got the lie of the ship. Of course this would have to be confirmed by bearings and measurements.

The following week-end I returned with Dumas, and we both dived with Girault. We concentrated on the wood, and I took notes. To my embarrassment,

Dumas lifted the lowest plank, which was just under 2 metres long and 40 centimetres wide [Fig. 48 (3)]. In the normal way this 'lift' would have been a crime against scientific method, but it was pardonable on a site which had been dug for eight years, where nothing had been recorded and where there was little prospect of reform. The plank made an awful mess on the white roof of the cabin, its lower side being covered with soft, black lead of toothpaste consistency, about half a centimetre thick. Then and there, in duty bound, I had to dissect and draw it. It could not be taken off the boat and was too big and dirty to get into a small, French car. I felt my popularity ebbing with every moment it remained on top of the white paint. To make matters worse, my interest proved infectious, and other divers surfaced with sometimes meaningless and always filthy trophies, from the hole where they had all been working; among these were crumpled sheets of lead of the type to which Cousteau had referred. All these sheets came from the same place and one, for certain, from below the plank which Dumas raised.

What was the explanation: why was the consistency of the lead sheets as good as new, while on a contiguous timber the lead was in paste? Had there been two layers of lead covering the bottom of the ship? As I worked on the plank, trying to see the pattern of the dowels which had held the tenons, and also the nails which had fitted the ribs, another peculiarity came to light. The black paste had to be scraped off in places, so that I could see the insertions of the dowels or treenails. In doing this, I noticed the imprint of woven fabric where the paste had been removed. Some sort of cloth had been laid over the hull under the lead. Girault said the samples of linen had been found and analysed earlier in the excavation. At Nemi there had been felt impregnated with tar between the lead and the wood. I cut a section of plank and sent it off for analysis.

Archaeological laboratories are overworked and cannot always tackle jobs connected with excavations that do not directly concern them. The two different kinds of lead found on the Congloué present possibilities that are worth investigating. Either the black paste on the plank had once been lead sheeting, which had contracted a kind of metal disease from long contact with the hull and the copper tacks with which it was affixed (a disease which it escaped when torn from the hull on sinking), or this black paste was lead paint. This possibility was suggested by fibres[1] which were found embedded in the paste; these might have

[1] I am indebted to Dr M. L. Ryder for the opinion that the fibres found on this wood were vegetable; this would be consistent with the earlier, French findings of linen fibres.

been caught up when the paint was being laid directly on to the linen. On the other hand, they could have got into the paste after the ship was wrecked and during its process of decay. In building a roof it is common practice to isolate lead from wood by means of tarred felt. In the case of this wreck it seems most likely that lead sheets were laid over linen, especially as the paste proved on analysis to be almost entirely lead.

When in the course of the original excavation, wood from the Congloué hull was analysed, keel and planks were found to be of a soft conifer, probably Aleppo pine. The mortises and tenons were, as always, made from a hardwood like oak or olive. If the wood I had found differed from the original analyses it might provide an answer to the crucial question: two ships or one? The samples are still in the hands of experts. By this time my care-free tourism was a thing of the past. One way and another, it seemed that enough evidence remained on this wreck to answer some of the questions that had so troubled the experts, and induced in them a mistrust of submarine archaeology.

It was at this stage that Girault announced that, a little higher up the slope, there was a third area of wood with double planking and ribs. So far I had seen only single planking backed by lead, and one rather battered rib [Fig. 49 (2)] (though of course the presence of other ribs had been clearly indicated by copper nails through the planks). The single rib was in too bad a state to draw. I was doomed to a busman's holiday and poor M. Girault to a dirty boat, for I could not leave France without seeing this last lot of wood and finding out whether all three groups were *in situ* and interrelated.

The following week-end was my last opportunity to visit the Congloué. I carefully planned my two dives. On the first, with the help of M. François Clouzot, a very active local diver, I would plot the relationships of the three groups of wood to each other. On the second dive this triangulation would be checked, and another bearing taken on the new set of planks and ribs, to see whether all three sets were parallel. If they were it would give a further, and possibly confirmatory, indication as to the lie of the ship. During the second dive that day I would check depth measurements which, on that particular site, would not be difficult.

On the first dive I got another bad bottle, which was tiresome, as my task was exceptionally energetic. Knowing my own predetermined fixed points, I had to swim from one to the other at the mobile end of the tape; Clouzot remained at the base of each triangle, marking the distances as I measured them until, at a signal from me, he proceeded to the next pre-arranged point, where we repeated the process. My bottle was so uncomfortable that I had to give up before finishing the list. Happily my notes, written on a sheet of plastic, were comprehensible to a second party. They were partly diagrammatic and read: 'from basket to rake to hole on mid-lower plank', and so on; Clouzot stayed down and completed the list. Later, Girault made an excellent photographic overlay of the area. This was useful as a cross-check, though in itself it would have been incomprehensible to any outsider who did not know the site, because the wood, which was almost buried in sand, did not show. However, on Girault's photographs such things as the modern rake (goodness knows why it was there!) and the basket, which were my key points, tallied with the drawings I made.

On the second dive I was to take the short measurements alone on the bottom, while Clouzot, swimming on the surface, sounded at agreed points. As I have said, depth measurements were easy; indeed, they were the one thing that was never in dispute among the *habitués* who had worked on the same spot for eight years. Depth on the Congloué was important to us all for reasons of safety; after 40 metres every extra metre counts against the diver's working time. Clouzot could not see me from the surface, but he followed my bubbles, and we communicated by pre-arranged signals on the sounding line, which was attached to a small piece of lead. When this fell near me I would note its position, then by pulling on the line, signal to Clouzot to move on.

It took me only a few minutes to check the short measurements before going to the marker-float attached to another lead (identical with the one on Clouzot's sounding line) that Girault had placed over the new area of wood which was covered with sand. I started to clear the sand with my hand, and was so astonished by what I saw that I settled down to draw it and take as many intricate measurements as I could, even if I had to outstay my allotted time on the bottom. In vain did Clouzot drop his sounder on and around me. I was so absorbed that I absent-mindedly signalled back to him by pulling the string on Girault's marker float. Far above, Clouzot diagnosed a narcosis, but while my bubbles tickled his stomach, he knew there was life.

According to the bearings, the new planks were exactly parallel to the other two groups, lower down the slope [Fig. 48 (1)]. Moreover, this new planking was double; I could see that the edge of the lower plank was thinner than the one above it. The two together measured about the same width as the lowest plank which Dumas had raised from the hole. No less than seven ribs in good condition were nailed on top of the double planks. They were neatly broken off along the edge of the planks. The three westernmost ribs emerged from a timber which had been cut to receive them. It must have run the whole length of the planking, but what remained was broken, again quite cleanly, after the third rib. What was this timber?

M. Benoît wrote in his *Premiers Résultats des Fouilles Sous-Marines*:

> The absence of the bottom of the Congloué hull makes it uncertain whether the axial keel was not repeated in secondary, bilge keels which reinforce the rigidity of the hull, below the water line, as on the Nemi ships.

This statement is misleading on one obvious point: a significant part of the Congloué hull is there today, even after eight years of digging. Perhaps one side of the ship had collapsed over the cargo and, when this side was found, in the early days of the excavation, the diggers assumed that there would be no more hull below. Alternatively, in the absence of underwater records, the reports which reached the surface (where they were then interpreted) may have been incoherent. In any case, here for certain was a rider [Fig. 48 (1)]. Without removing this rider, the ribs and double planking, there was no way of telling whether a bilge keel had also existed. The salvage of this bit of hull would, however, have taken several dives and several divers, which was out of the question.

The three parallel groups of planking taken together suggest a transverse section of hull running from the keel to a rider. Other intervening parts of this hull may still be buried under the sand or, after eight years of digging, they may have been dispersed. The topmost planks, under the rider [Fig. 48 (1)], were double. The lowest planking [Fig. 48 (3)] by the keel was single. It would have been logical to assume double planking by the keel, for the plank Dumas raised corresponded with the keel facets [x 4 on Fig. 48] and a thinner plank might have been carried by the garboard filling piece (*y* on the same figure). This hypothesis is, however, contrary to the evidence, for the thick plank Dumas raised had copper tacks and traces of lead sheeting on its underside; it must therefore have been the outside of the hull. Whatever the explanation, the transition from single to double planking could not have taken place without some intervening timber, such as a bilge keel, for the wide single planks were still too narrow to have taken a double row of mortise holes at their juncture with double planking. Incidentally, if the three groups of wood do constitute a transverse section of part of the hull, then, allowing for the collapse and spread of the waterlogged wood, the rider is about the same distance from the keel as the outer bilge keel is from the main keel on the Nemi ships. This suggests the possibility that double planking may have started on this hull, above the water-line, where the lead sheeting ended.

These are valid questions, raised by the analysis of documents. That I cannot give the answers is tantalizing but accidental; I was not in a position to undertake continuous research. The answers are there, buried in the sand. The point at issue is: will normal methods of archaeological recording give results underwater as they do on land? I think the answer is 'yes'.

In favourable conditions much could be learned about ships' structure, even at the eleventh hour, after the cargoes had been salvaged from the wrecks. When one considers the number of cargoes that have already been removed, on that coast alone, it is tempting to imagine an expedition called 'operation hulls'. The comparative information produced by even a survey of these structural remains would be impressive.[1]

The above is sufficient to show the kind of factual detail that can be found on a site even after years of digging. It is interesting at this juncture to re-examine the opinion of divers who have known the Congloué throughout the excavation. On the small area which I have described, I personally had seen nothing to suggest that there had been more than one wreck. After my first dive I had an intuitive conviction that the ship lay parallel with the base of the cliff; the notes I made subsequently confirmed this impression. However, the question still remains: were there two ships? or one carrying some amphorae that were 80 to 100 years older than the rest of her cargo? Dumas had dived on this site from the day of its discovery, throughout the years of Cousteau's excavation. Before showing him my drawings, I asked him whether he had had any reason to suspect the presence of a second ship, and what he estimated was the lie of the main ship. His answer to the first part of my question was a categorical negative, while his description of the axis coincided with my own deductions. He had kept a daily log while he worked on the site; there were no measured drawings to substantiate this record, but that did not invalidate it. Other divers held similar views: none had seen evidence of more than one ship. Without sifting what evidence there was, I would not have dared to state an intuitive judgement; nevertheless, these hunches are too often right to be dismissed.

[1] I presented a list of the drawings I had made at the Congloué (I had no time to make copies) to the local museum before I left France.

In practice, someone like Dumas who has a wide experience of wrecks, makes unerring diagnoses. When, for instance, the *Calypso* was on the Anticythera site, many dived and, one after another, they reported that no trace of the hull remained. Then Dumas went down; on surfacing he told them that if they put their *suceuse* on the sand at a certain place they would find the wood of the hull. They did. The same thing happened in Turkey when we were looking for traces of the Bronze Age wreck which, the year after Mustafa and Throckmorton had seen it, seemed to have disappeared from the bottom. After the other searchers had lost hope Dumas diagnosed two large portions of cargo which were entirely camouflaged by concretions. Sometimes even its author cannot explain this kind of assessment; when committed to action there is no time for analysis. Yet someone who is familiar with different kinds of wreck-formations and has always examined them in relation to their geological surroundings unconsciously notes any anomaly on the bottom. The sea-bed is in some way unnatural, and a slight variation in its line betrays an alien, buried obstruction.

Judging from its contents, the Congloué ship must have measured at least 60 metres; the excavated area of cargo covered, according to Cousteau, 300 square metres. On the face of it, it is hard to deny that somewhere in this vast area may lie traces of an earlier, Cnidian ship, and it might not be too late to verify this point. From his first dive in 1951, Dumas was convinced that there was only one ship, lying parallel to the base of the island. This does not entirely contradict Cousteau's assertion that the axis of the keel ran uphill, as the bottom has a north-westerly to south-westerly slant. This slope was probably more apparent on the virgin tumulus than it is now that the level has been lowered by 3 or 4 metres. However, it does not look as though the axis of the keel could possibly have been at right angles to the cliff. Had records been kept from the outset, there would have been no dispute.

CHAPTER 16

Land Archaeology and Marine Problems – The Interpretation of Existing Reports – Awareness of the Limitations of Underwater Work and Divers' Craftsmanship

ARCHAEOLOGY can only be practised by archaeologists. Underwater, when archaeological control has existed at all, it has been tenuous, perhaps because maritime problems old and new are not only complex but different in kind from those that exist on land.

Harbour machinery, ships and wreck-formations are new to the world of archaeology. Only the objects carried on a ship constitute a 'closed group' which can be diagnosed on land in a routine manner; an entirely fresh approach is needed to understand the mechanism that surrounded and enclosed these objects. Intellectual aspects of the problem apart, the material difficulties of underwater excavation make it impossible for a landsman to direct fully efficient research unless he uses divers who are not only professional but who also have experience of Mediterranean sites and wreck-formations. '*Si le plongeur savait, si l'archéologue pouvait* . . .' summarizes part of the present dilemma. Divers of a new breed who have, for various motives, been probing Mediterranean antiquities for the past twenty years have gained experience. Their knowledge is precious, and it would take more than a generation of archaeologists, with the limited time they have in the field, to reach the same degree of understanding. Unless more evidence is to be destroyed, the two groups must come together and evolve satisfactory methods of excavation.

The personal records I have given of the state of affairs on a particular site at a specific time will have been useful if they have demonstrated the type of archaeological question that can be posed. Anchors, amphora and tile-carrying wrecks are found throughout the Mediterranean, and there is reason to suppose that there is a Phoenician port as far west as the Narbonnaise in France. In order to keep the material within the limits of this volume, all but the most representative examples of submarine remains have had to be omitted. Until land and sea techniques are co-ordinated and systematized there is no reason to dwell on exceptional phenomena.

A passing reference to oddities is, however, justified, because, paradoxically, exceptions are characteristic of the sea. For example, human remains have recently been found on the wreck of a ship that was carrying breech-loaded cannons (such as were used in the fifteenth and sixteenth centuries). It was an electrifying experience; for apart from a few animal bones, presumably from a stew pot, these were the first remains of a living creature found on a Mediterranean wreck. A body was found on the *Vasa* and others on the Dutch wrecks excavated by Dr van der Heide, but from long and sometimes grisly experience, we in the Mediterranean had supposed that bodies would have been eaten by fish, or would have disintegrated after a few months as a result of chemical action. Nor did the comparatively late date of this ship explain the mystery, since preservation on a wreck becomes stabilized after a short time and then remains unchanged for centuries. In this case the build of the ship, the way it collapsed, the amount of copper objects near the remains and the chemical make up of the surrounding bottom may account for the bodies; again, only meticulous excavation of the site would give the answers.

Not surprising for their preservation, but equally difficult to explain, were seven stone sarcophagi lying in a line along the base of the seaward wall of the Hellenistic port of Side in southern Turkey. I found them when I was examining the ancient harbour-works (which incidentally, do not correspond with the plan of this harbour in *die Hafenanlangen*).[1] 'Mast stones' are another recent discovery: two have been found *in situ* on a wreck with dolia between and amphorae packed around them. Of the hundreds of amphora-carriers on record, this was the first to contain these curious stones. Torr, who sifted classical texts for references to ships' structure, does not mention mast stones in his *Ancient Ships*. The only hint of their possible existence may be found in the 'stone boats' of Celtic saints like Brendan, or in Breton legends concerning 'sacred stones' from boats. One can imagine a chronicler looking down at the huge stones which must have almost covered the bottom of a boat, then with poetic licence describing the boat as 'of stone'.

Strange finds would fill a volume, but I quote them not only as proof that

[1] See footnote 1 on p. 94.

exceptions exist but also as a caution. The urgent need is not for volumes, but for one or two factual reports: reports that will stand comparison with records of land excavations. Miss Kathleen Kenyon has pointed out that: 'excavation, however well executed, without adequate publication is wanton destruction'—an axiom that is true on land or sea.

Reports on underwater excavation, if they are to carry conviction, will have to devote considerable space to technicalities: an analysis of the site, a statement of the total diving times on the bottom, a description of the machinery used and the reasons for its choice, the gross and net weights of the objects lifted (especially when these constituted the cargo of a ship) and so on. If such facts are omitted the report becomes suspect. This is a very real danger, for whereas land excavation methods are open to inspection, it is difficult to check the efficiency of underwater work, or to judge whether it could have been done better. Moreover, it is only by a comparison of techniques that a fairly standardized and efficient method can be evolved.

Most of the available reports on submarine remains have not been written by archaeologists. They are difficult to evaluate unless the reader is in a position to question the divers who actually worked on a specific site: it is therefore dangerous at present for a scholar to interpret and draw conclusions from published evidence. On the basis of such reports it has, for instance, been suggested that ancient hulls can be classified and even dated according to the presence or absence of a keelson (that is to say the large timber inside the hull that lies above and reinforces the keel). It has been argued that whenever keelsons have been found there has been no lead sheeting on the hull, and conversely, that when floor-timbers are substituted for a keelson lead covers the outer planking.[1] This is an extremely interesting idea and may well be true, but let us examine the reports on which it is based.

The Congloué ship was lead plated, and from elements that were raised a reconstruction was drawn of a transverse section through its keel, garboard filling pieces and floor-timbers. So far so good, but the point along the length of the keel which this section represents has never been stated. Was it taken amidships or from an extremity? Transverse sections of hulls vary with the curve of the ship. If we are to assume that keelsons ran the entire length of these ships and followed their curve up into the bows, then there may be some justification for such vague sections. Otherwise it might be argued that keelsons gave place to floor-

[1] *Actes du IIème Congrès International d'Archéologie Sous-Marine*, Albenga, 1958, pp. 347–8.

timbers or some other kind of reinforcement in different portions of the hull.

It is essential to know where a transverse section was taken, but on the Congloué wreck it is unlikely that this evidence will be forthcoming, since the very axis of the keel is still in dispute. Furthermore, as no records were kept, transverse sections could not be related to the hull, even if its axis were known. In the early days of the excavation Cousteau reported a timber (mentioned earlier) which he took to be the keel, but which, from subsequent experience of these ships, sounds more like a keelson. Again, at what part of the site had this timber been found and what relation did it bear to the reconstructed section?

There is in fact a reason to suppose that keelsons did not run the entire length of these ships, but to my knowledge it has never been stated in print in a report. On the Drammont and Chretienne 'A' wrecks, divers said they noticed 'one end of the keelson sticking out of the sand'. The ends of the timbers they saw were not broken, but cut vertically. The Chretienne 'A' keelson disappeared three months after it was reported and before I could get there to examine it (Appendix). A partial plan was made of the Drammont hull, but it does not show the extremity of the keelson. The cut end of this timber was, however, recorded in a photograph.

Incomplete reports invalidate interpretation. The essence of scientific recording is a non-selective statement of all the evidence: both the discoveries and the circumstances surrounding them. Incomprehensible or apparently irrelevant events may turn out to be significant when sets of records are compared after a lapse of time. So far, wreck excavations have been virtually unrecorded.

We must admit that it would be psychologically difficult to maintain a degree of scientific impartiality, underwater, during the long months of heavy manual labour on a buried wreck. This is another reason why preliminary analysis of the site is so essential. Providing a wreck has been thoroughly understood, there are certain aspects of the formation where some compromise is justified during recording. Of course, when wood, that is to say the structure of the ship, is concerned no effort should be spared in noting detail. The limits of absolute accuracy in recording are difficult to define, but in his excellent report on the wreck at Spargi, Dr Roghi (himself an experienced diver) has put some of the practical problems into words:

> After a diagrammatic plan, whether photographic or drawn, has been made, the diver who consults it will still have difficulty in finding his way about the bottom.

> The sea-bed is harder to decipher than a field on land, and this for a multitude of reasons which it would take too long to enumerate.
>
> The material appearance of the sea-bed can be entirely changed by the displacement of a single object, particularly as the bottom is composed of so many heterogeneous elements. The mere displacement or removal of a couple of amphorae from a deposit can cause the heap to shift and so alter its appearance that the diver will lose his bearings.
>
> It is illusory to aim at a perfect enumeration of amphorae, since, particularly in the first layer of the deposit, they will not be arranged like books on a shelf. They are in such disorder that the diver cannot tell which come from the accidentally deranged first layer and which belong to the second layer (where they may well be *in situ*); in these circumstances one has to be content with a good approximation.
>
> When the grid was removed so that a layer of amphorae could be lifted, the attempt we made to mark its four corners with pickets proved impractical. When divers started to extricate some of the heavy jars the remainder shifted, the sand slid downwards and the fins of the divers, who were forced to grope about, displaced everything.[1]

The difficulty of maintaining fixed points would, of course, be minimized if Dumas' method of excavation by coring and trenching were used. Dr Roghi has given a transparently honest and vivid picture of what happens on the bottom when teams of divers have to work in relays. He proceeds to describe solutions to the problems he understands so well, and his report does not end on a despairing note. I have quoted this passage as an antidote to theoretical schemes. Paradoxically it is the simplest things about the sea, its movement and the force of water itself and the differing equilibrium of sand or objects, that are the most difficult for beginners to appreciate. They govern every operation underwater, yet their significance can be learned only through individual experience. A diver is a craftsman in the same sense as a highly trained ballet dancer. The qualities required to work effectively underwater are more those of an artist, with his subjective turn of mind, than a sportsman. The latter may move with ease in the water, but it does not follow that he will have the disciplined awareness required for activities other than the shooting of fish.

It is my personal belief that archaeological discipline can be practised undersea, but this only if scientists and divers are aware of what is involved. It must always be remembered that human beings are contending with a strange element. The mental effort required from a man working in deep water increases in proportion to the physical effort he makes. It is amusing to hear professional

[1] Gianni Roghi, 'Note Tecniche', *Bollettino e Atti*, 1958–59, pp. 16–17.

divers harping on the big 'holes' they have dug. In a discussion on technique it sounds, from the archaeological point of view, comic and faintly naughty, yet their insistence on exertion illustrates a basic fact. A diver pits himself against a force of nature; work is concentrated into a few, brief minutes, during which he undergoes an emotional test. In the early days he had to suck for every breath of air; now demand-valves have been improved; but he is still limited by a small bottle and knows that he dare not get out of breath. Digging his 'big hole' with an air-lift, he has to hold this powerful machine, then set himself an objective: such as freeing a certain amphora in one dive. He sucks and he pulls, until his objective becomes an obsession; judgement, already impaired by depth, hardly governs his actions. If he is experienced he will realize what is happening to him; if not, being alone on the bottom, he may wrench the amphora and break it. Land archaeologists have tests and tribulations of a different order: they do not 'take it out' on their trench. The diver becomes emotionally part of his big hole.

APPENDIX

THOSE interested in the structure of ancient ships can now regard the Chretienne 'A', like the larger and better-known wreck at the Grand Congloué, as a cautionary case history. In a period of thirteen years since the discovery of this Chretienne wreck, and in the intervals between the bona fide investigations listed below, the hull of the ship and its cargo of amphorae have disappeared, leaving only unanswered questions. The ship's structure remains a mystery, though there was every indication that wood was *in situ*. The destruction of this site seems to have resulted more from a desire for amphorae than from the imperfect techniques associated with pioneer excavations.

It can be argued that amphorae from the Chretienne 'A' now give pleasure to private owners, whereas the entire cargo might not have justified the museum space it would have occupied. Nevertheless, there is a principle at issue: when a wreck is being pillaged for its cargo the individual who digs fastest stands most chance of private profit; this is incompatible with scientific investigation.

The following reports of bona fide research give an idea of the potentialities of the site before it was destroyed.

1948

M. Henri Broussard, president of the *Club Alpin Sous-Marin de Cannes*, discovered a wreck which became known as the Chretienne 'A', lying along the landward base of the safety beacon off Anthéor Point. Fishermen had for some time been finding pottery in their nets at that place. Broussard visited the spot with Dr Denereaz, reported the wreck to the appropriate authorities and received permission for his club to dive on the site.

In its virgin state the wreck was covered with concretions and overgrown with poseidon grass. Samples of surface cargo had to be extracted from the stony crust that soldered them together, while, to gauge the size of the wreck, it was necessary to clear the weed. Broussard describes this early stage in the *Bulletin Officiel du Club Alpin Sous-Marin*, No. 8, 1956. It is also mentioned in Philippe Diolé's *4000 Years Under the Sea*.

1949–50

During the two following summers the *Groupe de Recherches Sous-Marine* of the French Navy also made several visits to the site (see Philippe Tailliez' *Nouvelles Plongées sans Cable*).

Frédéric Dumas dived on the wreck five times in 1949 and four times in 1950 and was able to make a sketch of the site while it was virtually undisturbed (Fig. 50). He has extracted the following observations from his log books of that period:

> We made a sounding on the site, through the cargo to the hull. The hole was rather less than the height of a man. The surface amphorae were lying on their sides; the second layer, held together in sand, were more upright, being at an angle of about 45° with their mouths facing north-east; many of the jars were broken. The third layer was in much the same state, though the amphorae were slightly less inclined and the proportion of broken specimens was smaller. In layers two and three I saw no jar upside down.
>
> The flanks of the amphorae were worn: presumably they had rubbed together to such an extent as to cause grooving in the pottery.
>
> On August 24, 1950, we saw the hull at the bottom of our excavation: it consisted of inner floor-boards and one rib. The rib allowed me to estimate the approximate axis of the ship; the surface appearance of the wreck had been an oval field of amphorae running from east to west. Below the cargo, I gauged the axis of the keel to be running from south-west to north-east, that is to say at an angle of about 45° in relation to the axis of surface remains of the wreck.

1953–54

Members of the C.S.S.-M. made frequent visits to the site during the winter of 1953 and the summer of 1954. They discovered the large lead anchor stock and cleared it of weeds and concretions (Plate 4). On June 13, 1954, I dived with Barnier and other club members to raise the stock. The following is a résumé of my diary notes:

As we were preparing to dive, fishermen belonging to the *Syndicat de la Pêche* put out from the port of Agay and accosted us, asking to see our papers. They did not leave until they were satisfied that we had official permission to work on the site. When I dived I saw an area of coarse sand (mainly crushed shell) covered with broken amphorae. The lie of the buried ship seemed obvious to me, but I was told that there could be no basis for my assumption, as the surface had been too disturbed when the pie-crust of concretion had been removed. Nevertheless, when I pointed out on a photograph (taken, I think, by Rebikoff) where I should have expected to find a flank of the ship, Barnier said that they had in fact discovered ribs on that spot. He had lifted one of these, but it soon shrank and became distorted. This rib was not from the excavated area mentioned by Dumas.

The lead anchor stock (which had been cleared during the winter) was now lying on sand with the crown of its wooden stem in place (Plate 4). While clearing the stock, Barnier had found and raised the concretions that contained iron implements in the form of hollow moulds (to which we will return later). The lead stock, over 2 metres long and weighing 300 kilograms, was salvaged. Photographs of this operation were published in the *Illustrated London News* of August 21, 1954.

On June 24 I made a second visit to the wreck.

Two points deserve comment: the first is the axe head and the adze found in concretions near the anchor. They were the first indication divers had that metals 'disappeared', eventually leaving a void and no more than a thin brownish skin on the inner surface of a concretion that formed as this was going on (Plate 2). Parts of rigging must be hidden within the seemingly meaningless lumps that are scattered over the surface of most wrecks.

A local potter took casts from the voids inside the concretions that were found at the Chretienne 'A'. Results were satisfactory, but the method somewhat archaic. Mr L. Biek, of the Ancient Monuments Laboratory of Great Britain, who is interested in the rate of corrosion in metals, was able to show the shape within one of these concretions from a Mediterranean wreck in an X-radiograph. He is of the opinion that such natural moulds could be recorded by most medical or industrial X-ray sets. It is an important finding in relation to these vital but hitherto neglected parts of wreck-formations.

Barnier had discovered by accident that the concretions he raised were hollow; when he split one open a black and evil smelling liquid spurted into his face. M. Marcel Rousseau (Rebikoff's assistant) examined the concretions as they were being broken; both men agree that, before casts were taken, part of the mould of the axe was mislaid. It had contained a spike; they realized later that this would have been an extension of the blade, an extension which is still

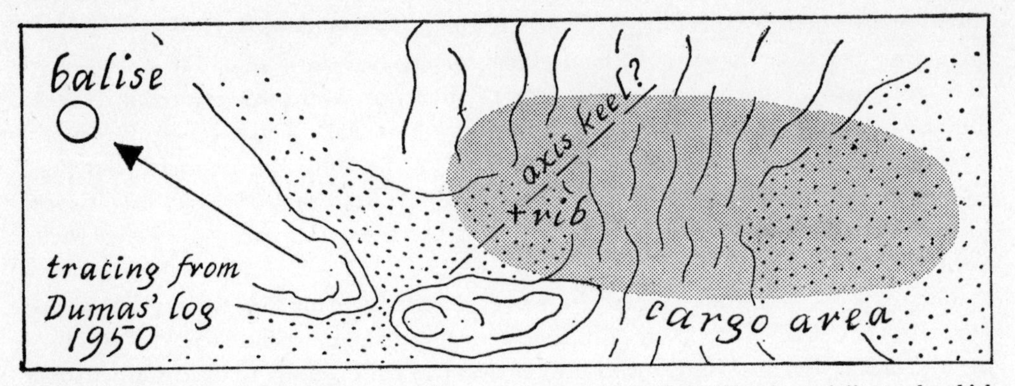

50 (above) *and* 51 (opposite) *are tracings of the drawings of the Chretienne 'A' wreck which Dumas and I made, independently, and with an interval of eleven years between them. The axis of the keel (relative to the rocks and the Balise) is the same in both. In Dumas' sketch the shaded area denotes spilled cargo, whereas in mine it represents the hull of the ship; these estimates are not incompatible, as the cargo would have tipped and spread downwards if one extremity of the ship had indeed been propped up on the rock to the east. In the 1961 drawing, note the larger area of sand due to the concretions (shown in Dumas' version) having been removed during excavation.*

characteristic of woodcutter's axes in parts of Italy and which serves to fix the tool into a wooden surface when it is not in use.

The second fact worth noting reflects on the sad lack of recording on underwater excavations. In his book quoted above, Commandant Tailliez published a very helpful list of underwater sites in France, giving the dates and most important discoveries. He was, however, misinformed about the parts of the anchor raised from the Chretienne 'A'. He lists a lead assembly piece, though no such part was found, nor could the crown we lifted be accurately described as 'the anchor stem'. Such slight inaccuracies reflect neither on the excavators nor on Commandant Tailliez, but they are unfortunately symptomatic of the lack of normal excavation routine that characterizes submarine archaeology.

1961

In June 1961, seven years after the anchor was raised, I received a letter saying that all the amphorae had been removed from the Chretienne 'A' but that, in the middle of a desert of sand and sherds, the cut end of a sizeable timber, like a Roman keelson, was emerging from the bottom.

Two months later I returned to have a look at it; by then the tourist season was

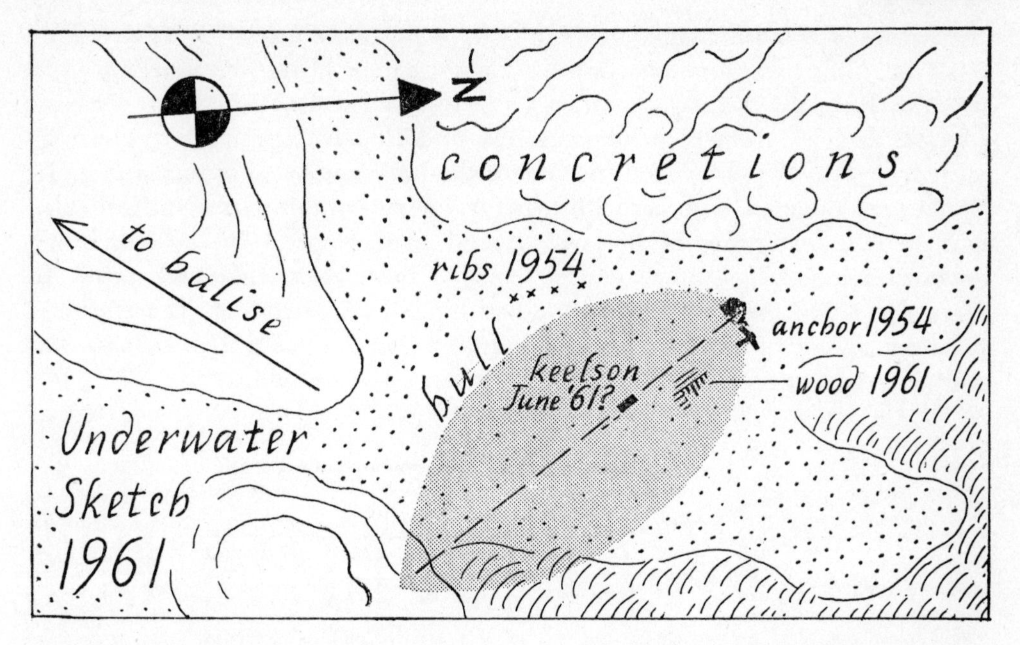

over and even the wood had disappeared. According to people living on the opposite shore, who watched the diving boats that anchored near the Beacon, holiday-makers from a nearby camp had taken the wood because of the copper nails it contained and which they prized as souvenirs. Despite this, I dived on the wreck five times between August and October of that year. At no time did fishermen or coastguards come out to inspect our papers, nor was there any attempt to protect the antiquities as there had been in 1954. The following is extracted from the notes I made in 1961:

The wreck had indeed changed; now it was a clean flat expanse of sand contrasting with the dark surrounding rocks and weeds. Though the timber had disappeared, Dumas, who was also diving, discovered a portion of hull under about 60 centimetres of sand at the north-eastern extremity of the excavated area (Plate XX). He cleared as much of this wood as he could by hand, revealing inner floor-boards, five ribs and the outer planking of the hull. This he photographed (Plate XX) while I made measured drawings of the wood underwater. I also noted its relation to the site and to the Beacon rocks (Fig. 51). The latter were well known to all who had dived on the site over a period of thirteen years.

Analysis of the drawings showed that we were on an extremity of the ship; this was confirmed by comparison with photographs of the site that had been taken by Rebikoff and Barnier in 1953 and 1954 when the anchor stock was discovered. Indeed, from these photographs, and in Barnier's opinion, the stock must have lain above this very portion of the hull that we were seeing in 1961. The overall sketches, together with structural details of this part of the hull, also indicated an extremity of the wreck; and furthermore, the last remaining anchor on a sinking ship was most likely to have been left in the prow. In Dumas' opinion the timber which he had himself seen two months earlier had been the keelson of the ship; its position in relation to these ribs and planks was another confirmation that they were an extremity of the hull.

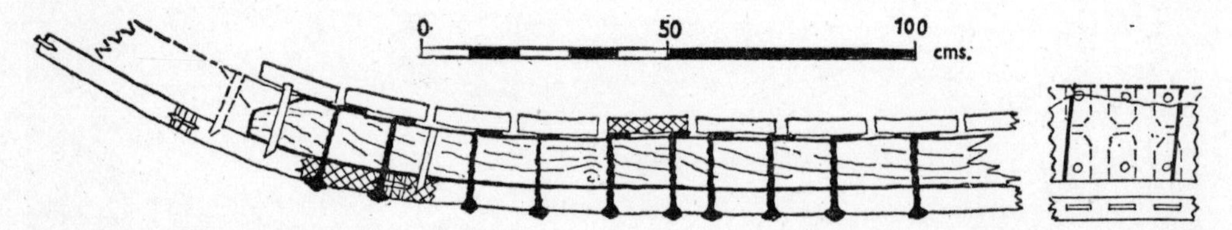

52. The centremost of the five ribs found in 1961 (drawn on land). Copper nails shown in solid black. Cross hatching denotes the floor board and section of a plank that were lifted. A plan and elevation of this plank is shown to the right; notice the lines scored across it by a Roman carpenter as a guide for its assembly with the ribs.

The relationship of the ribs to the planks showed a tapering in the structure. The ribs crossed the planking of the hull and also ran under the floor-boards at an angle of 84°. This slant, very apparent to the naked eye, was also seen in the contactual imprints of the ribs on the planks. Lastly, and most important, there were carpenter's markings on the planks which allowed the angle to be measured with a protractor. Like the wood which Dumas had seen in 1950, this portion was also astonishingly well preserved. On the inner surface of the hull the carpenter's guide lines had been scored on the softwood planks with some pointed implement, so that the ribs could be assembled and nailed in the right place.

From these five ribs I was again able to judge the axis of the keel and consequently the way the ship and its cargo had settled on the bottom. I recorded this estimate on a sketch (Fig. 51) which I later compared with the one Dumas had made in his log book eleven years before (Fig. 50). They tallied. I also compared these sketches with early photographs of the site taken at the time when Barnier found ribs; again all the documents agreed.

The ribs which we found in 1961 were nailed to the hull in pairs. The interval between each pair was 17·5 centimetres, while the coupled ribs were separated by only 6·75 centimetres. In later times ribs were grouped to give additional strength, but this arrangement had not been noted on classical ships. On the Nemi and London Museum ships all the ribs are equidistant. This would also seem to be the case on the *Titan* wreck [Fig. 46 (1)] and on the set of ribs which I myself measured at the Congloué [Fig. 48 (1)]. It is, however, unwise to compare the rare records which have hitherto been made underwater, because these details have not been related to a precise point along the axis of the keel, and we cannot assume that the structure of a hull, or the intervals between ribs, remained identical from stem to stern.

The centremost of the five Chretienne ribs (Plate XX and Fig. 52) had several interesting features. The wood was so hard that it had retained a curve; without corroborative evidence we cannot say whether this was the original curve of the hull at that particular point, but it remains a possibility. On my last dive in 1961 I picked up a loose fragment of rib from this part of the wreck. When I attempted to take samples from both ribs I found that the second had been so softened by waterlogging that it could be cut with a knife, whereas no saw could get through the curved rib. The two may have been made of different kinds of hardwood; I finally managed to take samples, and they are now being analysed.

Another interesting feature of the curved rib was the oblique cut, pierced by a treenail at one end. Similar cuts are illustrated on p. 157, Fig. 159, of Guido Ucelli's *Nave di Nemi*. Their purpose was to make an end-to-end join between timbers; oblique cuts at the extremities were joined by a wedge-shaped piece of wood which was secured at either side by treenails.

Lastly, we found brushwood over the floor-boards at one side of the excavation (twigs can be seen emerging from the sand at the top right of Plate XX). We had no time to examine these twigs closely; they might have come from a rustic broom; alternatively, they may have been laid over the floor-boards to protect them from the pointed ends of the amphorae. The latter hypothesis may explain the undamaged state of the bilge. Waterlogged softwood usually moulds itself over protuberances (in this case the ribs), but as can be seen from the photograph, these floor-boards had not caved in.

I, personally, did not see the wreck of the Chretienne 'A' in its virgin state, but I did see the second layer after weed and concretions had been removed when the surface was covered by broken amphorae, and then again later when the site had become a flat and empty desert. It is apparent that the ship had been preserved in the sand.

The wreck was dated, from the objects raised during those bona fide visits, as being of the first century B.C. Pozzuolane stoppers from the amphorae were stamped with Oscan letters. The amphorae themselves are comparable with those from the Albenga wreck (this latter site is now being excavated systematically by Dr Nino Lamboglia, who is directing professional divers, so for the first time in history, a marine excavation may provide information about structure). I have also seen in private possession the rim of a jar from the Chretienne 'A' incised with the letters 'AM', cooking-utensils and a folded bit of lead sheeting.

Despite this sheet, the Chretienne hull could not have been plated. On leaded wrecks the sheets are so numerous that they cannot be ignored during even the most uncontrolled excavation. MM. Broussard and Barnier, who are certainly observant and careful divers, agree that such sheets were not found in quantity on this wreck, nor was there any lead plating on the part of the hull I saw, but I cannot be certain that the extremity of the ship came from below the water-line.

It can be concluded that there is very little doubt that had the Chretienne 'A' wreck been subjected to methodical research, sufficient structural parts would have been found for this ship to have been at least partially reconstructed.

GLOSSARY OF TURKISH WORDS

Ada, island
Amca, uncle; a respectful term of endearment
Arak, alcoholic drink flavoured with aniseed

Balik spor, fish sport
Bekci, guardian of antiquities
Bodrum, a cellar

Çai, tea
Congoa, sponge trawl
Çorba, soup

Dalguç, diver
Dolmuş, full; used of a taxi which only leaves its rank when every seat has been hired

Gasinosou, casino
Gümrük, customs post

Halva, a sweet made out of honey and nuts
Hamam, a turkish bath

Iskariot, parrot fish

Kaÿmak, cream
Kara, black
Kebab, skewered meat, or meat balls cooked over charcoal
Keffal, mullet
Kulaç, 5 feet; Turkish equivalent of a fathom
Kurbağa (*Adamlar*) *Kulübü*, frog(men's) club
Kuruş, small coin; equivalent of a farthing

Lucoum, Turkish delight

Mercan, bream
Mese, snacks served with drinks
Müdür, head man of a village

Narghile, hubble-bubble; also used to describe a method of diving whereby air is supplied through a hose, from a compressor on the surface, to a demand valve worn on the diver's back

Orfus, grouper

Paplama, a kapok quilt

Sünger Kooperatifi, sponge Cooperative

Tata Koyu, Wooden Village
Tura, a sultan's stylized signature

BIBLIOGRAPHY

The subject of marine archaeology is seldom treated directly; in this short list books have been selected either because they are essential to the subject or because they are of indirect interest and might otherwise pass unnoticed.

Actes du IIème Congrès International de l'Archéologie Sous-Marine, Albenga, 1958.

BENOÎT, FERNAND, *L'Epave du Grand Congloué*, XIV Gallia supplement, Paris, 1962.

— *Premiers Résultats des Fouilles Sous-Marines; Typologie des Amphores et Construction Naval*, Paris, 1960.

BOREUX, CHARLES, *Etudes de Nautique Egyptienne*, Cairo, 1925.

BOUCHAYER, AUGUSTE, *Marseille, ou la Mer qui Monte*, Paris, 1931.

CASSON, LIONEL, *The Ancient Mariners*, London, 1959.

CLUB ALPIN SOUS-MARIN, *Rapport du Ier Congrès International d'Archéologie Sous-Marine*, Cannes, 1955.

Drammont Wreck: duplicated technical report made by the Office Française de la Recherche Scientifique for the Ministère de l'Education Nationale, 1959.

DUMAS, FRÉDÉRIC, *Deep-Water Archaeology*, London, 1962.

FAHMY, ALY MOHAMED, *Muslim Sea Power in the Eastern Mediterranean from the 7th to the 12th centuries*, Alexandria, 1950.

FRANZEN, ANDERS, *The Warship Vasa*, Stockholm, 1960.

GRACE, VIRGINIA, *Amphoras and the Ancient Wine Trade*, Princeton, N.J., 1961.

HOLMES, ARTHUR, *Outlines of Physical Geology*, London, 1948.

JAL, A., *Archéologie Navale*, Paris, 1840.

— *Glossaire Nautique*, Paris, 1848.

JONDET, GASTON, *Les Ports Submergés de l'Ancienne Ile de Pharos*, Cairo, 1916.

KENYON, KATHLEEN, *Beginnings in Archaeology*, London, 1961.

LANDSTRÖM, BJÖRN, *The Ship*, London, 1962.

LEHMANN-HARTLEBEN, KARL, *Die Antiken Hafenanlangen des Mittelmeers* (Klio, Beiheft XIV), Leipzig, 1923.

MARCHIS, E., *La Pêche des Algues Marines, des Eponges et des Coraux*, Paris, 1929.

MARINE NATIONALE, G.E.R.S., *La Plongée*, Paris, 1955.

MOLL, F., *Das Schiff in die Blinden Kunst*, Bonn, 1929.

MOLLAT, MICHEL, *et al.*, *Les Sources de l'Histoire Maritime*, Paris, 1962.

POIDEBARD, A., *Tyr*, Paris, 1939.

— and LAUFFRAY, J., *Sidon*, Beyrouth, 1952.

Le Plongeur et l'Archéologue, ed. François Clouzot for the Confédération Mondiale des Activités Subaquatiques; Barcelona Congress, 1960.

— *60 years of Underwater Archaeology*, ed. J. du Plat Taylor for C.M.A.S. (in preparation).

RODRIGUES SANTAMARIA, BENIGNO, *Diccionario de Artes de Pesca de España y son Possessiones*, Madrid, 1923.

Royal Naval Diving Manual, Underwater Warfare Division, Naval Staff, Admiralty, London.

TAYLOR, E. G. R., *The Haven Finding Art*, London, 1956.

THOMPSON, D'ARCY WENTWORTH, *A Glossary of Greek Fishes*, Oxford, 1947.

TORR, CECIL, *Ancient Ships*, Cambridge, 1894.

UCELLI, GUIDO, *Le Navi di Nemi*, Rome, 1950.

UNZE, OTTO, *Frührömische Amphoren als Zeitmarken im Spätlatine*, Marburg, 1958.

U.S. Navy Diving Manual, Navy Department, Washington 25, D.C.

WHITAKER, JOSEPH I. S., *Motya; a Phoenician Colony*, London, 1921.

PERIODICALS

Articles in scholarly and, to an increasing extent, in adventure and diving magazines are the main source of information on marine antiquities. These publications are so numerous that they cannot all be listed. The following selection gives examples of periodicals and some articles that have a direct bearing on submarine archaeology.

Acta Archaeologica, Copenhagen. (Olaf Olsen, 'The Skuldlev Ships'), Vol. XXIX, 1958.

American Journal of Archaeology. (George Bass, 'The Cape Gelidonya Wreck; Preliminary Report'), Vol. 63, No. 3, 1961.

American Philological Association; Transactions and Proceedings. (Lionel Casson, 'The Isis and her Voyage'), Vol. 81, No. 1, 1950, p. 43.

Annales de Bretagne, Rennes. (R. Y. Creston, 'Construction des Navires Venètes', and P. Emanuelle, 'César et les Venètes'), 1955–58.

Antiquity, Newbury, Berkshire. (A. Merlin, 'Submarine Discoveries in the Mediterranean'), Vol. 4, 1930, pp. 405–14.

Antiquity and Survival, The Hague. (G. D. van der Heide, 'Zuyder Zee Archaeology'), Vol. 3, 1955.

Archaeology, U.S. (George Karo, 'Art Salvaged from the Sea'), No. 1, 1948.

Athenische Mittelungen. (M. Verdelis, 'The Isthmian Shipway'), Vol. 71, 1956, p. 56.

Atti del VIII Congresso Internationale di Archeologica Classica, L'Erma di Bretschneider. (M. F. Benoît, 'Une Nouvelle Etape de l'Archéologie; les Recherches Sous-Marines. Méthodes et Résultats. Architecture Navale'), Vol. 1, 1959.

Atti del VIII Congresso di Studi Bizantini. (M. Dolley, 'Naval Tactics in the Heyday of the Byzantine Thalassocrasy'), Vol. 1, p. 324.

L'Aventure Sous-Marine; Techniques et Exploration, Paris. Archaeological Number: 36, 1962, also periodic reports.

Bollettino e Atti, Centro Italiano Ricercatori Subacque. (Gianni Roghi, 'Note Tecniche sul Rilevamento e lo Scavo della Nave Romana di Spargi'), 1958–59.

British Academy Proceedings. (O. M. Dalton, 'The Brescia Astrolabe'), Vol. 12, 1926.

Bulletin de l'Institut Français d'Archéologie Orientale, Cairo. (Georges Foucart, 'Pharos et Mariotis'), Tome XV, 1918.

Bulletin de l'Institut Océanographique de Monaco. (Brouardel et Vernet, 'Variations en Mer de la Teneur en Oxygène Dissous au Proche Voisinage des Sediments'), No. 1111, 1958.

Bulletin de la Fédération Française d'Etudes et de Sports Sous-Marins. Marseille. Annual lists of sites and frequent reports on discoveries.

Bulletin de la Societée Française Minér. Crist. (Goni, Guillaumin and Perimond-Tronchet, 'Description d'Espèces Minerales Néogènes Formées sur les Jas d'Ancres Romaines Immergées'), Vol. LXXVII, 1954.

Bulletin de Correspondence Hellénique. (Braemer and Mercadé, 'Céramique Antique et Pièces d'Ancres'), 1953; (On Nirou Khani, Crete), Vol. L, 1926, p. 574; (J. Paris, 'Contribution à l'Etude des Ports Grecs'), Vol. XV, 1916.

Ephemeris Archaiologiki, Athens. (In Greek) 'The Anticythera Wreck', 1902.

Etudes Ligures (see *Studi Liguri*).

Expedition, University Museum Pennsylvania. (George Bass, 'A Bronze Age Shipwreck'), Vol. 3, No. 2, 1961.

Explorers' Journal, New York. (Stanton A. Waterman, 'Three Thousand Years Under the Sea'), Vol. 38, No. 3, 1960.

Gallia, Imprimerie Nationale, Paris. (F. M. Benoît, 'Nouvelles Epaves de Provence'), No. 16, fascicule 1, 1958; (Jean Chauffin, 'Les Tuiles Gallo-Romaines du Bas Dauphiné'), No. 14, 1956.

The Geographic Magazine, London. (N. Flemming, 'Apollonia Revisited'), Vol. XXXIII, No. 9, 1961.

Illustrated London News. Weekly archaeological articles.

Informations Sous-Marines. (W. Haag, 'La Recherche Archéologique dans nos Lacs Suisses Offre-t-elle le moindre Intérêt?'), No. 6, 1958.

Isis, International Review of Science and Civilization, Harvard U.P. (O. Neugebauer, 'Early History of the Astrolabe'), Vol. 40, 3, No. 121, 1949.

Journal of Hellenic Studies; British School of Archaeology at Athens. (J. M. Cook, 'Old Smyrna'; John Leatham and Sinclair Hood, 'Submarine exploration in Crete'; John Boardman, 'Excavations at Pendakis in Chios'), Vols. 53–54, 1958–59.

Mariner's Mirror, Society of Nautical Research, Cambridge U.P. (F. Moll, 'History of the Anchor'), Vol. 13, No. 4, 1927; (J. W. van Nouhuis, 'The Anchor'), Vol. 37, No. 1, 1951; (R. C. Anderson, 'Italian Naval Architecture about 1445'), Vol. 11, No. 2, 1925, etc.

The National Geographic Magazine, U.S. Frequent articles on underwater archaeology.

Präehistorische Zeitschrift (von Hans Günter-Büchholz, 'Kefti Barren'), Vol. XXXVII, 1959.

Revue Biblique. (R. Savignac, 'Une Visite a l'Ile de Rouad'), Vol. XIII, 1916.

Revista di Gerona. (Frederico Foerster, 'El Yacimiento Arqueologico ante Isla Pedrosa (Estartit)'), Vol. IV, No. 13, 1960.

Revista del Mar, C.R.I.S., Barcelona. (Frederico Foerster, 'Recopilación de Métodos de Medición Utilizables en Agua para Planos de Yacimientos y Excavaciones'), No. 33, 1962; (Clemente Vidal Sola, 'Arqueologia Submarina'), No. 31, 1961, etc.

Revista Sagauna e Ventimiglia. (N. Lamboglia, 'La Prima Campagna Sottomarina del 'Daino' nelle Acque Ligure'), Vol. XIV, 1959.

Revista de Studi Liguri (*Etudes Ligures*), Musée Bicknall, Bordighera. (N. Lamboglia, 'La Nave Romana d'Albenga'), No. 18, 1952; (F. M. Benoît, 'Jas d'Ancres et Pièces d'Outillage des Epaves de Provence'), Vol. XX, No. 2, 1955, etc.

Scientific American. (Dennis Price, 'The Anticythera Clock'), June 1959.

Zephyrus. (Henkin, 'The Huelva Hoard'), Vol. VII, 1956.

INDEX